D1643059

LEO PANITCH is Professor of Political Science at York University in Toronto. His major publications include *Social Democracy and Industrial Militancy* (1976), *The Canadian State: Political Economy and Political Power* (1977) and *From Consent to Coercion: The Assault on Trade Union Freedoms* (1985). Leo Panitch was a founding editor of the Canadian journal, *Studies in Political Economy: A Socialist Review*, and has recently become a co-editor of *The Socialist Register*.

Leo Panitch

Working-Class Politics in Crisis

Essays on Labour and the State

VERSO
The Imprint of New Left Books

**British Library
Cataloguing in Publication Data**

Panitch, Leo
 Working class politics in crisis : essays
 on Labour and the state.
 1. Labour Party. Great Britain
  I. Title
  324.24107   JN1129.L32

First Published 1986
© Leo Panitch 1986

Verso
15 Greek Street, London W1V 5LF

Typeset in Garamond by Spire Print Services Ltd
Salisbury, Wilts

Printed by the Thetford Press
Thetford, Norfolk

ISBN 0-86091-142-X
ISBN 0-86091-849-1 Pbk

Contents

Dedicated to the memory
of my parents,

Max and Sarah Panitch

Preface

The essays collected in this volume were written over the span of the past fifteen years. Although the opening essay, which is the most recent, speaks most directly to the current crisis of working-class politics in the West, and particularly in Britain, my work over the whole period has been centrally concerned with analysing those very limits and contradictions in the practices of working-class parties and trade unions which have led us to today's impasse. All the essays, therefore, may be seen as anticipating and exploring the roots of our current troubles.

The central theme that runs through most of the essays concerns the irreducable importance of political and ideological structures in determining the limits and possibilities of working-class advance. As opposed to those past and present sociological reductionists who proclaim the 'decline of the working class' on the basis of trends in occupational structure or cultural homogenization, I have sought to discern the extent to which the Labour Party's own ideology has contributed to a decline in class politics and working-class identity. At the same time, however, I have tried to develop an understanding of the continuing salience of class struggle and the strains and contradictions it yields for the integrative practices of social democracy. In particular, through my study of the corporatist political structures which social democratic governments have sponsored as a means of accommodating the trade-union movement to the capitalist state, I have pointed to the recurrent instability of modern corporatism and sought to warn against the authoritarian capitalist response that has attended this instability in the face of recurrent trade-union militancy and the absence of a viable socialist political alternative.

The concentration of these essays on the predominant practice of working-class politics in the West, that of social democracy and corporatism, may strike a discordant note in a period when the crisis of working-class politics is often attributed to, or at least taken as proof of, the failures of Marxism. Their republication today is intended to do so, and I hope they will provide a useful corrective to this trend. This is not to say that Marxist theory and strategy is not in need of substantial revision and development. The reader will find in these essays an appreciation of Marxism for the attention it pays to class struggle in its analysis and practice and for the recent development of a Marxist political theory which has considerably enhanced our understanding of the operation of the capitalist state. But the reader will also find a critique of an economic determinism which seeks to read off the generation of the current capitalist crises from the immutable laws of Marxist political economy; and a critique of Marxist state theorists for their neglect of the complex and contradictory relationship between the trade unions and the capitalist state. Perhaps most important, a number of these essays discuss Marxism's traditional failure to address adequately the necessary institutional forms of a democratic socialist state, as well as the need for a new socialist politics that would seek to develop such political agencies in the struggle against capitalism as would presage such a state.

I am grateful to the original publishers of these essays for their permission to reprint them in this volume. Two of the essays, 'The Impasse of Social Democratic Politics' (1985) and 'Socialists and the Labour Party: A Reappraisal' (1979), first appeared in *The Socialist Register,* the former article having first been presented as a paper at the Centre for Socialist Theory and Movements' conference on 'Does Socialism Have a Future?', Glasgow, April 1985. 'Ideology and Integration: The Case of the British Labour Party' appeared in *Political Studies,* vol. 14, no. 2, June 1971; 'Profits and Politics: Labour and the Crisis of British Capitalism', in *Politics and Society,* vol. 7, no. 4, December 1977; 'The Development of Corporatism in Liberal Democracies', in *Comparative Political Studies,* vol. 10, no. 1, April 1977; 'Recent Theorizations of Corporatism: Reflections on a Growth Industry', in *The British Journal of Sociology,* vol. 31, no. 2, June 1980. 'Trade Unions and the Capitalist State' was presented as a paper at the International Conference on the State and the Economy, University of Toronto, in December 1979 and subsequently revised and published in

New Left Review, no. 125, January–February 1981. 'The Importance of Workers' Control for Revolutionary Change' was presented as a paper at the Second International Conference of Self-Management, Cornell University, June 1975, and subsequently published in *Canadian Dimension,* vol. 12, no. 3, June 1977, and reprinted in *Monthly Review,* vol. 24, no. 10, March 1978. 'The State and the Future of Socialism' was presented as a paper at the Third International Colloquium of the Interuniversity Centre for European Studies in Montreal, March 1978, the proceedings of which were published as *The Future of Socialism in Europe?,* edited by André Liebich, and the paper was republished in revised form in *Capital and Class,* no. 11, Summer 1980. I have not substantively altered any of the essays, although I have made minor corrections and excerpted a few passages that seem repetitive in the context of their collection in a single volume. Except in a very few instances, I have not added more recent references, nor have I attempted to update the material in the texts. For this reason, I have thought it best to indicate at the end of each essay the year in which it was written.

Over the course of the fifteen years during which these essays were written, I obviously relied for intellectual, political and emotional support on a good many people. Melanie Panitch, Donald Swartz, Sam Gindin, Ralph Miliband, Colin Leys and Reg Whitaker have been especially important to me in this respect. So were many of my students and colleagues at Carleton University from 1972 to 1984 and more recently at York University, as were my comrades in the Ottawa Committee for Labour Action. Many others contributed as well to particular essays, through their encouragement, help and criticism. Particular mention should be made here of Greg Albo, Perry Anderson, Chris Boyle, Tony Benn, Stephen Hellman, Laurence Harris, Michael Goldrick, Jane Jenson, Stella Lord, Steven Lukes, Lewis Minkin, Dennis Olsen, Angus Stewart, Adam Przeworski, Philippe Schmitter, Ian Taylor, Sid Tarrow and Ellen Meiksins Wood. I am grateful as well to Robin Blackburn for having suggested the idea for this collection, and especially to Neil Belton of Verso for his help and encouragement.

Leo Panitch
Toronto
November 1985.

1.
The Impasse of Social Democratic Politics

There are three stages through which every new notion in England has to pass: 'It is impossible: It is against the Bible: We knew it before. Socialism is rapidly reaching the third of these stages. We are all socialists now,' said one of Her Majesty's late Ministers; and in sober truth, there is no anti-socialist political party. That which has long formed part of the unconscious basis of our practice is now formulated as a definite theory, and the tide of democratic collectivism is upon us. (Sidney Webb, *English Progress Toward Social Democracy*, Fabian Tract, no. 15, December 1890.)

Introduction

The notion of gradual but inevitable progress toward socialism through the vehicle of a paternalist parliamentary state has always entailed a historical determinism far more myopic than could ever be properly ascribed to Marxism. The rude shock administered by the establishment of the new right's 'market populism' as the governing ideology of the 1980s appears to have clearly and definitively shattered the complacency associated with the phrase, so oft repeated over the past century, 'We are all socialists now.'

At the same time it must also be recognized that the emergence of market populism amidst the current crisis of capitalism has simultaneously exposed in its wake the impasse of working-class politics in the West. The long-standing assumption that a return to mass unemployment and an abandonment of bourgeois commitment to the

Keynesian welfare state would lead to political instability and a crisis of capitalist legitimacy, an assumption as common among liberals as among many Marxists, has been cast into doubt. For the moment at least, it is the weakness of the political forces associated with the working class—whether trade unions, or social democratic parties, or revolutionary socialist parties—that has come to the fore and brought home an old lesson: there is nothing automatic about the development of socialist consciousness when the capitalist economy is not generating material benefits or job security for the working class.

Indeed, the impasse that has been reached would appear to be the obverse of the one that many thought characterised the working classes in advanced capitalism since the Second World War. Whereas it was earlier argued that the ability of the system to generate immediate material rewards foreclosed the possibility of developing sustained and broad interest in socialist ideas, today it would appear that the absence of widespread socialist conviction or understanding among the working classes in advance of the crisis has made many working people vulnerable to the new right's ideology and amenable to the 'common-sense' remedies of restraint and sacrifice as a means of restoring capitalism's health. If the 'objective' economic conditions are present today, the no less 'objective' political and cultural conditions are not. In other words, the failure to generate socialist consciousness in the period of capitalist boom appears to have laid the grounds for a further failure in the period of bust.

The consequences of this have proved severe not only for socialist politics but for working-class reformism. Reformism was able to retain popular support and programmatic direction when it appeared the system could support it, but it lost a good deal of both when economic conditions and the bourgeois onslaught against previous reformist gains in these new conditions combined to demonstrate how utterly dependent the system—and every individual within it—is on meeting the requirements set by capitalists for when and where they will invest. 'Common sense' has told all of us that reforms conceived and implemented within the logic of capitalism have to be re-examined once they really do begin to have the effect of scaring business away. At a minimum, a new defence of old reforms becomes necessary; inertia alone cannot be counted on. In the elaborate and complex poker game that is capitalist democracy, the new right used monetarism to call the old left's—including the unions'—bluff with regard to the hand it had been holding for some forty years. And it turned out that we had little strength in any suit. It has been hardly surprising, therefore, that there has been a good deal of socialist 'rethinking' going on in recent years. In so far as the primary form of working-class politics in the West was that of reformist parties, this rethinking initially took the form (often drawing on the new intellectual revival of Western Marxism since the 1960s) of attempting to understand and transcend the limits and contradictions of social democracy both as state policy and as political and ideological practice. This inevitably involved an assault from the left on the 'we are all socialists now' ideology to match the one that had emerged from the right. This in turn produced considerable internal party strife as battles were fought out over the very meaning of socialism and democracy, amidst the heady revival within these parties of a form of radical discourse which the predominant leadership of these parties had long before stopped to take seriously. At the root of it all was the perception that if the history of the modern state was not one of inevitable gradual progress toward socialism this had much to do with the effective abandonment of the socialist project by working-class parties. Tony Benn characteristically captured the spirit of this development in the British context at the beginning of the 1980s: 'We have persuaded the Labour movement that one of the reasons we have made so little progress over seventy years is the weakness of the Labour Party. That is the real issue that has been raised.'[1]

With rather astonishing haste, and long before the project of transforming these parties could be said to have been achieved, a remarkable shift of direction has taken place in the general orientation of leftist intellectuals towards understanding the roots of the impasse. Increasingly, this rethinking has placed under scrutiny the very nature of the socialist project itself, above all as it has been classically conceived by Marxism. Brought into question has been the centrality, or at least the relative salience, of the working class as the agency of social change, whether because of the declining proportion of manual industrial workers in the labour force, or because of the inherent inability of workers to transcend militant trade-union economism. At the same time, the vision projected by Marxism—and especially by 'actually existing' socialism's practice—of a centrally planned non-market economy has come under increasing attack for associating the notion of socialism with authoritarian statism. While by no means unimportant issues have thus been raised, sometimes with considerable insight, the irony of this orientation to the problem is that it not only shifts attention away from the primary modern practice of the Western working class—reformist social democracy—but actually replicates, both in its critique of Marxism and in its strategic proposals, many of the essential tenets of that very practice.

The response of workers to the crisis must not be seen mechanistically or ahistorically as something inevitable, or as 'natural' or 'given'. It is rather a product of a range of previous practices that fostered certain structures and ideas that blocked the development of a viable socialist response to the crisis, and that excluded socialist options as 'unrealistic'. If we see the impasse in this way, as something constructed rather than given, we may also see that *the impasse pertains not only, indeed not so much, to the drag that the working class or Marxism imposes on the socialist project, as many would have it today, as to the drag that social democracy continues to exercise on the working class and the intellectual left.* For even though the Keynesianism and corporatism of social democracy have exhausted the limits of their reformist and electoral possibilities in the current crisis, they retain deep ideological and organizational supports which recent intellectual and party political experience indicates cannot be easily transcended.

Therefore to speak of the impasse of working–class politics rather than the impasse of socialist politics involves a deliberate decision. It is designed to establish at the outset the problematic of the link between the achievement of socialism and the working class as its progenitor; and it is to emphasize that, contrary to much current misconception, *it is not only the viability of revolutionary socialism that is open to question as a result of the current crisis. The impasse we have been speaking of pertains far more to reformist gradualism precisely because this has been—and remains —the primary practice of Western working-class parties.* This is not to deny the need for Marxian socialists to engage in a profound re-examination of a strategic kind with regard to their own forms of political practice, but this is hardly to be achieved through putting aside all of the difficult questions about how a transition to socialism in the face of bourgeois opposition is actually to be effected, which, as we shall see, the new revisionism is wont to do. Before turning to a critique of the latter, however, it will be necessary to define in more concrete terms the exact nature of the impasse of working-class politics.

The Contradictions of Social Democratic Governments

To understand properly today's impasse, we must locate it in the historical context of the rise and fall of post-war social democracy. Until the post-war era, the socialist aspirations and rhetoric of social democratic parties had stood uncomfortably alongside their strategic commitments. How could public planning and control over the economy—which was the principal case offered not only for distributive reforms but for public ownership—be effected without offending the principle of inter-class compromise and co-operation upon which the gradualism, parliamentarism and tripartism practised by these parties ultimately rested? When a party like the British Labour Party finally committed itself to socialism in the sense of clause four—the taking into public ownership of the means of production, distribution and exchange—it never answered the question that arose over how this could be achieved while at the same time retaining its long-standing commitment to class co-operation as opposed to class struggle. As for the classic social democratic parties of the Continent, their dilemma after the First World War was no longer how their vulgar economic Marxism could be made consistent with their tepid political parliamentarism, but how their triparite 'functional socialism' could retain its relevance when the bourgeoisie refused to co-operate in it (at least once the immediate revolutionary threat at the end of the war had passed.) This difficult question of how economic planning might be introduced without causing a massive political fissure was either avoided or it was answered in the face of capitalist opposition by the abandonment or marginalization of such economic planning structures as had been initiated by social democratic governments at the end of the war.

After the Second World War, on the other hand, in the context of the experience of the Depression, the defeat of fascism, and above all the onset of the greatest boom period the world economy has probably ever known, the conditions were established for social democracy's apparently successful resolution of the above dilemma. With Keynesianism and the welfare state coming to provide new substantive content to 'state intervention' and being accepted as such by significant sections of bourgeois opinion, it was no longer necessary for social democratic parties to emphasize public ownership as the centrepiece of planning or control over the economy. Indeed, to do so would involve throwing away the opportunity for class co-operation through tripartite indicative planning and, as was so often repeated at the time, confuse means with ends. Social democratic leaders discerned the emergence of an efficiency-oriented managerial class which had come to appreciate the limits of an unregulated capitalism and the virtues of macroeconomic planning, welfare reforms and stable industrial relations. In turn, capitalists and senior bureaucrats discerned a party leadership anxious to prove their 'soundness' and 'responsibility' by playing the key role of securing trade-union co-operation in incomes policies so as to obviate the inflationary pressures of full employment capitalism. To one side this meant that we were all socialists now; to the other—and with rather more justice—that we were all capitalists now. But what did it matter? The terms were misleading in any case, were they not? This was after all the era of the end of ideology.

Or so it seemed. The so-called post-war settlement between labour and capital in the West may have concealed to some extent, but it hardly closed, the contradictions that give rise to class and ideological struggle and to economic instability under capitalism. In particular the resurgence of industrial militancy in the late 1960s threw into sharp relief at one and the same time the economic strength of workers under the conditions of near full employment and the political weakness of labour *vis-à-vis* capital even under the tripartite economic planning arrangements of social democratic governments. Moreover, the drawing to a close of the post-war boom in the 1970s underlined the instability of corporatism and revealed the fragility of the Keynesian welfare state. A combination of special conditions had produced the high investment ratios of the 1950–73 period: the cleansing of unproductive and less dynamic capitals during the depression and the war; large post-war pools of skilled cheap labour; clusters of technological innovations favouring productivity growth and mass consumer demand; the weakening of trade-union militancy during the Cold War; the abundance of cheap raw materials and the availability of new markets and relatively open trade under United States economic leadership. Each of these ran out, however unevenly, by the early 1970s. This made particularly problematic for the economy and the state the consumerism and confidence of the workers which the boom had generated and which combined to sustain industrial militancy in the 1970s even as unemployment levels began their disastrous ascent. At the same time, the explosively expansive potential of public employment and state social expenditures became increasingly clear as the employment and growth performance of the private sector declined.

The collapse of the Keynesian era in the stagflation of the 1970s meant that the old 'settlement' had to be renegotiated—and not only between capital and labour, but also within labour, that is, between social democratic leaderships and their trade-union base. How to generate new capital investment while simultaneously extending the limits of reform so as to provide effective quid pro quos for new rounds of wage restraint by the unions became the central question for social democratic governance in the 1970s. This did not in itself appear to entail an impasse for reformist working-class politics. On the contrary, it seemed to provide the opportunity for a new testing of the limits of reform within capitalist democracies. And, indeed, a shift to the left, a resurgence of parliamentary *socialism,* was visible in one country after another. What was now taken up was what had been largely foregone in the post-war settlement in the way of industrial democracy and effective control over private investment decisions: the sphere of production rather than that of distribution became the primary focus of legislative reform. This was seen, for instance, in the turn by the DGB unions and the Social Democratic Party (SPD) government in West Germany towards *Strukturpolitik* and investment planning as well as the attempted extension of co-determination beyond the iron and coal industry. It was seen in Sweden in the famous Meidner Plan and in the legislation in the mid 1970s which provided a legal framework for union challenges to managerial prerogatives on the shop floor and for worker participation schemes on works councils and company boards. It was seen in Britain in similar progressive labour legislation and the proposal of the Bullock Inquiry on industrial democracy as well as in the planning agreements and National Enterprise Board elements of Labour's 1973 programme. And it was seen, of course, in the emphasis on autogestion and nationalization that characterized the phenomenal revival of the French Socialists under the umbrella of the Common Programme.

What has now become apparent after a decade is that in one country after another the much-vaunted social partnership, in so far as it ever existed beyond the most superficial and conditional levels, simply could not be reconstructed on a firm foundation. As social democratic parties took up demands for industrial democracy and investment planning, it now turned out that it was capital that balked at co-operation on such revised terms. In Germany and Britain this became clear very quickly in the mid 1970s, even though the SPD and Labour governments adopted conventionally restrictive, virtually monetarist, macroeconomic policies. The German employers' constitutional challenge to the co-determination law and their 'taboo catalogue' on negotiations over work-time reduction led to the complete breakdown of concerted action in economic policy-making in 1977 and to the six-week metal workers' strike and lock-out in 1978 which presaged the even more protracted and bitter conflict of 1983 and shattered the myth of social consensus. In Britain, the radical thrust of the planning agreements and enterprise board proposals was quickly jettisoned in the face of business opposition, but neither this, nor the extensive wage restraint practised by the unions under the social contract until 1978, allayed capital's fears of 'union power'. Above all, as Colin Leys's interviews with

Confederation of British Industry leaders have shown, the Bullock Report's majority recommendation on parity representation on company boards, although not taken up by the Labour government, became the rallying point for the conversion to Thatcherism by British industrialists regardless of its destructive implications for manufacturing industry. 'It was at this time that opinion among the CBI leadership shifted from a defence of collaborative relations with the state and the labour movement to one of more or less open rejection . . . In the mid-1970s a majority of manufacturing executives had come to feel that the survival of capitalism was at stake. They judged that unless trade union power was drastically reduced, control of capital would pass out of owners' hands and profits from manufacturing would progressively disappear. Consequently short-term business interests, and even the long-term interests of individuals or firms had to be sacrificed. Even those who were unconvinced by the Thatcherite project saw no realistic political alternative.'[2]

Just how widespread, and how fundamental, is the breakdown of the post-war consensus can be seen by looking at the Swedish case. Despite the defeat of the SAP in 1976, it seemed to many that the elaboration of the Meidner Plan laid the foundation for Swedish social democracy's inauguration of a new 'middle way' socialist society without having to disrupt economic growth and class harmony. These hopes have been disappointed, not only by the severe watering down of the wage earners' funds scheme after considerable strife in the social democratic party, but by the real and growing disenchantment shown by Swedish capital with the social consensus approach. This has been seen not only in the vociferous opposition of the Central Employers' Federation (SAF) to the wage earners' funds even in their watered down versions as little more than forced savings schemes; it could also be seen in the Swedish employers' determination—and their recent success—to break the wage solidarity practice on the Landsorganizationen (LO) unions and the system of centralized bargaining upon which it was based. After the massive general strike of 1980, and the extensive strikes of the following year, protracted negotiations in 1982–3 were only concluded after the crucial metal sector settled separately without regard for the wage solidarity principle. Finally, in 1984, centralized bargaining was abandoned altogether in favour of sector by sector bargaining. This was a major victory for the employers and was achieved even in the face of the LO granting major concessions. This dramatic change in labour–capital relations has occurred in spite of the social democrats' re-election in 1982. And it has occurred in spite of the introduction of a version of the wage earners' funds that pose no challenge whatsoever to capital in terms of economic democracy and the socialization of industry and in spite of the expressed hopes of the government that the funds will 'secure acceptance for a high level of profit in enterprise', 'reduce distributive conflict' and 'encourage restraint in collective bargaining'. Swedish capital's mobilization against the funds and their dismantling of centralized bargaining shows that capital's own interest in social consensus is a highly conditional one: the attempt by working-class institutions to pose fundamental challenges to managerial prerogatives or private ownership as a quid pro quo for wage restraint finds capital withdrawing from the process. [3]

What this means is that the old dilemma has reasserted itself: those social democratic parties which remain in office in the 1980s are primarily engaged in managing the crisis in a form increasingly reminiscent of the inter-war years. Where unemployment levels have been kept relatively low (as in Sweden and Austria compared with France) considerable credit is due to the cushioning effect of public sector institutions and practices forged during the era of consensus. But concern with reviving business profits and reducing the deficit have been the main themes of recent budgets in Austria and Sweden; and this, along with the accelerating trend to decentralized bargaining in these countries as capital exploits and exacerbates labour's divisions and insecurity in this era of capitalist 'restructuring', clearly indicates that there is little prospect for a stable or unproblematic revival of the old consensus politics. And if this is the case for Sweden and Austria, it is most certainly the case for Britain where the crisis—economic, ideological and political—is incomparably more severe.

Labourism and the Working Class

To begin an examination of the impasse of working-class politics by stressing the historical dilemmas of social democracy and the limits they impose on political practice, as we have done, stands in sharp contrast with current intellectual trends on the left. [4] From André Gorz's *Farewell to the Working Class* and Eric Hobsbawm's *The Forward March of Labour Halted?* the starting point for analysis of the impasse has been what it tells us about: first, the nature of the working class, and second, the errors of 'orthodox' Marxist notions of class struggle as the focal point of socialist politics. Consequently, in so far as the practice of working-class parties is criticized, it is for too close an attachment to traditional forms of class politics.

One must, of course, be careful to distinguish between a Gorz and a Hobsbawm, between a 'Green' and a 'Eurocommunist' analysis of the impasse. Gorz's polemic against 'Saint Marx' involves a fundamental displacement of the working class as a potentially revolutionary subject (by a vaguely defined and rather amorphous 'non-class of non-workers'). Counterposing his position against a caricatured presentation of Marx as believing that the development of capitalist forces of production would directly give rise to a spontaneously unified, inherently 'universal', revolutionary class of industrial workers, Gorz presents an exactly opposite picture of an 'actual' working class which neither is, nor can be, anything more than a pale, and increasingly fading, reflection of capital itself, incapable of doing more than bargaining over the price of its labour. In this fashion Gorz belittles the enormous stress Marx put on the role of unions and parties in 'the formation of the proletariat into a class'[5] and he ignores the actual historical experience of the attachment of large sections of the working class to socialist parties. He shows little interest, therefore, in examining the practices of these parties to discern the extent to which they fostered or constrained its revolutionary potential. The matter is settled by his denial of this potential in face of the original Marxist sin of having based its political practice on chasing a false god. A rather more nuanced argument, but with a similarly one-sided reading of Marxism's alleged forces of production determinism, is offered by those 'discourse' theorists who grant the conjunctural pre-eminence of class conflict in certain historical periods but attack Marxism for its *a priori* classism, its tendency to privilege the working class among a plurality of possible hegemonic subjects 'whose forms of constitution and diversity it is only possible to think if we relinquish the category of "subject" as a unified and unifying essence'.[6]

The remit of these critiques of Marxism (apart from their misinterpretations, to which we shall return) obviously can have little salience in explaining the impasse in those countries where social democratic parties, which have long since rejected—or never adopted—Marxist analysis, have been the focal point of working-class politics. Whatever their relevance to the Second International's practice before the First World War or to the contemporary politics of the French Communist Party, they are largely beside the point if we are trying to understand the impasse today in Britain or West Germany or Sweden. Far more germane, therefore, is the interpretation of the impasse offered by Eric Hobsbawm in his attempt to confront the crisis of British Labourism. Hobsbawm has consistently identified a declining secular trend in Labour Party voting corresponding with the relative numerical decline of the manual working class and a growing sectionalism among trade unionists as the two fundamental problems which socialists had to analyse and overcome. Neither engaging in the caricature of Marxism so evident elsewhere, nor calling for the abandonment of the working class (his model is clearly the Italian Communist Party which 'is and wishes to remain a classical mass socialist labour party, attempting to rally the widest range of forces around its essential core of the working class'), Hobsbawm nevertheless insists that the old formula that governed socialist strategy in the first half of this century (that is, 'class = support for the worker's party = being against capitalism = for socialism') no longer automatically obtains. Even among the core of Labour's traditional manual working-class support, as Hobsbawm increasingly has come to argue since the disastrous results of the 1983 election, and as Stuart Hall repeatedly warned before it, the long-standing pull of traditional loyalties have considerably frayed, especially under the impact of the dissolving effects of consumerism and mobility on working-class communities.[7]

Although the tenor of the argument sometimes gave the impression of sociological reductionism regarding the declining working class, and of a remarkably uncharitable portrayal of trade-union behaviour (which largely ignored the unrequited wage restraint practised under the social contract), it needs to be recalled that Hobsbawm insisted that what he was describing was an avoidable crisis:

> Marxists are not economic and social determinists, and it simply will not do to say that the crisis of the working class and the socialist movement was 'inevitable', that nothing could have been done about it. . . . If we are to explain the stagnation or crisis, we have to look at the Labour Party and the labour movement itself. The workers, and growing strata outside the manual workers, were looking to it for a lead and a policy. They did not get it. They got the Wilson years—and many of them lost faith and hope in the mass party of the working people.[8]

Because Hobsbawm was looking for, nay, insisting on, more than superficial analysis of the impasse and solutions to it, one might have expected that a serious and sustained analysis of the role of the Labour Party would have been undertaken, not as an academic exercise nor one directed at finding the appropriate culprits to blame, but in order to lay the basis for a truly innovative way forward. As sensitive and acute an historian as Eric Hobsbawm could hardly have imagined that the Wilson years or the Callaghan years which followed were accidents of

Labour's history rather than products of it, nor that fundamental change in the leadership, and more importantly, the long-standing orientation of political parties is something that might be affected smoothly, without the pain and cost associated with rancour and division. Yet apart from the kind of passing comment offered above, this analysis of the party's historical contribution to the construction of the impasse has not been forthcoming. On the contrary, the brunt of Hobsbawm's attention (and ire) has been directed towards a polemic against those very forces in the Labour Party which have sought such changes in organization, personnel, ideology and policy as would forestall a continuation of the practice of the Wilson/Callaghan years. The thrust of change is portrayed as irresponsibly divisive in the face of the need for a popular front against Thatcherite reaction. The attempt to require of the leadership a commitment to mobilization and education towards a socialist transition is caricatured and derided as an ultra-leftist attempt to establish a 'correct position and wait for the British people to recognize how wrong they are in not agreeing with it.' And, despite his insistence that the 'solution lies not in changing the workers, but the party' (as if the whole brunt of his analysis on economism and sectionalism does not belie such false polarities and does not implicitly require that the workers as well as the party be changed), it is he who insists that Labour return to the traditional presentation of itself as a 'broad people's party' as the fount of its politics. He demands that the party define its socialism in terms of 'a fair, free, socially just society', realistic policy, awareness of the conflicting sectional interests of workers, and, above all, in terms of Labour having an electoral chance to immediately form a government. This may indeed presage a different politics than practised during the Wilson—Callaghan years, but it is cast in such familiarly general terms as to invite the question of what is new?

Precisely because Hobsbawm no longer undertakes a serious examination of the Labour Party's role during what he takes to be a long period of decline rather than a sudden fall from grace, precisely because he levels his political critique against those who call for a more explicitly socialist orientation for the party, his intervention does indeed bring to mind the earlier revisionist debate at the end of the 1950s when it was argued that Labour had to abandon outmoded socialist nostrums to catch up with an embourgeoisified working class. The parallel has been repeatedly drawn in the debate that has raged around the new revisionism, but it is really only germane in one respect, and that is for a common crude determinism which moves directly from socio-economic changes to the orientations of the electorate, without a serious examination of the role of the party as an intervening variable. James Cronin has gone to the heart of the matter in contending that what is at issue is not the empirical validity of the new revisionism's descriptions of changes in social structure or voting behaviour, but rather that 'they remain embedded in a form of analysis which . . . is distinguished by the simplicity of its understanding of the link between politics and class structure'. In other words: 'The recourse to social structural explanation is had, therefore, even before the political dimensions of the problem are recognised and discussed, and certainly prior to the development and testing of any argument that assumes that the political crisis might in fact be rooted in factors that are themselves primarily political in nature.'[9] This recalls Frank Parkin's riposte to the earlier revisionist contention that the de-radicalization of socialist parties was a necessary response to changing attitudes on the parts of its supporters. His point was that this approach ignored the extent to which parties are themselves critical to the formation of working-class political perceptions: 'It seems plausible to suggest that if socialist parties ceased to present a radical, class-oriented meaning system to their supporters, then such an outlook would not persist of its own among the subordinate class . . . This is really to assert that the mass party has a potentially more formative influence on the political perceptions and understanding of the subordinate class than is generally acknowledged.'[10]

When cast in this light, it immediately becomes clear that Hobsbawm's equation regarding the period of 'forward march' ('class = support for the worker's party = being against capitalism = for socialism'), which captures so much of the new revisionism's assumptions regarding the historical trajectory of working-class politics before the socio-economic changes that allegedly produced the impasse, actually represents a form of class reductionism which fails to acknowledge how indirect and tenuous the posited identities actually were. Hobsbawm acknowledges that even when a growing number of workers could have been relied on to accept the equation, that itself 'was not enough, as the history of the Labour Party shows'. But what he does not do is analyse to what extent the historical practice of the party, during the period of 'forward march' no less than later, was not merely 'not enough' but actually served to render the equation invalid.

The first point that must be made in this respect is that the primary association between class identity and workers' party was always far more ambiguous in the case of the Labour Party than is currently admitted. It must be remembered that the attachment of the dense network of pre-existing working-class institutions to the Labour Party in the first decades of this century took place in a manner, unlike the case in much of Western Europe, whereby the party was itself little involved as an agency in the formation of class identity and community. As Cronin puts it, the trade-union leadership came to attach its organizations to Labour, thereby making it a mass workers' party, by virtue of the political vacuum left by the Liberals' resistance to growing union strength:

> Into this vacuum the Labour party stumbled. I mean stumbled in a very serious way, because it is impossible to detect any particularly keen political intelligence running though the party's organization or appeal in this period, nor can one find any particularly dramatic transformation of consciousness among working people. . . . The Labour Party, in short, won the allegiance first of the leaders of the working class and its organizations and then of the workers as a whole, but less by its own organizational efforts than by default on the part of the other parties. This would mean, of course, that the fit between the outlook and policies of the party and the attitudes and beliefs of working people would be highly imperfect, and in general much less close than the organizational links between the party and the class. Only to the extent that the party's thinking was itself fuzzy and unclear and to the extent that its appeals were based upon class identity rather than program did it reflect what might be called the underlying consciousness of its supporters. This rather vacuous and negative compatibility would serve Labour well enough when the fortunes of the party and the class were for one or another reason on the rise, but it would do far less well in periods when the climate was unfavourable. [11]

It must immediately be added, moreover, that Labour's own ideological self-identification as a class party (and hence its very 'class appeal') was always a particularly tortured and ambiguous one, despite its manifest organizational, financial and electoral working-class grounding. Hence the extent to which it reinforced and extended class identity vis-à-vis its supporters—actual and potential—is by no means something to be taken for granted. Labour's predominant ideological orientation was consistently one of presenting itself as a national party, not in the Gramscian sense of formulating and leading a hegemonic class project, but in the conventional idealist sense of defining a 'national interest' above classes. Fabianism and Macdonald's 'organic' conceptions of socialism (the watchword of which was 'not class consciousness but community consciousness') most clearly represented this 'national' as opposed to class ideological orientation. This is not to say that the party did not represent and even formulate working class demands, but it did so in a manner that *a priori* conceived these demands as inherently partial and sectional. Labour certainly lived off, electorally and organizationally speaking, the existing consciousness of the class, but far from carrying it to a hegemonic political plane it attached itself to it through reinforcing and on many occasions actively inducing those values of moderation, responsibility and class harmony that encapsulate class identity within a subordinate framework. This orientation was never ubiquitous in the party and intra-party conflict very often could be traced to implicit challenges to this predominant thrust. But it gathered strength through the course of the century rather than attenuated, particularly so long as social democracy was able to conceal the fundamental contradiction contained in its planning plus class harmony strategy by virtue of the conjunctural inter-class collaboration that emerged around the mixed economy and the welfare state after 1945.

The broad-based alliance that produced the 1945 Labour government's massive majority did indeed contain within it considerable popular radicalism. But, Gareth Stedman Jones is by no means wrong to point out that 'the present appeal of 1945 is not primarily based upon an assessment of its policies, but rather upon a nostalgia for the social and political alliance upon which it was based'. From Morgan Phillips's concern as general secretary of the party during the 1945 electoral campaign to 'remove at the outset any lingering impression that the Labour Party is a class party'[12] to the predominance of Beveridge's liberalism and Durban's Fabianism in the programmatic and ideological framework of the new government, the ideological orientation which promulgated planning and class harmony as the embodiment of socialism remained dominant. This foreshadowed a series of reforms which, with great consequences for future developments, foreclosed rather than opened up a 'forward march for labour'. Stedman Jones, who shares a good many of the new revisionism's prescriptions for current strategy, is correct when he points out regarding the 1945 government that 'the assumption of social reform and post-war reconstruction for the welfare of, rather than by the agency, power and intelligence of, the working class remained deeply ingrained.'[13] Hobsbawm, of course, has contributed much himself to such an understanding of the historical limits of Labourism. Indeed, on the landslide of 1945, he once wrote: 'This does not mean that the reformist leadership of the labour movement has become any less wedded to the status quo; if anything the opposite has been the case. It is quite easy to justify a moderate policy in socialist as it is in conservative phrases; the former may be even more effective.'[14]

What Hobsbawm did not recognize then and fails to acknowledge now is that Labourism is a practice that has had no little bearing not just on reproducing reformist attitudes among workers but on the actual withering away of the party's class base. *And here we come to the nub of the matter.* The discourse theorists are by no means wrong to place enormous stress on ideological and cultural factors in the formation of social and political subjects. Class identity, class consciousness, class politics, are indeed but one of a number of possible forms of collective expression even in a capitalist society, and it is by no means an automatic and inevitable outcome of economic locations in productive relations alone. Where the discourse theorists falter is in their utter relativism. They fail to recognize that the salience of relations of production provides great potential, by virtue of their central place in the constitution of social arrangements in general as well as their inherently exploitative and hence contradictory and conflictual character, for struggles about and around the formation of class subjects; and that in turn the possibility of realizing a socialist project cannot conceivably do without working-class identity, consciousness and politics forming its mass base and organizational core. This is not only because of the potential size of a collectivity which draws on those who occupy subordinate positions in production relations, but again because of the centrality of such a collectivity to the constitutive principle of the whole social order. If the issue is in fact social transformation, the supercession of capitalism as a system, then the mobilization of the working class's potential range and power is the key organizational and ideological condition. It is hardly sufficient, but it *is* necessary.

But here is where the Labour's 'discourse' precisely comes in. There was indeed no basis for an assumption that the class identities formed among manual workers in their trade unions and local communities through their experience of and struggles against an earlier industrial capitalism ('the making of the working class') would *automatically* persist, let alone extend to new occupational strata of workers or to new communities. Much less was there ground for thinking that left to itself this old class culture would transcend occupational, industrial or local particularisms or the economism and sectionalism that so often are their trade-union expression. And least of all should it have been thought that a hegemonic class self-identification and political orientation *vis-à-vis* other groups and classes, including that aspect of it that involves being 'against capitalism and for socialism', would directly flow from the numerical growth of workers (manual *or* other) or even their electoral 'support for a workers' party'. The whole point of inserting the working-class party into the equation as a mediating factor between class and socialism—and, putting it less abstractly and formally than equations allow, the historic importance of the formation of *mass* working-class parties around the turn of the century—was precisely that they were potentially more than the electoral aggregators of individual expressions of pre-existing class identity, projecting them into the state arena as conduits for the attainment of governmental office by party leaders (socialist or otherwise). Mass working-class parties were rather the essential condition in the twentieth century for the reinforcement, recomposition and extension of class identity and community itself in the face of a capitalism which continually deconstructed and reconstructed industry, occupation and locale. They were also the essential mechanism for the transcendence of sectionalism, particularism and economism not only through the national identity given to the class through its association with the party's project of winning state office, but through their potential role in socialist education and mobilization. Ater all, if the notion of a hegemonic class project means anything, if the struggle for socialism *was* to be more than elitist, vanguardist, a war of manoeuvre (pick your anti-Leninist adjective), then it above all required class identity and community of a new kind. This had to include widespread understanding of how capitalism worked in general, of why supporting a workers party meant being against capitalism as a system, and of a socialist vision that meant more than 'more' in the particular and economistic sense, all leading to a self-confidence on the part of a very great number of working-class activists to provide leadership in their wider communities in relation to multifarious forms of subordination, deprivation and struggle.

That the Labour Party has not played this role has a great deal to do with the impasse of working-class politics. In so far as non-manual workers in the service, commercial or retail sectors do not see themselves or politics in class terms, this has something to do, if we do not have an economic reductionist view of class formation (whether of a vulgar Marxist or modernization school variety), with Labour's discourse. Labour tended, especially in the critical post-war period that witnessed the growth and even the unionization of these new strata of workers, to define working class in terms of an old 'sectional' manual industrial stratum, to define white-collar occupations as 'middle class' in the conventional bourgeois terms of income, education and status, and to take as evidence for the need to move even further away from the language of class politics the expansion of this grossly conceived 'middle-class'. As old manual working-class communities declined and the locus of a new manual working class shifted to new industries and locales, a privatized 'instrumental collectivism' replaced old communal solidarities and became the fount of a largely apolitical trade-union militancy. This cannot be separated, however, from the failure of the party even to try to refashion new class communities by engaging the 'affluent' worker in class terms—that is, other than trying to use the old class loyalties of the union leadership to prove that Labour could secure wage restraint from the unions where the Tories could not. It is all too often forgotten that Goldthorpe and Lockwood ended their famous study with this very observation, and one may perhaps be forgiven therefore for quoting them at length in this regard:

> It is . . . difficult to accept entirely at face value the argument typically advanced by those advocating a 'centrist' strategy that this is made *necessary* by the changing nature of economic and social conditions—that it represents the only realistic and responsible line of development of Labour politics within the affluent society. Rather, we would suggest, such advocacy must be understood as being itself a political initiative—an attempt at political leadership—intended to take the party away from radical politics of a class-oriented kind because a move in this direction is regarded as inherently desirable. . . .
>
> However, the fact that the strategy in question is *not* empirically well-grounded has significant consequences. It means, for example, that Labour has in one sense underestimated the potential firmness of its support among the working class and thus the possibilities offered by retaining—and developing—its class base. On the other hand, though, it means that the effects that affluence and its concomitants most probably *have* had on the working-class Labour vote have been neglected. That is, the tendency for a purely affective or customary attachment to Labour to give way to one of a somewhat more calculative kind: an attachment likely to be more dependent on Labour clearly and consistently demonstrating it *is* the party of the working man. This neglect would appear to have become particularly far-reaching in its implications in the course of the second Wilson administration. Government economic policies—notably in regard to prices and incomes and industrial relations—have not been manifestly favourable to working-class interests, and there have been few compensating measures of a radically redistributive or otherwise egalitarian kind. Under such circumstances, it is not hard to envisage the frustration of the affluent worker's private economic ambitions leading to still further attenuation of the links between localised trade union collectivism and electoral support for the Labour Party. [15]

The terrible irony of this prediction is that its coming to fruition, as manifest in the decline in the Labour vote in the 1970s and early 1980s, is now taken as the basis for a renewed determinist reading of electoral trends (what might now be called the 'Crewe–Hobsbawm School of Psephology') which asserts the necessity again for a centrist strategy and an attack on radical politics of a class-oriented kind. If any critique of this new revisionism is to be more than facile, however, it must be recognized that the perverse electoral consequences of Labour's rejection of class politics are the remit, not merely of the policies of the previous Labour government or the one before it, not even of the revisionism of the 1950s, but of the much older and deeper practice whose effects in terms of the withering away of working-class political identities are by now very difficult to reverse. The long term socio-economic changes, in other words, have had many of the effects it was claimed they would precisely because of *long-term* political and ideological practices, and immediate electoral tactics are actually framed in terms of *their* all-too-real effects. The two most systematic studies of working-class attitudes which actually compare British workers with Swedish and French (Scase and Gallie)[16] *do* find that British workers are far less class conscious in any sense that is meaningful for the prosecution of socialist politics *and that the long-standing ideological and organizational practices of the working class parties in each country are among the primary determinants of this difference.* This should hardly be surprising. Apart from the ambiguous and tenuous and defensive nature of Labour's class appeal, the very fact that a mass party of Labour's size and importance has not been able to sponsor or sustain throughout the post-war years a mass readership socialist newspaper speaks volumes to the failure of the party in defining the language and terrain of politics in distinctive enough terms to make class politics viable. This is not only a matter of failing to provide a class and socialist discourse for new potential supporters, but of the consequences for traditional supporters. Raymond Williams tells the story of his mother who took the old Labour *Herald* because she was a trade unionist. When Hugh Cudlipp took it over and changed its name and orientation in the 1950s with the Labour Party's blessing to 'modernize' it, she continued taking it. And when it was again taken over by Rupert Murdoch and changed its name in 1967, she also kept taking it. Whenever asked what happened to Labour 'opinion', Williams points to the history of the chauvinist newspaper, the *Sun*. [17]

What all this means is that the roots of the impasse do indeed extend very deep in British society. Those who would point to the growth of trade-union membership and the extensive militancy through the 1960s and 1970s as evidence for the continued salience of class and class conflict are by no means wrong to do so. But the fact is that the main expression of class struggle took place on the limited terrain of the industrial sphere and was not attended by a politicization which could overcome the sectionalism and economism of instrumental collectivism. This certainly belied romantic assumptions regarding the direct revolutionary implications of this militancy even as it increasingly confirmed the inherent instability and contradictory character of the Keynesian social democratic state. To be sure, the constant tendency of the Labour leadership—in and out of office and including the 1945 government no less than subsequent ones—was to see this militancy entirely as a 'problem' for the macroeconomic management of the economy. It was something to be restrained and co-opted via centralized corporatist arrangements with the union leadership designed to insulate them from membership pressures and instil capitalist growth criteria within the formulation of union wage policy. This needs to be stressed as one of the major long-term practices that contributed to the construction of the impasse. Far from support for the workers' party equating itself into being 'against capitalism', Labour governments took any indications that trade-union militancy involved such a dimension as the evil product of 'tightly knit groups of politically motivated men'.

The issue is not one of 'betrayals' by this or that government. Of course there were many betrayals, not least the promise of full partnership for union leaders in the making of economic policy alongside capital and the state or of the promise that wage restraint would be compensated for by controls over investment and prices, and by income and wealth redistribution. But the union leadership's readiness to practise wage restraint short of these conditions being met, and the second-order prioritization they gave to these aspects of the social contract under each post-war Labour government as compared with industrial relations reforms which facilitated what Richard Hyman has recently pointed to as the *passive* growth of union membership ('boosting union numbers without winning workers' active commitment') must be counted in as part of the equation. [18] Yet, even given all this, it can hardly be said that the Labour leadership betrayed mass socialist aspirations, for these were far from the direct source either of the Labour vote or of union militancy. On the contrary, the very identification of socialism with the corporatist and bureaucratic practices of an increasingly cramped Keynesian welfare state certainly did create considerable popular space for what finally became embodied in Thatcher's market populist appeal amidst a politically privatized and only instrumentally collectivist working class. The appeal of less taxation, law and order and chauvinism can be a strong one, even if only temporarily, when reformism has little else on offer.

The Challenge from the Left

If the foregoing argument would seem to indicate that the obvious strategic alternative to an increasingly cramped and beleaguered collaborationism lies in the attempt to turn social democratic parties towards a more explicitly socialist orientation, as was undertaken by the left in the Labour Party after 1979, it must at the same time be said that here is where the full awesome measure of the impasse becomes visible. For what the British experience indicates is that the very attempt to transform the party in such a way that it becomes a vehicle for socialist mobilization is no easy task, however discredited pre-existing practices have become. This is because the prerequisite working-class identity and self-confidence, let alone the mass popular support for socialist ideas and alternatives, can hardly be said to be ready made after decades of social democratic practice but have in good part to be constructed anew. It is also because the very attempt to change the party in such a fundamental manner inevitably results in such severe internal party divisions as to undermine the immediate defensive role which such parties play against right-wing forces, at least in immediate electoral terms. It is in no small part the recognition of this that has led many socialist intellectuals to turn against the Labour left with considerable vigour. Unfortunately, in their apportioning of blame for Labour's divisions they fall wide of the mark, as they do, moreover, in their facile promise of the viability of a return to reformist gradualism and consensus politics.

What took place in the Labour Party after 1979 was certainly the best organized, most inspired and most sustained attempt in the party's history at turning it from a party of defensive and tepid reform and integration into a party of socialist mobilization and transformation. The profundity of this challenge has less to do with the specificities of the Alternative Economic Strategy, the constitutional reforms, or the changes in defence policy, than with the strength of determination and the degree of talent and skill that was unleashed by a new understanding on the part of so many activists of the severe qualitative limitations of Labourism as ideology and practice. It was precisely Tony Benn's remarkable ability to articulate this understanding that allowed him to represent the disparate forces that composed the new Labour left. Whereas the old Tribune left tended to see its project as returning the party to its traditions, when the party was allegedly more socialist, the new Bennite left came far closer to defining its goals in terms of wrenching Labour out of its traditions, of breaking definitively with the class harmony orientation that from the inception of the party determined the integrative kind of parliamentarianism and the non-transformative kind of reformism that Labour practised.

It was the very novelty of this challenge, and the fact that it emanated from a far larger group of activists than could be directly associated with 'entryism', that ensured that far more was at stake than a slight alteration in the distribution of power in the party. The *grand peur* induced by the British press with regard to what was happening in the Labour Party, fed and encouraged as it was by much of the old guard, may have been caricature but it was not mirage. The propaganda campaign against the Labour left—Tony Benn became for a period the most vilified man in the media next to the Ayatollah Khomeini—was not undertaken for nothing. Like all effective propaganda it had just enough of a rational kernel of truth to it to make plausible the dire warnings of the imminent victory of the socialist hordes over the old responsible and reasonable Labour leaders.

Perhaps the most superficial and damaging aspect of the new revisionism has been its *parti pris* attack on the Labour left as bearing primary responsibility for Thatcher's re-election in 1983. Whereas the 1979 defeat was portrayed in terms of the direct effect of long-term socio-economic changes on Labour's traditional vote, the 1983 defeat is attributed very largely to the immediate electoral effects of the Labour left's campaign to change the party. According to Hobsbawm, the left thought 'a Thatcher government was preferable to a reformist Labour government'.[19] According to many others the left sought a continuation of the old 'orthodox socialism' which, with an astonishing gloss on Labour's actual history, they see as the root of Labour's long-term failure. The misrepresentation this involves, even if one agrees that Labour's divisions were a real factor in the defeat, is familiar enough for those acquainted with the heat generated in splits on the left, but this hardly makes it acceptable. This is not just a matter of insisting that the assault on the old leadership and ways of the party after 1979 were not just a product of the strategy of the Campaign for Labour Party Democracy much less of Militant and even less of Tony Benn all by himself, but were a decade-long outgrowth of the severe crisis of

Labourism and the spectacular disappointments which the Wilson and Callaghan governments represented for so many Labour and trade-union activists. Nor is it just a matter of insisting on the genuineness of the belief on the part of these activists that unity around a radical socialist programme—which obviously had to include, if unity was the condition for success, trying to ensure that the parliamentary leadership would subscribe to, campaign for and attempt to implement it—would alone create the popular understanding of the causes and dimensions of the economic crisis and hence renew Labour's credibility so that Thatcher could be defeated next time. Even if the immediate appeal of such a programme was over-optimistically presumed, any adequate reappraisal of the thrust for change and the direction it took after 1979 must surely put it in the context of the proximate failure of Callaghan's tired corporatist, 'give-the-social-contract-another-chance' appeal in the 1979 election, the high number of working-class abstentions in that election, the poor showing of Thatcher's government in the opinion polls until the Falklands episode, and the fact that socialist parties won elections in Greece and France in 1981 on the basis of programmes more radical than the Alternative Economic Strategy.

Without denying the severity of reaction that the ideology that became known as Thatcherism represented, or even its ability to galvanize certain popular attitudes, it should at the same time be remembered that even those who first drew attention to the hegemonic potential of Thatcherism, most notably Stuart Hall in 'The Great Moving Right Show', insisted that 'the contradictions within social democracy are the key to the whole rightward shift in the political spectrum'. Hall identified Labour's corporatist practice, which 'requires that the indissoluble link between party and class be used not to advance but to *discipline* the class and the organisations it represents', as lying at the core of these contradictions: 'The rhetoric of "national interest" which is the principal ideological form in which a succession of defeats has been imposed on the working class by social democracy in power, are exactly the sites where this contradiction shows through and is being constantly reworked.'[20] To accuse the Labour left of bad political judgement for not taking Thatcherism seriously enough, as Hobsbawm did after the 1983 election, misses completely the understanding that was shown on the left of the basis for Thatcher's populist anti-corporatist appeal. It misses as well the importance of the Labour left having placed at the centre of its objective not more nationalization (this was a minor strain after 1979, when most of the left was quite prepared to live with what had been articulated in the 1973 programme) but the democratization of the party. The hardly ambiguous manner in which so many socialist intellectuals who have now taken their distance from Benn were earlier prepared to see Benn as their standard bearer had a great deal to do with Benn's own populist arguments for democratization against a Labourism which had not only become enmeshed in the state apparatus, but which had used parliamentarism as a means of stifling the socialist aspirations that constantly resurfaced in the party.

But even if all this is granted, the truly astonishing aspect of the new revisionist quickie history of the 1979–83 conflicts in the party is the extent to which it forgets that it takes two to tango. The resistance of the preponderant part of the parliamentary leadership to the constitutional reforms; the fuelling of the press hysteria on these reforms by labelling them as undemocratic on the basis of the most narrow parliamentarist nostrums; the readiness with which not only those MPs who left the party, but so many who stayed used adjectives like ultra, extremist and crazy with abandon—all this can hardly be ignored in assessing the 'suicidal civil war' in the party. Are socialist historians suddenly to cast themselves in the mould of those who understand political instability and conflict in terms of the responsibility that those who challenge the powers-that-be must bear for it?

A proper history of this period in the party obviously cannot be presented here, but perhaps the most critical illustration of the need for a more nuanced assessment of the causes and electoral consequences of the intra-party divisions may be signalled. What becomes especially clear as one re-examines the flow of events in this period is that the primary strategic consideration of the right wing of the Labour Party, the predominant part of which stayed in the party rather than joined the Social Democratic Party, was not unity but rather the belief that Labour could only win if it could be shown that the left were defeated inside the party before the election. This was particularly seen after Benn's narrow loss to Healey at the 1981 conference. The 'peace agreement' insisted on and provisionally secured by the Trade Unions for Labour Victory at Bishop's Stortford in January 1982 was followed by a series of initiatives, most notably the drive to expel Militant, in which right-wing union leaders like Sid Weighell, Terry Duffy and John Boyd took the lead, and whose inflammatory speeches against the left were echoed by Hattersley, Shore and Healey in the context of trying to block reselections in the ensuing months. It was Benn who was led to warn in this context at a National Executive Committee meeting in March 1982: 'The media will have a field day if we throw people one by one to the lions. I don't think we can gain by it.'[21] And so they did. For the last year and a half before the election, it was the left in the party that was on the defensive against a right that tenaciously clung to the view that the key to electoral success was to prove that the Bennite, Marxist, Marxist–Leninist, or Trotskyist left (the terms varied, but the scope assigned to them was commonly sweeping) had been marginalized in the party.

It is hardly anything new in the history of the Labour Party that on the basis of immediate electoral calculations it has been the left rather than the right which has tended to assume the burden of party unity. The tide in the party changed not after the disastrous defeat of the 1983 election, but a year and a half before, as not just the revolutionary entryist left but the Labour Co-ordinating Committee and the Campaign for Labour Party Democracy ran up against the most formidable barrier to change in the Labour Party: the need for party unity in order to maintain Labour's immediate electoral utility as a defensive agency for the working class. This is a real need always policed by the unions and one whose primacy was felt all the more urgently as the unions proved increasingly unable to provide, under conditions of mass unemployment, their own defence against Thatcherite reaction of the kind they had been able to mount against Heath's 'Selsdon man' a decade before. The case that unity around a radical socialist programme would alone renew Labour's credibility could not carry enough weight in the party, particularly because the leading agents in the drive for defensive unity, that portion of the old Tribune left ranged around Foot, had a very strong base in the party. Their position rested, as always needs be in the case of the Labour Party, on a considerable part of the union leadership, but it also had a degree of appeal to constituency activists of a kind that the right wing of the party could never muster on its own. This determined, moreover, that the shift in the balance of forces in the party after 1981 would outlast the run up to the 1982 election. Tariq Ali's and Quintin Hoare's judgement in this respect that 'the Foot/Kinnock recipe of fudging all issues in order to restore the old *status quo ante*' could not achieve longer-term success was severely mistaken: '[The] option, favoured by Foot and the bulk probably of the union leadership, is to strive to restore the Grand Old Party as before . . . . It involves fudging over unwelcome conference policies and minimising the practical effect of recent constitutional changes, rather than defeating them as the right would like . . . . At bottom, this option is a short term one, unlikely to survive either Foot himself or the next general election.'[22]

The strength of the Foot–Healey/Kinnock–Hattersley alliance, wherein the paramount concern for defensive unity is conjoined to the tenacious belief that the key to electoral success lies in marginalizing the left, has very great implications, moreover, for the 'popular front' strategy advanced by the new revisionism. The impression is sometimes given that this strategy primarily entails the forging of alliances with the new social movements, articulating the demands of women, blacks, and the peace movement to Labour's working-class base in a hegemonic socialist project. Yet however attractive this may sound in abstract terms, this is not the substantive element of the strategy actually being advanced, the key component of which entails ensuring that the old Gaitskellite right, with its enormous presence and respectability in the media, adheres to a broad anti-Thatcherite front centred around the Labour Party. This is not in the first instance a matter of entering into an electoral or parliamentary coalition with the Alliance (as, for instance, Hobsbawm's detractors have been too quick to insist) nearly as much as guantanteeing that the hazy compromises struck in the Foot–Healey era, which involved limiting the electoral damages done by the SDP split and preventing further defections by the Labour right, are fully stabilized in the Kinnock–Hattersley era. What the alliance with the parliamentary right means, however, is that the very attempt to restructure the party so that it might become a central site and vehicle for struggles by women and blacks as well as rank-and-file workers must be effectively constrained. The persistent refusal of the leadership and their trade-union allies to proposals to give the Women's Conference effective powers in the party even if only to elect directly the women's representatives on the National Executive Committee) notably supported by the National Union of Mineworkers alone among the unions at the 1984 conference), their opposition to black sections, their inaction on the establishment of work-place branches (passed by the 1981 conference)—all this tells us a great deal about the true nature of the alliances being (re)constructed in the Labour Party.

The critical factor that must be recognized is that the popular front strategy, as was so often the case with popular fronts in the past, has far less to do with the activation at the base than with alliances at the top among parliamentary and union elites. The centre of gravity necessarily rests with those elites closest to the centre of the political spectrum whose adherence to an anti-Thatcher coalition is the central condition of success for the whole strategy. The main issue is not the question of the viability of popular fronts in the past, although it is tempting to point out as against the gloss that Hobsbawm puts on them that the parallel with the 1930s and the war is, to say the least, strained; that the fact that it was the Labour centre and right that rejected the popular front in the 1930s (to the point of expulsions of those on the left of the party who advanced it) goes strangely unmentioned; and that Hobsbawm astonishingly asserts that it was the popular front strategy that 'produced ten new states setting out to construct socialism' without mentioning the role of the Red Army in Eastern Europe or the readiness with which Communists were dropped from post-war governments in Western Europe when it suited their erstwhile partners. But the main issue is the here and now, and in this respect the real choices are not between an abstract 'broad alliance' line and an equally abstract 'class against class' line. What is on offer, what is available in the 'defensive unity' model Labour Party, is a parliamentarist alliance under the hegemony of a party leadership whose centrist political strategy precisely embodies Bernard Crick's disarmingly honest prescription that 'however inadequate and over-empirical the old Butskellism was, we have to win the country back to that middle ground before we can move forward from it'.[23] Unfortunately, that very practice, as we have seen, precludes moving forward.

Theorists of the New Social Contract

The widespread shift in opinion among socialist intellectuals towards a less 'orthodox' and more 'realistic' approach has been remarkable for its virtually exclusive concern with the tactical considerations involved in the formation of 'broad alliances' and for its relative silence and vagueness on programmatic questions. To Raymond William's charge that the anti-Thatcher 'coalitionists' appear basically content with reviving old Butskellite policies which are inadequate 'for any sustained recovery or advance', Hobsbawm has replied that the question of developing policies that go beyond 'trying to make the best of a bad job and give capitalism "a human face"' by trying to 'envisage a British socialism' is indeed a crucial one. But he consistently sets aside any further discussion of this for the prior tactical one of re-electing a Labour Government. However, a few others (all too few) who share the view that the failures of socialist politics have mainly to do with the narrow class-centredness of its practice in the face of a changing class structure have attempted to address the difficult issues involved with the development of programmatic alternatives that would complement the 'realism' involved in the 'broad alliance' position. As Mike Prior and Dave Purdy argued in 1979:

> It cannot be too strongly emphasised that the politics of hegemony are not to be equated with the winning of allies, whether socially in terms of the broad democratic alliance, or politically in terms of an alliance of political parties. What must underpin any such alliance, and is the only safeguard against the degeneration of hegemonic politics into backroom deals and electoral manoeuvres, is a firm commitment to the *policies* of hegemony and the transformation of social practice. [24]

Far less ink has been spilled on this since 1979 than on tactical questions, but as we shall see what has emerged in policy terms from this perspective evinces a clear tendency to return to slightly amended versions of those very reforms that were thrown up in the 1970s and failed to generate those crucial ingredients which would make them viable—the co-operation of the bourgeoisie and the commitment of the Labour leadership to them. Moreover, it is one of the paradoxical aspects of these programmatic discussions that, although they insist that the working class can no longer occupy the exclusive or central place in socialist strategy, they nevertheless concentrate their attention very largely on developing policies for the participation of organized labour in national economic and enterprise-level decision making. A cynical explanation of this would be that, having abandoned the perspective that organized labour can be the fount of a socialist 'solution', they have come to the view that the trade unions are the central 'problem'. Yet it would appear that this is in fact a reflection of the fundamental ambiguity of the new revisionism in its attitude to the working class. Its hostility to trade-union militancy and its insistence on the decline of the working class is uncomfortably conjoined with an appreciation (even an exaggeration) of the salience of organized labour in the economy and of its potential power as an agency for extending economic and industrial democracy.

This ambiguity is most clearly seen in the proposals that have re-emerged on the left for the development of a new social contract as the programmatic centrepiece of socialist strategy. In the view of Dave Purdy, Paul Hirst, Gavin Kitching and Geoff Hodgson, among others, the traditional trade-union obsession with economistic wage demands and their defence of unfettered collective bargaining has been reinforced by a romantic and pseudo-revolutionary perspective among socialists which condemns outright any involvement by the unions in the management of the capitalist economy, denies any responsibility for unions in causing—or solving—economic crises, and naively views the defeat of incomes policies by a militant wages struggle as a political as well as economic victory which presages a decisive confrontation. Although such a sweeping critique is a patent caricature both of past union behaviour and of the socialist opposition to incomes policies, it must nevertheless be said that many elements of their argument do contain important insights, even if these are not nearly as heretical nor as novel on the left as they insistently claim they are. Kitching, for instance, goes to the heart of the matter when he argues that: 'The tragedy of the British working class in fact is that it is neither radical enough nor self-confident enough to wish to change the system, yet it is too well-organised and economically militant to allow it to function "properly".'[25] The argument that he, like all the other advocates of incomes policy, makes to the effect that consistently high wage demands cannot be accommodated within an internationally competitive capitalist system without corresponding increases in productivity and profits is utterly conventional, but that in itself does not make it wrong, as Glyn and Sutcliffe, among many others, have insisted for a long time. Nor is Paul Hirst wrong, in making his case for 'national income planning', to insist on the importance in electoral as well economic terms of overcoming the irrationalities of the wages structure:

> To see a minority enjoying a constant or increasing standard of living whilst one's own is declining or stagnant, and simply because of the accident of the trade, firm or place where they work will be generally unacceptable. . . . Pensioners, the unemployed, recipients of social security have votes too. Unless the Labour Party can provide a credible alternative to either a wage freeze or a 'free-for-some', it could well find itself excluded from power.[26]

The well-worn insistence that collective bargaining is not in itself socialist, and that the planning of incomes has to be a feature of any socialist economic programme, may by now be tiresome, given how often it has been used by conventional Labour politicians to justify their equally conventional wage restraint policies, but again it is not wrong as cast in such general terms. All one can say is that it calls to mind once more the point made by Hobsbawm himself a long time ago, that 'it is quite easy to justify a moderate policy in socialist as it is in liberal or conservative phrases: the former may be even more effective.' Or, as he put it more recently, 'that what most Labour leaders have meant by "socialism" is rather different from what is in the minds of socialists'.[27]

Thus the fact that the advocacy of a social contract by socialist intellectuals provides a verbal meeting ground with those elements of the Labour leadership, such as Hattersley and Shore, for whom striking a wage restraint agreement with the union leadership along traditional Keynesian lines remained as much their central strategic concern through the early 1980s as it had been for Wilson, Brown and Callaghan in the early 1960s and 1970s does not invalidate such advocacy itself. The real question is whether this socialist advocacy provides different and better grounds for accepting the claim by both groups that the social contract they have in mind this time will indeed be different from what went before and was such an important element in producing the popular confusion, discord and disillusionment that led to Thatcherism.

The argument for why it is essential to premise a socialist strategy around a social contract rests on the view that it alone provides the opening within capitalism for a series of compromises between capital and labour that will both meet capital's need for wage restraint and labour market flexibility and at the same time lay the grounds for a major extension of control by workers and their representatives over economic decision-making at the national and enterprise levels. Kitching has posed the issue most clearly and deserves to be quoted at length:

> The central issue of economic policy in all advanced capitalist societies today is that of wage regulation—the need to keep wage rises broadly in line with productivity increases in order to ensure sustained growth without inflation. Monetarism is the capitalist class's response to the conviction that wage restraint cannot be attained 'voluntarily' under conditions of full employment. Yet it is also clear that wage restraint cannot be maintained with a highly unionized and compartmentalized labour market without a continuing level of mass unemployment that would threaten the very stability of capitalism, or at least would require the drastic abridgement or even the ending of democratic freedoms.
>
> It is quite likely therefore that after the monetarist experiment, advanced capitalist societies will return to Keynesian demand management and 'pump-priming' for one more and perhaps final experiment with more 'moderate' solutions. In doing so, they will once again, confront the necessity of winning mass working-class compliance with wage restraint, and various forms of 'social contract' will be born again. . .
>
> In short, capitalism in Britain may not need a 'responsible' and self-disciplined working class in order to survive. In the end, dictatorial solutions are always a possibility. But it is conceivable that capitalism in conjunction with parliamentary democracy needs such a class in order to survive. We may therefore see, in the not too distant future, a crucial

historical moment in which the British working class has an opportunity to extract major, indeed transforming, changes in the capitalist system in return for its cooperation.[28]

What Kitching proposes is that the unions seize this opportunity with both hands upon the ascension of a Labour or Labour/SDP government which he correctly discerns 'will want, sooner or later, to negotiate a "wages policy" (i.e. wage restraint) with the unions'. Instead of pushing for improved wages and conditions in the forlorn hope that capitalism's limitations in this respect will somehow radicalize workers, they should 'quite consciously offer whole-hearted cooperation to capitalism but demand in return for such cooperation concessions which aim quite consciously to change the fundamental nature of capitalism'. What he has in mind is that the unions go far beyond the usual price and dividend control and macro-economic policy demands on the social wage and unemployment, and undertake a radical 'pre-emptive unionism' by which long-term wage restraint bargains and redundancy agreements are exchanged for very precise demands, industry by industry, on 'investment policy, marketing, health and safety conditions, manning levels, retraining, an 'open books' policy.' This would entail developing within individual unions an extensive research and planning capacity (his model being the Lucas Aerospace Shop Stewards' Combine and its alternative corporate plan in the 1970s), with union initiatives for joint management of enterprises being framed in overtly 'cooperative' and 'reasonable' terms 'for the good of the industry as a whole'. In this way management resistance can be portrayed as unreasonable and authoritarian, and tactical ideological advantage can be gained by unions in management—labour relations. 'The essence of the matter is really very simple. If the British working class is to sell itself to capitalism, it must sell itself in a planned, thought-out and expensive fashion; in a fashion which, as its conditions are met, explores the limits of the concessions which capitalism can make without changing its fundamental nature'.[29]

A similar position is taken by Paul Hirst. He discerns that previous incomes policies have been rendered unstable by virtue of their effect on pay differentials that workers have struggled to maintain rather than their inequity in terms of the lack of equivalent controls on prices and high incomes. He argues that a 'socialist-egalitarian' incomes policy should explicitly seek to close differentials among workers (by erasing them 'upwards') while offsetting workers' discontent over their loss of relative status and benefits through 'a strategy of progressive increases in workers' control'. To this end he proposes linking incomes policy to the implementation of the Bullock Inquiry recommendations, so that unions can extend collective bargaining to include questions of enterprise policy and operation. Since management will not strike such bargains unless they limit the scope of trade-union struggle, this will mean that the bargains will have to 'limit the right to strike, involve the reorganisation of jobs, etc. . . [and] commit the organised workers to the enterprise in a way that limited wage negotiations never did'. But extending the scope of bargaining would mean that 'the unions recognise that changed economic conditions and their own strength necessitate and make possible . . . new forms and methods of struggle' through joint representation committees, company board representation and the development of management and economic policy knowledge and skills at the enterprise level among union personnel. Legislation by a Labour government along the lines of Bullock could serve as a catalyst for unions to enter this process as well as a means of compelling management to accept it. 'Bullock and incomes policy together represent a great lost opportunity for the trade unions and the Labour Party. It is a failure of political thinking which will have to be overcome if democratic socialism is to succeed in its objectives.'[30]

As Hirst acknowledges, this approach is very similar to that taken up by the Eurocommunist wing of the British Communist Party in the late 1970s at the time when Hobsbawm first enunciated his analysis of the crisis of British working-class politics. Although Hobsbawm was then—and has remained throughout the ensuing debate—remarkably vague with regard to programme or even policy, Mike Prior and Dave Purdy published at the same time a strong defence of the principle of the social contract ('as distinct from the Labour Government's current degenerated pay policy'). The novel element in the social contract, they claimed, was that it embodied the notion that 'the trade unions should not accept or be expected to accept responsibility for the performance of the economy without a corresponding extension of power to influence national policy':

> This quid pro quo principle presents a major opportunity for subverting capitalism by linking the issues of pay and inflation with those structural issues—the volume, pace and composition of investment, the pattern of production and consumption, the scale, direction and composition of foreign trade, the character and consequences of technical innovation—which under capitalism are determined anarchically as the outcome of private action and decision beyond the scope of social control. Correctly used a social contract becomes an instrument for the assertion of a coherent working class strategy

for the national economy. If offers a lever for shifting the terms of public debate and welding together a progressive social and political alliance.[31]

What are we to make of this programmatic alternative, which does indeed appear to be the one that will inform—at least in terms of the face it presents to the Labour Party—a Kinnock—Hattersley-led strategy for the next election? It must be said, first of all, that it is not quite as novel in many respects as its various authors claim. For the first two or three years of the 1945 Labour government, it was the left in the labour movement, and especially in the unions, which insisted on the importance of a wages policy, manpower planning and the democratization of the administration of the newly nationalized industries as part of a strategy for transforming wartime planning into socialist planning. In the late 1950s and early 1960s a group of socialist intellectuals on the Labour left—Royden Harrison, Michael Barratt Brown, Ken Alexander and John Hughes—issued a series of pamphlets which presented a sustained argument for a wages policy as part of a socialist strategy for the Labour Party along very much the same lines as is being heard today. Nor is it the case that the unions did not try to make their support for the wage restraint they have undertaken for every Labour government in the post-war era conditional upon 'a corresponding extension of power to influence national policy'. Even if all too few of them were as clear as Frank Cousins in insisting that fundamental change from what he called the 'trade union function' in the existing system was conditional on a Labour government actually trying to 'change the system', it should be recalled that the 1964 Trades Union Congress's support for an incomes policy was not only made conditional on 'the planned growth of wages' as opposed to conventionl wage restraint, but on 'the extension of public ownership based on popular control on a democratic basis at all levels'. It is certainly true that the unions' conditions for participation in the social contract a decade later were set out, under the influence of Jack Jones, much less vaguely and with less bombast and more detail than conference speeches and resolutions promote, particularly in terms of going beyond demands for Keynesian reflation and formal price and dividend controls to insist on the planning agreements, the closing of wage differentials and the industrial democracy proposals (that directly led to the Bullock Inquiry), all of which came to compose the social contract. The fact that the unions practised wage restraint under every Labour government before these conditions were achieved and despite their not being achieved, may indeed say something about their priorities. But if so, it has as much, if not more, to do with the importance they have attached to the tactical considerations of getting and keeping a Labour government in office as with any unbending obsession with untrammelled wage bargaining.[32]

Just as those who are concerned primarily with such 'realistic' tactical considerations fail to grant sufficient weight to the historical role of the Labour Party in trying to understand and compensate for the decline of working-class political identity, so those who concentrate on programmatic reform fail to appreciate the extent to which Labour's previous practice underlies, *especially among left-wing union leaders and activists,* the opposition to incomes policy today. The tendency to read this opposition off, in a quite reductionist and direct manner, from a natural or at any rate traditional trade-union economism or a knee-jerk pseudo-revolutionary leftism, is all too easy and belittles the actual political experience of participation of incomes policy at the national level (or joint representation committees and their ilk at the industrial level). There can be no question that a socialist party that actually tries to undertake a radical programme involving a significant diminution of the power and privileges of capital would have to depend on, and be either dishonest or naive if it did not demand and prepare for, some considerable material sacrifice and extensive change in the heretofore established adversarial industrial practices of its working-class base. No serious socialist could argue against this, or fail to take this into her or his strategic concerns. There is far less originality about this insight, even on the British left, than our new socialist social contract theorists flatter themselves with. And there is at least some basis for thinking, especially regarding the 1945 period but also more recently, that had a Labour government actually set out on this path they could have counted on a considerable body of support in the trade unions. To put the onus on the unions for failing to realize what socialist potential existed in the social contract is perverse. As we have seen it was the danger that the unions in the mid 1970s were pushing Labour into too radical directions, *especially around Bullock* (and at a time when the wage restraint under the social contract had not yet broken down) that drove industrialists to identify their interests with Thatcherism.

What promise this gives for the future accommodation of British industrialists, even after the experience of Thatcherism, to a strategy which involves going beyond corporatist macroeconomic management to challenge their very control of their firms and the disposition of their capital by their own workers is unfortunately slight. It is not improbable that in the face of the experience of mass unemployment, the defeats that have been suffered, and the tenacity of the new right, that the unions might be prepared to yet again go quite far in practising wage restraint under a Labour government. Even if pre-election commitments remain characteristically vague, such co-operation would be enhanced especially if the government is in a minority situation, and the restraint may find no little compliance from an insecure and demoralized rank and file. In such a situation, it is even possible that capital will co-operate in a Keynesian reflationary policy again, although how far this can remedy the British economy's deep structural uncompetitiveness remains as dubious as ever. *If* the passivity of workers is great enough, something along the lines of the quality control circles and Quality of Working Life participatory schemes so widely being applied in American industry might find further acceptance and even encouragement in British industry. And if Labour's 'controls' over investment are vague and flexible enough, they too might find a co-operative response. But all this falls very far short of the kind of challenges to capital's managerial and investment prerogatives as our new realists propose. To imagine that wage restraint and plant level flexibility will forestall a major confrontation with capital in the face of *such* challenges, or that a Kinnock–Hattersley Labour government will risk them, is to stretch credulity to new limits.

The foreign examples which are so superficially adduced (Australia is a new vogue; Sweden and Austria remain mainstays, despite the latter's extremely centralist and top-down union structure) offer no evidence whatever for capital's preparedness to countenance co-operation in such a strategy. Indeed as we have seen it has been capital which has withdrawn its co-operation from long-established corporatist wage bargaining in the face of such challenges. In so far as such countries have managed to maintain lower levels of unemployment their corporatist arrangements bear looking at seriously, although to what extent it is the strength of the labour movement in such arrangements as opposed to other factors that are at work here (Japan and the United States also have low levels of unemployment relative to Britain after all) needs to be examined seriously as well. In any case, one might wish for rather more of the kind of candour that one gets, for instance, from Göran Therborn when he recommends Swedish or Austrian policy to the British left. Therborn points out that not only the Eurocommunist and Latin socialist strategies for a move to the left did not bear fruit, but also that Scandinavian 'left-wing social democracy never materialised—a bitter lesson which Swedish social democrats . . . are learning now'.[33] He therefore admits that the policy pursued by the Swedish and Austrian governments 'is not a socialist one, and my socialist comrades may ask where socialism comes into all this if at all'.[34] His answer that socialism is not an overnight achievement but a long complex historical process and that full employment is necessary for further advances is a serious one if it can be shown that the conditions are now being put in place for the ascendancy of left-wing social democrats in the Swedish or Austrian labour movements rather than foreclosed as they were in the previous era of corporatist full employment. But in any case his tone is remarkably sanguine in comparison with the promise of the 'transformative' and 'subversive' phraseology of Britian's new social contract advocates (not least those British Eurocommunists who, having been inspired in the late 1970s by the Italian Communist Party's own version of the social contract at the time of its abortive alliance with the Christian Democratic government, are strangely silent regarding its failure and the reasons for the subsequent abandonment of this approach by the Italian Communist Party).

In fact, there is a marked ambiguity in the radical twist given to the social contract today. Hirst speaks in terms of a radical change in Britain's entire wage and salary structure yet he does not concern himself with whether and to what extent this is compatible with the continuing existence of a capitalist labour market. And is the closing of differentials 'upward' compatible with the increasing exposure of domestic labour markets to low foreign wage rates in an era of massive changes in the international division of labour brought about by competitive restructuring of industy in the crisis? Kitching, it may have been noted above, speaks on one page of aiming 'quite consciously to change the fundamental nature of capitalism' in exchange for the extensive co-operation he wants workers to give to capital, and on another page of 'exploring the limits of the concessions capitalism can make without changing its fundamental nature'. A similar ambiguity is seen in the 'realistic strategy' advanced by Geoff Hodgson, who does not explicitly advocate an incomes policy at the national level, but promotes extensive workers' participation within the capitalist enterprise as opposed to 'free collective bargaining' very much along the lines of Kitching and Hirst. Hodgson's case is based on the argument that workers' participation will raise productivity and thus be beneficial to both capital and labour, and that participation within the capitalist firm will presage and lay the ground for mobilization around a 'wider and more egalitarian transformation of society as a whole' on the grounds that there always is 'room for manoeuvre under capitalism'. But Hodgson does not ask what the limits to this room for manoeuvre are today in Britain and what costs to the autonomy of working-class organization are entailed in the reforms he advances.[35]

The failure to ask these questions is the hallmark of social democratic discourse and it is no less present in the gradualist parliamentary democracy plus workers' participation in the enterprise strategy than it is in the exclusively parliamentarist strategy itself. What if capitalists do not agree to more than minority representation in management or company boards or to workers' representatives being solely accountable to those who elected them and subject to recall (which Hodgson suggests, almost in passing, are the conditions that will prevent loss of autonomy and co-optation)? Will participation still be promoted on a weaker basis and will such participation 'within the capitalism of the present' still prefigure 'the participatory socialist society of the future'? Rosa Luxemburg's litmus test of dead-end parliamentarism, which is not to oppose participation but to ask whether it fosters illusions, is by no means inapposite here as well. The new realists have no more managed to square the circle of how to transform capitalism while co-operating fully with it than did traditional social democracy.

All this must reintroduce the old thorny question of for how long the issue of the socialization of the means of production can really be put off in any serious socialist strategy. There are no easy answers, to be sure. Hodgson criticizes 'orthodox socialist thinking' for insisting that an extension of public ownership must be the first step before any extension of participation in enterprise management and he quotes Wainwright and Elliot's study of the Lucas plan to the effect that 'the extent to which public ownership is an advance towards fuller socialism depends on the extent to which workers create a changed relationship between themselves and management in the course of achieving public ownership'. The point is well taken although it would again appear to be a more relevant criticism of the Morrisonian form of public ownership than of 'orthodox socialist thinking'. It is indeed remarkable that Hodgson fails to point out that this quotation from the Lucas study emerges in the explicit context of a critique of the 'traditional Labourist formula' and of a discussion of what a socialist government would have to do to make the implementation of workers' plans possible, the *first steps* in their view being:

> the imposition of exchange controls, the nationalisation of the banks and legislation for trade union control over pension funds. In addition a socialist government would back workers bargaining over proposals based on these plans, with financial and other sanctions on the companies concerned. Where

this met determined resistance, a socialist government would need to be prepared to socialise the company and/or industry under workers' control.[36]

This inevitably brings us back to the nature of the Labour Party and the meaning of the failure of the Bennite left to change it. Without this, the reissued calls for incomes policy and workers' participation must represent nothing really new. In an important article in 1981, Dave Purdy soberly examined the experience of Labour's 1974–8 social contract and argued that, apart from the 'cloud of haziness' which hung over the government's economic policy targets and its vulnerability to external events and pressures, its failure could be traced to the government's dependence on

> the active collaboration, or at least the tacit consent of private industrial and finance capital. The outcome of this dependent relationship is not automatically predetermined in favour of private capital. Nevertheless, it does set limits both to what any government can promise and on the extent to which it can deliver on its promises . . . there is no way in which private capitalist enterprises can be forced to invest against their better judgement. Governments can persuade, cajole, create a favourable climate, provide incentives and exert pressure. But they cannot compel unless they acquire the legal rights of disposition over privately owned assets; that is, requisition or nationalise them.[37]

In light of this, Purdy endorsed the 'standard left response to these difficulties . . . [which] envisages a radical and comparatively rapid shift in the underlying balance between public and private economic power' encompassing an extension of the powers and scope of the National Enterprise Board, compulsory planning agreements, controls over private banking, extensive restrictions on international flows of capital, while insisting that it is inconsistent for the left to demand all this and defend free collective bargaining. But the relevant point here is that the left that counted for something in the Labour Party and the unions *did* accept, for all practical purposes, wage restraint from 1975 to 1978 and even its obvious tacit inclusion in the framing of the social contract before the 1974 elections, while pushing for the very policies that Purdy agrees were essential to overcome the Labour government's 'haziness' of purpose and capital's power. And what would have happened, we may ask, if the unions had acted upon Jack Jones's warning that Benn's dismissal from the Department of Industry (precisely for insisting on these policies) would be 'a grave affront to the union movement' rather than accepting wage restraint as they did on the traditional basis? Would not the unions have then been subject to the 'realistic left's' attack for endangering a Labour government's survival, just as Benn was by his Cabinet 'colleagues' for insisting on policies that they, just as much as their Liberal parliamentary partners, saw as 'unrealistic' and 'dogmatic'?[38]

It was not Benn and the Labour left that were unrealistic, but those who clung to what Prior and Purdy themselves discerned in 1979 as the 'glaring and unresolved defect of the Labour Party . . . its inability to develop a strategy for socialism based on anything other than the equation between power and electoral success'. At this time they explicitly associated their strategy with 'the attempt, spearheaded by Benn, to develop a realistic alternative economic policy and to build popular involvement into the process of Government policy making around the themes of industrial democracy and planning agreements'.[39] The fact that so many socialist intellectuals have abandoned Benn today, indeed their denigration of him, appears to have much less to do with a change in Benn than in their own recognition of, and their accommodation to, the all too real logic of the equation between power and electoral success, even if it has little to do with socialism rather than minimal and temporary defence of the working class against the current reaction.

The truly innovative aspect about Tony Benn's personal development as a leading figure in the Labour Party lay in his realization that a realistic long-term hegemonic strategy of the kind Purdy applauds can only be undertaken by a party that is unified around, and whose leadership is committed to, the social ownership of the means of production, distribution and exchange. This requires a party prepared to see through the confrontation with capital that this will inevitably involve when immediate reforms and the building of popular understanding of the value and necessity for socialism combine to make winning such a confrontation a viable possibility. If Benn and those who supported him as the representative of this strategy were wrong or naive or unrealistic, it was in their underestimation of two things. The first, which we have already discussed, was not only how deeply hostile but how deeply entrenched were those in the party who opposed such a hegemonic strategy in favour of the old equation between power and electoral success. Given this, the constitutional reforms were not only bound to be inadequate but to be politically suicidal for Benn and the left as the immediate electoral costs of the conflict necessary to unify the party on a new basis became apparent. The second was the very deep incredulity among the British people that socialism could really be democratic and that those who proclaimed a determined belief in the need for socialism could really be democrats. This incredulity was the fount of the success that those inside the party and out eventually achieved in defeating and marginalizing the challenge and opportunity that 'Bennism' represented from its rise in 1971 to its eclipse in 1981. It is to this question of how to make a democratic socialist vision credible that we now need to turn.

Towards Socialist Reconstruction

To say that the new revisionists have failed to transcend the very limits of that social democratic practice which has in good part been constitutive of the impasse itself does not at all mean that they have themselves abandoned a commitment to socialism. On the contrary, their concern with 'rethinking socialism' has at least as much to do with the need to reconceptualize and reformulate a vision of a future socialist society so as to rid it of the centralist and authoritarian connotations as it does with their immediate tactical or programmatic concern to re-elect a Labour government. To insist that this was also Benn's concern as well as that of many Marxists who are now relegated to the orthodox, 'class-reductionist' camp by the new revisionism does not change the point except in so far as it should serve as a reminder that the debate over strategy should not be allowed to obscure what common ground continues to exist. Yet general agreement that socialism must involve some form of workers' participation or control in the socialist enterprise or an even more vague consensus that any socialism worth its name must be democratic has not carried socialists very far in overcoming the popular incredulity that socialism and democracy are really compatible.

The real lesson of Thatcherism is this. Social democracy, over the course of the post-war period, took upon itself the responsibility—and the credit—for the expansion of the Keynesian welfare capitalist state, and the solution it offered to the economic crisis that emerged in the 1970s was a defence of this state and a call for a further expansion of it. What came to be at issue ideologically and politically was not just the fact that the crisis itself had discredited this approach on its own prime criterion (the promise to end mass unemployment), nor the difficulty social democratic governments had in even maintaining previous reforms in this context. More important was the fact that this state had already become considerably unpopular in the eyes of most working people before the onset of the crisis. It *was* bureaucratic, inefficient and, above all, distant from popular control in any meaningful sense of the term. This was as true for those workers employed by the state as for the clients of its services. The word 'public'—whether attached to enterprise, employees or service—became in this context a dirty one in Western political culture after a decade of denigration by businessmen, politicians and journalists of various political stripes. And although this denigration clearly represented an aspect of a bourgeois strategy in the crisis that involved turning the screws on workers, women, radical and ethnic minorities and the poor, it came to have a popular resonance even among some members of these groups because it threw up images that related to their own alienation from the capitalist state.

It is quite understandable that social democratic parties—especially those that had recently held government office—should have become most associated in the popular imagination with this alienation. They had always insisted it was their pressure in opposition and their policies in office that led to the expansion of the state's role. It was symptomatic of their ideology that what socialist rhetoric they retained or picked up again in the crisis took the form of an insistence that the Keynesian welfare state had been a 'teeny bit pregnant with socialism' and that what was now needed was a further gestation period. It had always been strategically mistaken to think that welfare state reforms, macroeconomic fiscal policy and a few nationalized industries represented some way-station on a highway to socialism. It became for a period, and it is likely to become again at some point in the not too distant future, tactically disastrous even for reformist parties to seek to gain support by advocating the defence and expansion of such a state.

For socialists, the fact that a right-wing market populism representing the most blatantly reactionary elements of capitalist ideology rushed in to fill the vacuum left by the failures of social democracy and Keynesianism became, and must remain, a very great cause for concern. It underlines the urgency of our 'getting our act together', and it is the root of the new revisionism's tactics. But we must also learn from what the popular appeal of the radical right tells us. The strength of the monetarist assault should not have become the occasion for a knee-jerk defence of the Keynesian welfare state with all its ambiguous and constricted reforms, but rather treated as the occasion for proposing—for insisting on—the fundamental restructuring of the state and its relationship to society so that the communities it is supposed to serve and the people who labour for it together have great involvement in the public domain. Rather than leave the issue at 'less state' versus 'more state', socialists must recognize that popular antipathy to the state can also be addressed in terms of speaking of a *different kind of state*.

In this regard, the really novel element that has been brought into the debate among socialists in the West in the 1980s has not been workers' participation but rather the idea of 'market socialism'. Although the question of market socialism has for some two decades been central to the intellectual agenda regarding actually existing socialism, its extension to debates over socialist strategy in the West remained very much marginal. The impact of Nove's *The Economics of Feasible Socialism* has been such, however, as to have added an important dimension to the new revisionism. Although it is by no means yet clear to what extent its critique of Marxism and its perspective on the shape of a socialist economy is shared by all of those we have discussed above, Nove's concern to demonstrate that a socialist market is necessary for pluralism as well as efficiency is obviously intimately bound up with the common attempt to find a way out of the impasse of working-class politics in the West. And other less celebrated interventions, such as Hodgson's *The Democratic Economy,* have certainly made the connection even more explicit than Nove himself.

This is hardly the place, towards the end of what is already a very long essay, to undertake a full discussion of the case for market socialism. I raise it at this point only to ask whether the projection of the retrieval of the market does indeed help to establish the conditions for a democratic socialism and enhance its desirability and credibility. There are some, of course, who insist that a market socialism is no socialism at all. I would prefer to remain, at least for the sake of this discussion, agnostic on this question. Nove's model, after all, does envision the social ownership of all the major means of production and designates as state corporations, subject to central planning and administration, not only banks and other credit institutions but also all those sectors which operate in large, interrelated units or have a monopoly position. Even with regard to the socialized enterprises which would have 'full autonomy' as well as co-operatives and small-scale private enterprises (which would exist only 'subject to clearly defined limits'), central planning would have 'the vital task of setting the ground-rules for the autonomous and free sectors, with reserve powers of intervention when things got out of balance, or socially undesirable developments were seen to occur'. Major investments and the share of gross national product going to investment would be also centrally determined: this is no 'unplanned economy' obviously. Nove makes it clear that he expects that most final and intermediate goods and services will be bought and sold, but in so far as he explicitly designates that the management of the autonomous enterprises will be responsible to the workforce and establishes that a broader 'democratic vote could decide the boundary between the commercial or market sectors and those where goods and services could be provided free', this seems to put effective restrictions on the extent to which this 'market socialism' would be market *determined,* even if it could be said to be 'commodified.'.[40]

It would therefore seem churlish to dismiss Nove's market socialism out of hand. The same applies to Hodgson who is less clear but also insists that 'the planning system dominates the system as a whole'. This must temper one's view, even if it does not Hodgson's own, when he claims that in his advocacy of market socialism he is 'uttering heresy'. Indeed, one might wish that Hodgson was himself rather less ready to smoke out heresies as he is when he astonishingly cites Tony Benn's occasional use of the term 'market economy' ('the incompatibility of a strong political democracy with a market economy'; 'the market economy upon which British capitalism still relies for its motive force') as proof that Benn's *'bête noire* is markets *per se,* rather than capitalist hierarchy in industry, private ownership of the means of production, or the other integral features of a capitalistic economic system'.[41] Even the most determined exponents of democratic pluralism, it would appear, are not above a bit of witch hunting.

The question remains: to what extent does the market socialist model actually help resolve the socialism and democracy dilemma and aid us in the process of actually arriving at a democratic socialism? And here it must unfortunately be said that the answer is not very much. The transposition of the Eastern European advocacy of markets into a general model may be mystifying if the specific economic conditions and social forces involved there are ignored. The interest of managers in securing discipline over a workforce whose only power in the system rests on their ability to resist managerial authority by virtue of their job security cannot be left out of consideration; nor can the interest of the ruling party in these systems in having freedom defined in terms of market freedom rather than actual political pluralism. Hodgson's own quotation from Brus regarding Eastern European reforms is relevant here: 'It is not "depoliticisation of the economy" but the "democratisation of politics" that is the correct direction for the process of socialisation of nationalised means of production . . . the problem of socialisation turns into the question of the democratic evolution of the state, of the political system'.[42] Unfortunately, Hodgson does not seem to grasp the extent to which this represents a criticism of the turn to markets in some 'actually existing' socialist states as a means of solving their problems as well as a statement of the neccessity of not suppressing the question of the social ownership of the means of production in discussions of democracy as we have seen Hodgson is wont to do in his 'workers' participation within capitalism' strategy.

Unfortunately, Nove offers even less in his own brief treatment of how a transition to his market socialism might be effected in the West. Apart from the obligatory sweeping denunciations of the 'extreme left' and a critique of import and exchange controls and traditional nationalization as a recipe for driving the centre into the arms of the right, which occupy most of his discussion, his own proposals are remarkably slight. 'The biggest obstacle of all' to 'a gradual shift in economic power away from big business' are 'trade unions pursuing the narrow sectional interests of their members'. But while he advocates limits on wage increases, he is at the same time opposed to price controls, import restrictions and material allocation. He advocates a new approach to nationalization, whereby the nationalized firms would operate on 'normal commercial criteria' where competitive conditions exist, and where specific firms rather than whole industries are removed from the private sector. Industrial and service co-operatives would also be encouraged in so far as they also operated in a competitive environment. Both nationalized industries and private corporations would have to introduce 'elements of workers' participation into the management structures', a turn of phrase he apparently considers less vague than the 'totally undefined workers' control' he attacks the 'Marxist utopians' for advocating, since he provides absolutely no further elaboration of what this means except that to say there is much to be learned from West German *Mitbestimmung*.

In light of much careful argument and scholarship in the rest of the book, one cannot but be appalled at the slightness of Nove's chapter on the transition. West German capital's trenchant opposition to the extension of *Mitbestimmung* receives no mention. The Scandinavian trade unions' wages policies are adduced as proof that the regulation of incomes is a precondition for non-inflationary full employment without continuous conflict, but no note is taken of the Swedish general strike of 1980, or the employers' dismantling of the centralized bargaining on which the system rested, not to mention the previous instability that led to the wage earners fund proposals as a gradual means of socializing capital and the capitalist opposition that determined their subsequent sorry fate. Whatever this social democratic-sounding bombast, which goes far beyond the social contract exponents we examined above in its acceptance of existing economic arrangements within capitalism, has to do with Nove's model of socialism is by no means clear—until, that is, he concludes his discussion of what he for some reason calls the 'Transition from Capitalism to Socialism' with the following: 'Of course, all this would imply a mixed economy, with the stresses and strains that inevitably accompany it. But stresses and strains we have already!'[43] *And so do we have a mixed economy*!

It would seem as though the existence of a market in the Western capitalist countries makes irrelevant for Nove the need for a serious discussion of how a social democratic reform programme would lead on to anything like Nove's model of socialism and of why the bourgeoisie would come to acquiesce in the social ownership and control of the means of production even if its political administration were conceived as democratic and its economic dynamic as competitive. What is even worse, the connection posited between markets and pluralism seems to render irrelevant any discussion of the actual political institutions that would compose a democratic socialist state. The importance of the Brus quotation above and of Perry Anderson's comment on Nove's work, that 'only a *Politics of Feasible Socialism* could rescue it from the realm of utopian thought it seeks to escape', speaks precisely to this failure of the market socialists to cope with the socialism and democracy dilemma in a serious fashion.[44]

We come, finally, to the real issue posed by how to make socialist advance possible in face of the impasse of working-class politics today. If there is a really awesome gap in Marxism and a true need for revision, it is in its treatment of the state under socialism. Marx's three main concepts in this respect—the dictatorship of the proletariat, the smashing of the bourgeois state, the withering away of the state—all cover over the dilemmas involved in constructing a democratic socialist state rather than clarify them. The first conflates the notion of making the working class the dominant class (in the sense that the bourgeoisie is the dominant class in capitalist society) with the question of the limits that are imposed on democratic freedoms by a revolutionary confrontation and consolidation of power against the reactionary forces. The second has a destructive and negative connotation which conceals positive institution building of the kind envisaged by Marx on the basis of the experience of the Paris Commune, involving multi-tiered forms of representation, provision for the recall of representatives, elected officials, etc., and it discourages contemplation of the complex issues involved in the multiple sovereignties implied by this. The third seems to deny the very importance of the issue itself since the 'state' is apparently a passing socialist phenomenon anyway, even though in his dispute with Bakunin, Marx made it very clear that he saw some form of extensive public authority as necessary even in communist society (how could it be otherwise, even if this public authority is not conceived as imposed upon society, if people are to collectively determine their fate?).[45]

I have argued that a plan for achieving social control of the means of production and for building the mass popular support which will make such an achievement possible cannot be avoided if we are at all serious about a transition from capitalism to socialism. But such public support cannot be built if the limits of capitalist democracy cannot be demonstrated and if the difficult questions about the nature and form of democratic political institutions under socialism cannot be worked through. The terrible irony of the return in the 1980s to a widespread concern among 'realistic' socialists with the immediacy of the question of power is that it has embroiled itself in a beside-the-point attack on vulgar Marxism while ignoring and even caricaturing the enormous contributions that were set in motion in the 1970s by the developments in Marxist writings on the state which were just reaching towards breaking the theoretical logjam of Marxist politics when the tide among socialist intellectuals turned back towards reformism.

The initial purpose—and effect—of this work was to provide a nuanced counterpoint to conventional liberal and social democratic understandings of capitalist democracy which claimed that the state had freed itself of the domination of capital and to demonstrate that far from becoming external to capital, the state had become an ever more integral element in its development and reproduction. It did not deny the state's autonomy from immediate pressures from capitalists, but, on the contrary, set out to demonstrate that such autonomy was an essential condition, given the competitive nature of the economy and the capitalist class itself, for the defence and reproduction of capitalism. Above all, its outstanding contribution was to provide strong invitation and useful tools for understanding both the variations and the *limits* of this general autonomy of the state. It provided a framework for understanding positive state responses in given conjunctures to working-class (and other) demands while at the same time demonstrating the way these positive responses could be contained through the limits that the institutionalization of political status tended to impose and through the state's own reading of the requirements of capital accumulation in given conjunctures. Thus to have developed the notion of relative autonomy was an accomplishment precisely because it focused attention on the balance of class forces (to see how relative this autonomy was in particular situations) and because it also drew attention to the limits beyond which reform and 'intervention' in the capitalist economy could not go without inducing a political fissure reflective of a crisis of hegemony and capital accumulation. It is extremely unfortunate that so much of the new revisionism has forgotten or ignored the essential lesson of this work.

This development, which marked an important departure from the Marxist classics even as it built on them, was certainly long overdue. Nor should the debates between the various tendencies that developed be overblown. What I have just described was common to Miliband, Poulantzas, Offe and others, with the debates among them pertaining more to language and particular focus than substantive incompatibilities. If the development of Marxist political theory had stopped here, however, it would indeed have had defeatist implications given the stress on reproduction and limits. But it did not, as toward the end of the 1970s both Miliband (in *Marxism and Politics*) and Poulantzas (in *State, Power, Socialism*) turned their attention to a revision of classical Marxism's fragile, contradictory and incomplete approach to a theory of the socialist state. To be sure, there were predecessors (not least Macpherson's attempt to point to the possibility of the retrieval of liberal democracy within socialism). But in Miliband's critique of Leninist democratic centralism and the dictatorship of the proletariat (very different from the opportunistic grounds on which Eurocommunists rejected it and the orthodox insurrectionary grounds with which their detractors defended it), as well as in his use of the notion of structural reformism to counterpose a strategy of administrative pluralism to social democratic reformism on the one hand and to 'smashing the state' on the other, a new start was made. So was it in Poulantzas's trenchant critique of the utopian notions of 'direct democracy' and in his insistence on thinking through the place and meaning of representative institutions in socialist democracy.[46]

It was only a start, to be sure. But that it was made at all and then ignored in a panic rush to traditional reformism and popular-frontism and social contracts and workers' participation in the capitalist firm has been a great diversion. Benn's attack on the undemocratic character of the gentlemen's club of Parliament and Whitehall in which the Labour Party had become structurally as well as ideologically enmeshed certainly needed more ballast than his populist appeals and the intra-party supports for constitutional change could provide. In 1981,

48

as the struggle to change the Labour Party reached its climax, and while the TUC–Labour Party's Liaison Committee's subcommittee on industrial democracy and planning were examining five options for new planning structures, none of which involved any popular involvement in the process, Raymond Williams briefly set out some ideas on the radical reconstitution of the traditional forms of representation and administration of the kind that Marxist political theory was beginning to generate and was necessary if a socialist government in Britain were to have any chance of success.

> This is deliberately different from listing certain major political and economic policies. Of course these are crucial, but some of the best of them—the nuclear disarmament of Britain; the control of banks, insurance companies and pension funds for productive investment; exchange and import controls for the recovery of British industry—are typically presented as if they could be carried through on the basis of a parliamentary majority. This, even on the left, is the Labourist perspective which is at the heart of the problem. For to carry through any of these policies . . . would require a degree of popular understanding and support which is of a quite different order from an inherited and in part negative electoral majority. . . The very powerful forces it is certain to encounter, in any of these initiatives—over a range from national and international institutions and companies, through widely distributed organizations for influencing public opinion, to the confusions among its potential supporters—are not of a kind to be defeated from the parliamentary centre alone. . . The 'alternative strategy', that is to say, is no more than an intellectual exercise unless it carries with it, and indeed as its priority, an alternative politics. . . The defining centre of any successful left politics is the radical extension of genuine popular controls. . .It is an attempted break beyond the most benevolent or determined representative administration.[47]

To this end Williams presented a series of particular proposals for a Labour government's early priorities: to direct each nationalized industry to develop plans, based on the views of their workers, to democratize and socialize the 'nominally' publicly owned institutions; the direct election of national planning councils and consumers' advisory bodies in industry and service with direct access to Parliament as well as the relevant ministries; to break the 'system of monopolistic appointments to the control of public bodies which is in fact intended to ensure verticalism, concentration of power and dependence'; to supplement the responsibility of elected government for public finance and investment 'with alternative and parallel forms of public responsibility'; public hearings conducted by qualified planning groups with access to all available public and industrial information in order to 'develop visible and publicly approved investment plans'; to make the planning process open and public so that it is not 'swamped, as always before, by capitalist power and its highly experienced market forces'; a Freedom of Information Act on which all of the above would depend; major public investment in new electronics communications and their use for public information, discussion and decision; professional companies in the older communications sectors being leased, publicly-owned resources and made responsible to elected regional and local boards; the transfer of day-to-day administration of council housing to elected tenants' associations.

This much neglected article demonstrated precisely the enormous importance and immediate value of the kind of thinking that Marxist attention to the institutional forms of a democratic socialist state could provide—if there were a viable socialist party it could provide it to. To be sure, its immediate value seems now rather less clear given what has transpired in the Labour Party since 1981. A moderate Labour government elected on a negative vote and committed to the idea that a return to Butskellism is the best way of moving forward is no less likely to fail and to set the stage for a return to Thatcherite reaction or worse than is one with radical policies but unable to transform political structures in a way that would alone make its policies popular and hence possible.

We are, in other words, still left with the question of vehicle. The main theme of this essay has been that the impasse of the working class has much to do with the practice of social democratic parties: their acceptance of the structure of the state; their promulgation of class harmony; their concern with packaging policy programmes and mobilizing activists around the next election; their excessive focus on parliamentary timetables and debates; their acceptance of a division of labour between industrial and political organization with the necessary link between the two being cemented at the top of each structure—all this attests to their inadequacy. It must be said, however, that even if concentration on this kind of practice of working-class politics is justified by its sheer predominance, one cannot pretend that parties to the left of social democracy have pointed a way forward.

Even if these parties were clearer in their socialist purpose, they tended far too often towards an easy use of the term 'nationalization', leaving the impression that what was meant by this was merely state control of industry along the lines of what they themselves criticized as bureaucratically-run public corporations in which the relationship between workers and managers did not change and in which popular control was offered only in terms of a highly tenuated form of ministerial responsibility. Although one cannot dismiss these parties' capacity to develop a limited number of very committed and skilled organizers who have often played important roles in popular organizations, their greatest problem has been the adoption of an internal political structure which put far too much—or at least far too permanent—an emphasis on discipline as opposed to participation and discouraged creative interaction, rather than instrumentalism, with popular organizations. Any political party which puts such a high priority on discipline that pursuing a common line becomes a form of keeping its members and supporters *in line* is destined not to grow. This is entirely apart from problems associated with paying excessive attention to, let alone entering into a relationship of dependence on, foreign models of 'actually existing socialism' and defending too readily the tactical or even conjunctural positions taken by their governments. And not least problematic has been the tendency to search for immediate practical guidance and legitimation in the writings of Marx, Lenin, Stalin, Trotsky or Mao, which not only gave rise to a *practice* that was awkward in the Western context, but even a political *language* that had little apparent meaning to the uninitiated.

Fortunately, there is a notable awareness among a great many socialists today of the limitations of previous practice. At the same time, this has also induced a high degree of caution with regard to taking new socialist initiatives, of which the new revisionism is but one example. This caution is certainly understandable. It reflects the fact that the traditional Communist, Trotskyist and Marxist—Leninist forms of political practice have largely played themselves out by this point in twentieth-century history, at least in the English-speaking capitalist democracies and arguably in a good many other Western countries as well. It is not surprising that this should be so: they were the products of specific historical conditions and conjunctures, and it should hardly have been expected that they would crystallize revolutionary working-class politics into a permanent mould. This is not to say that all the organizations they spawned will pass away, or that some of their ideas and practices will not continue to be relevant or in some situations actually operative. It does mean, however, that socialism as theory and movement will have to evolve new forms and new substance. We are a new stage of socialist development and the confusion and hesitation that marks our time as socialist can only be seen in this light.

To this extent the new revisionists are right and although they are rather too ready to proclaim something new while clinging to the old, their caution does not necessarily reflect any lack of a sense of urgency or desire to move on. The promise of the attempt to change the Labour Party was that, especially through the voice of Tony Benn's insistent appeals for democratizing the party and the state, it began addressing itself to the unity of socialism *and* democracy, democracy *and* socialism. The promise of Marxist theory was that, while not losing sight of the very difficult process of trying to convince people that social ownership of the means of production was necessary, it began a revision of traditional Marxist thought that enhanced understanding of the limits of the capitalist state and promoted thinking on the democratic structures appropriate to a socialist state.

That recapturing this promise and moving beyond it will be very largely, if by no means exclusively, dependent on the struggles of working people and mean the revitalization and reconstitution of a political and cultural working-class identity seems to be incontrovertible. I argued earlier that the withering away of old working-class identities was indeed something real and would be difficult to reverse. To begin that process of reversal will mean, as this essay has tried to insist, not passively accommodating socialist politics to a fatalistic 'realism', but setting out to connect with and helping to broaden and deepen the experience of collective labour out of which working-class identity grows and can be nourished. The fact that older manual occupations have declined in relative numerical terms does not mean that exploitation has changed its character nor does it invalidate the classical Marxist project (based on its understanding of that exploitation) which, since the Communist Manifesto, has defined as the 'immediate aim' of working-class parties 'the formation of the proletariat into a class'. Capitalism's insistent recomposition of occupations and communities must make this immediate aim an ever present one for socialist politics, and one that is particularly pressing today. But it is hardly an ephemeral goal, least of all today as capitalists, aided by the state, increase the level of exploitation and managerial domination and subject newer industries and occupations, not least those in the service, commercial and public sectors, to the collectivizing experiences—in terms of low status, limited mobility, low relative pay, and lack of autonomy—wherein labour's common predicament and potential can be recognized and acted upon. One of the main reasons why social democratic incomes policies and participation schemes have to be looked upon with suspicion is that they can so easily become the basis for undermining the utility and autonomy of unions as primary organizational expressions of collective labour, devaluing the salience of class identity and struggle through their corporatist embrace.

Of course we must strive for a politics that seeks to transcend the sectionalism and particularism of trade-union identity. But this is something that is very different from a politics which pessimistically discerns the decline of the working class in the decline of the older industries and which promotes, on the basis of a presumed permanent minoritization of the working class, alliances with vaguely defined 'new middle classes' and 'new social movements' with slender social bases. In the sense of those people who are unpropertied workers and who are not involved in the supervision of collective labour, there is indeed a working-class majority in all advanced capitalist countries and the first task of a socialist party ought to be the nourishment of an understanding and consciousness of the existence and potential of this working-class majority. The socialist potential of such identity, while by no means foreordained, lies in the sense of collective power as well as the sense of collective deprivation which an understanding of the centrality of class relations to the whole social order entails. To demand a politics that envisions creating a working-class majority in terms of collective socio-political identity does not need to mean that other identities—of gender, or race, of ethnicity—have to be effaced. If anything, historical experience tells us that they cannot be effaced. And my own personal experience of working-class community tells me that it is possible for working people to think of themselves as workers and to act politically in a way that allows for, in fact obtains strength from, a simultaneous expression of their other collective identities in so far as a popular socialist culture provides a common terrain of understanding, purpose and activity. It has fallen to socialists in the last decades of this century to undertake the daunting task of establishing new political directions and institutions, much as our forerunners had to do in the last decades of the last. As before, and despite the very different conditions, these will not come out of thin air but will involve the breaking up and amalgamation and development of organizations that went before. That there will be enough immediate grievances and struggles, not least by workers, employed and unemployed, upon which to build in this terrible era of major capitalist crisis and restructuring there can be no doubt. Even if it is by no means inevitable, least of all when the terror of nuclear holocaust gives a new and horrible visage to the meaning of barbarism, socialism remains the only human alternative.

(1985)

Notes

1. Speech to Campaign for Labour Party Democracy meeting, 1981 Labour Party Conference, Brighton, 27 September, 1981.

2. Colin Leys, 'Thatcherism and British Manufacturing: A Question of Hegemony', *New Left Review*, no. 151, May–June 1985, p. 17.

3. For a full discussion of these developments, see L. Panitch, *The Tripartite Experience*, research study for the Royal Commission on the Economic Union and Development Prospects for Canada, Ottawa 1985.

4. It should be noted that the term 'the new revisionism', although put to good use recently by Westergaard and Miliband, has in fact a much wider remit than the Eurocommunist-inspired analyses of British Labour's crisis in the 1980s, or even than the more general retreat from traditional positions among Marxists that has been evident in this decade. The very academic revival of Marxism since the late 1960s has already begun to produce in the 1970s a 'new revisionism' emanating from various political institutions and intellectual circles that were themselves traditionally anything but Marxist. Among academics whose values and assumptions rarely strayed from the tenets of Fabian, Keynesian or Weberian analysis there was a tendency to recast their old conceptual gear in 'neo-Marxian' terminology, while continuing to explicitly reject the revolutionary implications of Marxism. And within social democratic parties, a good many of the new reformist strategies advanced in the 1970s were often formulated, even by elements of the old leadership and for the first time in decades, with the help of a vaguely Marxian vocabulary. What all this bespeaks, and has been far too little noted, is an important convergence of political and intellectual trends, coming so to speak from different directions, which has yielded a form of discourse and practice in our times that bears many of the earmarks of the revisionist and reformist Marxism of post-First World War social democracy. We are back at the original dilemma in more ways than one. For an earlier presentation of this 'new revisionism' see my review of C. Crouch (ed.), *State and Economy in Contemporary Capitalism*, London 1979, in the *International Journal of Urban and Regional Research*, vol. 5, no. 1, 1981, pp. 128–32. Compare J. Westergaard, 'Class of '84', *New Socialist*, January–February, no. 15, 1984; R. Miliband, 'The New Revisionism in Britain', *New Left Review*, no. 150, 1985; and B. Fine *et al.*, *Class Politics: An Answer to Its Critics*, London 1984, especially pp. 9–11.

5. 'Manifesto of the Communist Party', in Karl Marx, *Political Writings. Volume 1: The Revolutions of 1948*, (ed. D. Fernbach), London 1974–80. It is worth noting that Marx speaks not only of the role of communist parties in class formation here but of 'all proletarian parties' and of their expressing 'in general terms, actual relations springing from an existing class struggle, from an historical movement going on under our very eyes'. Gorz relies on a passage from *The Holy Family* ('It is not a question of what this or that proletarian, or even the whole proletariat, at the moment regards as its aim. It is a question of what the proletariat is, and what, in accordance with this being, it will historically be compelled to do.'). It is therefore interesting to note that Gramsci saw *The Holy Family* as 'an occasional work . . . a vaguely intermediate state' in Marx, directly contrasting it with *The Poverty of Philosophy* which he saw as 'an essential moment in the formation of the philosophy of praxis', and that he makes this contrast directly in the context of citing the latter work as his 'point of reference for the study of economism and understanding relations between structure and superstructure . . . where it says that an important

phase in the development of a social class is that in which the individual components of a trade union no longer struggle solely for their own economic interests, but for the defence and development of the organisation itself'. *Selections from the Prison Notebooks of Antonio Gramsci*, Q. Hoare and A. N. Smith (eds), London 1971, p. 162. A. Gorz, *Farewell to the Working Class*, Boston 1982, p. 16.

6. Ernesto Laclau and Chantal Mouffe, *Hegemony and Socialist Strategy*, London 1985, p. 181.

7. 'Labour's Lost Millions', *Marxism Today*, October 1983, p. 12; 'Labour: Rump or Rebirth?' *Marxism Today*, March 1984, p. 11.

8. *The Forward March of Labour Halted?*, London 1981, p. 18.

9. 'The Labour Party and Class Formation in Twentieth Century Politics', paper presented at the Conference of Europeanists, Washington DC, October 1983, pp. 8, 10.

10. *Class Inequality and Political Order*, London 1971, pp. 98–9.

11. Cronin, pp. 23–4.

12. *The Labour Party: The Party with a Future*, May 1945, p. 1.

13. *Languages of Class: Studies in English Working Class History 1832–1982*, Cambridge 1982, pp. 240, 246.

14. 'Trends in the British Labour Movement', in *Labouring Men: Studies in the History of Labour*, London 1964, p. 330.

15. John H. Goldthorpe *et al.*, *The Affluent Worker in the Class Structure*, Cambridge 1969, p. 191.

16. Richard Scase, *Social Democracy in Capitalist Society: Working-class Politics in Britain and Sweden*, London 1977; Duncan Gallie, *Social Inequality and Class Radicalism in France and Britain*, Cambridge 1983.

17. Speech to Socialist Society meeting, 1983 Labour Party Conference, Brighton, 3 October 1983.

18. 'Class Struggle and the Union Movement', in D. Coates *et al.*, *A Socialist Anatomy of Britain*, Oxford 1985, p. 119.

19. 'Labour's Lost Millions', *Marxism Today*, October 1983, p. 8.

20. 'The Great Moving Right Show', in S. Hall and M. Jacques, *The Politics of Thatcherism*, London 1983, pp. 26–7.

21. Quoted in The *Guardian*, 9 March 1982.

22. Tariq Ali and Quintin Hoare, 'Socialists and the Crisis of Labourism', *New Left Review* no. 132, March–April 1982, pp. 74, 80.

23. 'The Future of the Left–But What Then?', *New Socialist*, January 1945, p. 41. Hobsbawm's comments on the popular front experience are in 'The Retreat into Extremism', *Marxism Today*, April 1985, p. 10.

24. Raymond Williams, 'Splits, Pacts and Coalitions', *New Socialist*, March–April 1984, p. 33; Eric Hobsbawm, 'Labour: Rump or Rebirth', *Marxism Today*, March 1984, p. 11; Mike Prior and Dave Purdy, *Out of the Ghetto*, Nottingham 1979, pp. 170–1.

25. Gavin Kitching, *Rethinking Socialism*, London 1983, p. 111.

26. Paul Hirst, 'The Division of Labour, Incomes Policy and Industrial Democracy', in A. Giddens and G. Mackenzie (eds), *Social Class and the Division of Labour*, Cambridge 1982, p. 256.

27. Hobsbawm, 'Labour: Rump or Rebirth?', p. 8.

28. Kitching, pp. 128–9.

29. Kitching, p. 125.

30. Hirst, pp. 263–4

31. Prior and Purdy, pp. 129–30.
32. All this is discussed at length in my *Social Democracy and Industrial Militancy: The Labour Party, the Trade Unions and Incomes Policy 1945–1974*, Cambridge 1976.
33. 'Britain Left Out', in J. Curran (ed.), *The Future of the Left*, London 1984, p. 132.
34. 'West on the Dole', *Marxism Today*, June 1985, p. 10.
35. *The Democratic Economy*, London 1984, ch. 5.
36. *The Lucas Plan*, London 1982, pp. 263–4
37. 'The Social Contract and Socialist Policy', in M. Prior (ed.), *The Popular and the Political*, London 1981, pp. 108–9.
38. See my 'Socialists and the Labour Party: A Reappraisal', Chapter 4 of the present volume.
39 *Out of the Ghetto*, London 1979, pp. 183,187.
40. *The Economics of Feasible Socialism*, London 1983, pp. 200–20, 207–8.
41. *The Democratic Economy*, pp. 165, 181, 175.
42. Quoted in *The Democratic Economy*, p. 165.
43. *The Economics of Feasible Socialism*, pp. 160–75.
44. Perry Anderson, *In the Tracks of Historical Materialism*, Chicago 1984, p. 103.
45. I discuss this weakness of Marxism extensively in 'The State and the Future of Socialism', Chapter 9 below.
46. Ralph Miliband, *Marxism and Politics*, Oxford 1977, chs. 5 and 6; Nicos Poulantzas, *State, Power, Socialism*, London 1978, Part 5.
47. 'An Alternative Politics', *The Socialist Register 1981*, London 1981, pp. 1–10

2.

Ideology and Integration: The Case of the British Labour Party

A long tradition of political analysis has identified the British political system as harbouring a classic example of class-based party politics. British political parties, it was said, were divided, not along ethnic, religious or regional lines, but primarily reflected the social class divisions of an otherwise relatively homogeneous society. This analysis was to a large extent based upon the existence of the Labour Party, with its predominantly working-class origins and support, and its socialist ideology. It became increasingly commonplace in the 1960s, however, to qualify this analysis in a number of ways. Primarily, these qualifications derived from observations of the diminishing programmatic differences between the two major political parties and from a perceived change in the character, role and aspirations of the working class itself in modern British society in particular and in post-war Western societies in general. These changes are seen to make a working-class political party with an ideology that emphasizes its working-class nature as essentially anachronistic. Economic developments which create an affluent working class, social benefits from a 'collectivist welfare state', integration of working-class representatives into political and industrial decision-making processes, and an increasing cultural tendency to solve problems scientifically and in the light of expertise, are all seen as the conditions which, it is argued, are leading to a decline of class consciousness and class-based politics. [1]

British parties, it is claimed, are becoming more like American parties, fulfilling systemic functions like representation and brokerage, demand conversion and aggregation and the integration of individuals into the political system. The decline of class consciousness is seen to be attended by the rise of a multiplicity of groups, roles and occupations, and the political party is perceived to have developed as 'the agency that best linked a multi-group social structure with the government'. [2]

The significance of this theory of political parties lies in the under-lying conception of the role they play in the system in relation to 'organized interests'. Parties respond to the wishes of most such inter-ests, to some extent, for the dual purpose of securing election and ensuring recognition as a legitimate government which will take all major interest groups into account when formulating policies. Thus Robert McKenzie contended that 'elections in this country are primarily rough-and-ready devices for choosing between rival parliamentary teams' and went on to argue that the legitimacy of an electoral victory to one of these teams is maintained by the fact that organized inter-ests—even those allied with the losing team—are recognized by the win-ning party, which is open to their views. [3]

It is clear that if a party is to fit this model, its underlying ideological orientation—its conception of the social order—must be one of integra-tion. Its concern is ultimately with unifying the society by developing a policy of national and party interest which will be acceptable to a broad range of sectional organizations. It may recognize conflict within the society, but its role as a party, and especially as a government, is to facilitate compromise among the conflicting interests by means of a policy 'in the national interest' which overrides the uncompromised demands of any part of the society.

One major difficulty with this general theory of political parties is that particular parties are not well suited to 'brokerage politics'. Their origins, development and structure are such that they are closely allied with only one of the major sectional interests. In so far as the section in question is not dominant in the society, the party programme is less likely to stress a national interest based on a consensus among all parts of the community and is more likely to emphasize the legitimacy of given sectional demands. Theorists who emphasize the brokerage func-tions of political parties have of course not been blind to such examples. Macridis, for instance, notes that sometimes the function of representa-tion outweighs that of brokerage, as when a party represents the workers or the church. [4] Thus the party cannot afford to be as aggregative as the theory requires. By implication, however, most theorists see this as a problem of diminishing importance due to those social and economic developments which they believe are undermining class differences. In fact, the transformation of these parties is seen to have already occurred.

It is not the purpose of this essay to deny the socially unifying role the Labour Party plays in the British political system. Indeed it will be argued that the Labour Party exhibited an 'integrative ideology' long before the post-war developments which are presumed to have undermined class divisions in Britain. One of the outstanding American students of British politics, Samuel Beer, has presented the view, in recent years, that this aspect of Labour's ideology is in fact the product of the post-war period. As his interpretation has it, the Labour Party from 1918 to 1948 was characterized by a massive consensus on a socialist ideology that primarily existed to rationalize the 'thrust for power' of the working class; an ideology, the most important aspect of which was its view that the working class was the foundation for a party that would 'lead the whole nation to Utopia'. It was only the winning of power by organized labour after 1945 and the attendant social changes that reflected this power that led to the modification of this ideology and the emergence of the party as a national party. Although Beer recognizes that it is not easy for the Labour Party to abandon its class identification, he implies that this is only partly due to existing class divisions and gives more emphasis to the role that 'old' fundamental ideals and the 'language of class' continue to play in the 'new social order'.[5]

It may be, however, that this new conception of the role of the Labour Party is derived from the historically dominant strain in the party's ideology which has not stressed the discontinuities and divisions of British society, but has emphasized—albeit to a lesser extent than the Conservative Party—the unity of the society, the cohesiveness of the community. Assuming that it is possible to classify ideologies into those that are *integrationist* and *disintegrationist,* according to their portrayal of the existing society as either basically unified or basically fissured,[6] the Labour Party's ideology has long been essentially integrationist. The concept of ideology is being used here in the sense proposed by Clifford Geertz, that is, as 'schematic images of social order' with emphasis being given to 'the role that ideologies play in defining (or obscuring) social categories, stabilizing (or upsetting) social expectations, maintaining (or undermining) social norms, strengthening (or weakening) social consensus, relieving (or exacerbating) social tensions.'[7]

In recent years, political scientists have stressed the importance of political culture expressed in values, beliefs and symbols commonly held throughout a community as a determining factor of political behaviour. Whether a political culture is seen as the product of socialization processes involving family, school and peer groups, or as the product of broad historical and social forces like those which are used to explain declining class consciousness, it is presented as 'one of the main variables of a political system and a major factor explaining the political behaviour of individuals, groups and parties'.[8] The usefulness of an exposition based on political culture is circumscribed, however, to the extent that it is not an independent determining variable, that is, to the extent that values and ideas that are seen as determining are in fact created and maintained by the very structures they are supposed to determine.[9] To concentrate analysis on the way in which governments and parties respond to the desires, demands and political values of the populace is to neglect the possibility that political culture is largely a product of governments and political parties, and to overlook the degree to which many of the structures and processes that formally serve the purpose of aggregating and articulating demands are in fact tools of political mobilization which internalize existing authority patterns. In the case of the Labour Party, its integrative ideology may have served important functions in introducing and underlining the dominant values, beliefs and symbols of British society and thus contributed to the consensus which is presumed to have transformed the party itself.

Study of the British Labour Party suggests that the theory of declining class-based party politics is mistaken in a number of respects. It underestimates the impact on the party and the working class of that strain in its ideology which has *throughout its history* been aggregative and has minimized the party's class role. Conversely it overestimates the extent to which changes in social and economic conditions have facilitated a party system which does not reflect the class structure of the society. The former error allows the analysis to represent the 'transformation' of a social democratic party as more difficult and dramatic than it actually is; the latter permits the analysis to neglect current tensions between such a party and the organized working class.

II

One of the major themes of Labour's opponents has always been that the party cannot meet the systemic functions that are required of a 'national party'. This contention is based on the same appreciation as shown by modern analysts for the contribution of brokerage parties to the stability of the political system. Conservative politicians have often been ready to point out that Labour fails the nation because it is interested only in one class, while the Tory Party, although concerned with the interests of the working class, also considers the well-being of all classes and thus frames its policies so as to unite the nation. These views derive from a traditional theme of Conservative thought which depicts society as a living organism. A modern party theorist has expressed the theme in this way:

> It follows naturally from the Conservative attitude that one of the basic principles of the Party is the unity of society. Man is born into society, into a family and into a nation and, by the mere fact of existence, assumes inescapable duties towards his fellows and is endowed with the rights of membership of that society. The complexity of modern economic organisations serves only to emphasize further an aspect of the interdependence of the parts of society. Society is an organic whole. [10]

Labour's image as a working-class party remains deeply embedded as well in the minds of large sections of the working class. McKenzie and Silver found in their mid 1960s survey: 'The Labour Party is perceived overwhelmingly by its working-class supporters as the party of the working class and for the working class and pursues policies which are beneficial to it.' This attitude is also reflected in the trade unions where, as Martin Harrison noted, 'the belief that the party is "an agency for obtaining particular advantages for organized labour" is still deeply ingrained in the minds of the rank and file . . . Few of them would see that there could be a distinction between the good of the community as a whole and the demands of the organized working class.' [11]

Given the trade-union origins of the party, its working-class electoral foundation, its continuing structural alliance with the unions, and the emphasis which party doctrine has indeed placed on the inequalities that mark British society, it is understandable that such views abound. They are obviously inconsistent, however, with the theories of modern party analysts as well as with that strain in the Labour Party which presents the party as a national party which is sensitive to all group interests. In the 1950s and 1960s the party was subject to major (although not new) attempts to remove this inconsistency and to make explicit once and for all the party's aggregative character. Party intellectuals and leaders wrote extensively on the changed nature of modern capitalism, 'shopping lists' of industries to be nationalized were abandoned, and Clause Four itself was challenged. Central to this development has been the desire to remove from the party its class label, culminating in Mr. Wilson's appeal for middle-class votes in the 1964 and 1966 elections. The party was significantly affected by the theory that class divisions in Britain had disappeared. Thus Douglas Jay argued in 1959 that the party was 'in danger of fighting under the label of a class that no longer exists.'[12] And the party leaders were wont to turn the tables on the Tories by arguing that they were old-fashioned in representing only the upper strata while Labour was modern by virtue of its inclusiveness.[13]

One way in which the Labour Party has sometimes tried to surmount the conflict of values inherent in a national interest versus sectional interest, or community versus class dichotomy, apart from either denying the existence of class divisions altogether or accepting them as just, has been to differentiate between certain sectional interests and others. At times (particularly in the speeches of its fraternal delegates to the annual Trades Union Congress), the party has made such a distinction between its alliance with the trade unions and the Tory alliance with business. This is essentially an argument that party and unions are united in an entity more important than its parts—the labour movement, which is unlike other interest groups in that it is the 'spearhead of the aspirations and the repository of the loyalty of an economic and social class'.

However, this distinction has never been able to solve the national-class dilemma for Labour. For if the distinction is going to be intellectually and, more important to the party, politically convincing, it involves the acceptance of a certain view of the role of the working class as a historical force, so that its claims can be justified and legitimated despite the conflicting demands of other classes, with which it would othewise have to compromise. It involves substantially accepting the Marxist idea that the working class in its struggle with the capitalist class is the prime force for social change, and that it is through the conquest of political power by the working class that a new kind of society, giving a new status to the worker and based on integration rather than division, can be attained. The long-run interests of the community, if not of all humankind, are seen to depend on the rejection of policies acceptable to all parts of the existing community, and on the adoption of an ideology that helps to knit the social class together. Once one abandons this view of the working class as the prime mover, it may become impossible for any government, or even for any party, to see itself as class based, or at least to see the organized working class as essentially different from other interests.

The key to the development of the Labour Party as one of two 'teams' of British politics, therefore, may lie deep in its ideological roots. It may lie in the idea that as a society matured and individuals grew wiser, socialism—the obviously best means of administering the society—would gradually come to be accepted by *all sane people*. Until this happened it was a government's—any government's—duty to represent the myriad of interests in the community as fairly and as impartially as it could. For the expectation is not that the millennium will come when the working class matures, but that it will come when the society matures. One's fundamental aim therefore is to nurture the existing community as a whole; it is this value that takes priority over class.

It is generally thought that the critical element in Labour's ideology lies in its choice of means of action, in its self-confinement to the parliamentary machine. The turning point for social democracy, however, may not have been its decision to seek power through parliamentary channels, but its rejection of a certain view of the working class and its role in history. In order to ascertain how well suited Labour is to fulfil the systematic functions mentioned above, *and* to better understand its relationship—as a brokerage party—with the trade unions, it is necessary to examine Labour's conception of society, its assumptions of how society functions, and the views it has held with regard to class conflict and social harmony.

III

When examining Labour Party literature one cannot help but discriminate between various authors and works; there is no basic philosophy of the party that can be traced to one or two seminal texts. Richard Crossman once commented on the British labour movement's singular 'booklessness.'[15] Nevertheless, a number of themes can be found in much of the party literature which will substantiate our thesis. Certainly evidence of the party's rejection of the class struggle is not hard to come by: the inaugurating conference of the party (then the Labour Representation Committee) in 1900, defeated a resolution by a Socialist Democratic Federation delegate which called for 'a distinct party . . . based upon a recognition of class war'.[16]

Harold Wilson has noted that the Labour Party derived its socialist inspiration more from Methodism than Marx.[17] Sidney Webb expressed the same view forty years earlier on the negative influence of Marx on the party, although he found the roots of party thought elsewhere. Addressing the 1923 party conference, he argued 'that the founder of British Socialism was not Karl Marx but Robert Owen, and that Robert Owen preached not "class war" but the doctrine of human brotherhood.'[18] A survey of fifty-one Labour and Lib–Lab MPs returned at the 1906 general election indicated that still other influences were important. The forty-five MPs who replied to the questioner were influenced by Ruskin, Dickens, Henry George, Carlyle, Mill, Scott, Shakespeare and Bunyan. The Bible was mentioned more often than any author other than Ruskin. [19] Phillip Poirier's excellent book on the birth of the Labour Party cites Bellamy, Blatchford, Thoreau and Walden as the writers of note for ILP leaders, including Ramsay MacDonald. [20]

MacDonald's writing and speeches throughout his thirty years at the apex of the Labour Party are punctuated with a belief in the organic unity of society, often in terms not unlike that found in Conservative thought. 'Socialism', he contended, 'marks the growth of a society not the uprising of a class. The consciousness which it seeks to quicken is not one of economic class solidarity, but one of social unity and growth toward organic wholeness. The watchword of Socialism, therefore, is not class consciousness, but community consciousness.'[21] The influence of his thought upon the party was not only a product of his position of leadership but of his standing as a party theorist, on which grounds Keir Hardie described MacDonald in 1909 as 'the biggest intellectual asset the Socialist movement had in this country today'. [22] The other 'intellectual asset' of the Labour Party, its Fabian wing, expressed a similar view of the neuter political function of class. The touchstone of Fabian ideology, the theory of 'permeation', was concerned with 'the inculcation of socialist thought and projects into the minds of Liberals, Radicals and Conservatives, of Trade Unionists, and Cooperators, of Employers and Financiers'. [23] Their socialist thought consisted wholly of a gradualist programme of increasing public ownership; a 'thrust for power' by the working class had very little to do with it.

The first programme of the party to bear a socialist hue, the 1918 'Reconstruction Manifesto', *Labour and the New Social Order,* was drafted by Sidney Webb, and in fine British tradition spurned abstract theoretical formulations; it was essentially pragmatic and unanalytical. It expressed the belief that world war had dealt a death blow to capitalism, that the measures of a war economy heralded a socialist future and that any government to come would have recourse to socialism as the means of reconstruction. Above all, it abstracted its prescriptions from class. 'The first principle of the Labour Party . . . is the securing to every member of the community . . . of all the requisites of healthy life and worthy citizenship. This is in no sense a "class" proposal. . . It will be the guiding faith of any Labour Government.'[24]

This dedication no doubt appealed to a worker without the requisites in question in 1918, but as the passage indicates, it can be logically abstracted from the question of change in power relationships, or of the status of the worker. It is a crucial error to relate directly, as Samuel Beer does, the adoption by the party of a commitment to 'common ownership of the means of production, distribution and exchange' in the 1918 party constitution and programme to a commitment to a 'thrust for power' of the working class. In fact, the hostility of Fabians, like Webb, and Independent Labour Party leaders, like Snowden, to the ideas of workers' control and industrial democracy, then current, suggests the contrary. At a time when vociferous demands were being made by guild socialists, syndicalists and others to have workers take over and run their industries, *Labour and the New Social Order* only went so far as to vaguely commit the party to a system of administration in industry which would 'promote, not profiteering, but the general interest . . . in particular services and occupations'. In 1918, the Labour Party committed itself to socialist objectives in the sense in which socialism had always been advocated by the Fabian Society.

A sympathetic German observer of the period depicted the 1918 programme as 'the nearest approach to a theoretical formulation of principle known in the whole previous history of the Labour Party. . . In a world of drowning men clutching for straws, the programme was not without its effect, but as an example of theoretical insights and knowledge it remains . . . far inferior to the most elementary continental socialist programmes.'[25] In the light of this common response at the time to the party ideology it is surprising to find Samuel Beer today extolling the 1923 House of Commons debates on 'the Capitalist System' as an exercise in ideological thinking 'comparable with similar debates on the continent'.[26] Could Labour's leaders have been expressing in Parliament an ideological fervour they omitted from the party programmes? A reading of the debate shows it to be not out of line with party tradition. The speeches are almost devoid of the use of the concept of class; they indict an economic system and point to its defects and inequalities; but they do not deal with the assumption of power by the working class. Two non-Labour speakers in the debate realized the essence of the Labour 'attack'. Sir John Simon, the Liberal, perceptively commented on Snowden's introductory speech:

> He admitted in his speech that the evils of unrestricted capitalism have in many cases been met in the past, during the continuance of the capitalist system, by setting up minimum standards, by enforcing a common rule, by

carrying social legislation; but, says my hon. friend with a naiveté which is really charming, whenever that succeeds that is socialism! There is all the difference, however, between regulating a machine and pulling it to pieces.

A Communist MP, T. W. Newbold, scorned the Labour speaker's lack of theory. Why he wanted to know, did they assume that taking over Parliament was equivalent to taking over the state? Even if a Labour government could control the police, the army, and the navy, would it not have to use force to abolish private property? Or did the speakers 'employ the caustic device of assuming that force employed by the state is not force'?[27]

These speakers perceived, as Beer has not, the essence of the ideology of the Labour Party. It promulgated the coming of a new system, but it meant even then the humanization of the present one. Because the ideology presented socialism in terms of changes in organization which entailed changes in ownership regardless of the class context, the party was able to extol as socialism the introduction anywhere of publicly owned services. Thus Arthur Greenwood, just before becoming a Minister in MacDonald's second Labour govenment, heralded the 'socialist experiments in the Dominions', pointing to the taking into public hands of the bankrupt Canadian National Railway by Mackenzie King's Liberal administration.[28] The celebration of the policies of the most aggregative of political parties even then stands as concrete evidence of Labour Party tendencies. The question of force was not a problem for a party whose main goal was to be accepted as a *legitimate* government by all sections of the community.

After the First World War, the Labour Party was proving by its pattern of recruitment that it was a national party. Many middle-class and aristocratic individuals joined the party. Liberals and Conservatives dedicated to pacifism but not to socialism found a haven in the Labour ranks.[29] This infusion of people from other classes into the leadership was enhanced by local parties being given a free reign to select candidates *and* by the adoption of the Conservative and Liberal practice of giving first priority to winning the seat and seeing party loyalty and reliability as of secondary importance. Wertheimer suggests 'dozens of cases' where constituencies were handed over to people who declared themselves willing to finance their own election costs. Although the extent to which this plutocratic element was very important may be doubted, especially in view of the fact that many of these recruits were more 'socialistic' than trade-union leaders, their entry was combined with a feeling that men of the upper classes possessed qualities indispensable to the party. The rise of the party to official opposition, and to government in 1924 and 1929, encouraged this dependency on the traditional 'governing type' of British society. Most socialist parties about to come to power without experience face the alternative of taking office with leaders whose abilities are proven within the limits of leading the working-class organizations, or promoting experienced, or at least well-educated, newcomers of other classes to leadership positions. The Labour Party unhesitatingly chose the latter alternative. Wertheimer described how, at the 1928 party conference, George Lansbury, 'the old champion of the British working class and of society's outcasts, let these men take the field in a body as though he, and with him the whole conference, wished to show England that Liberalism and Conservatism has no longer the sole monopoly of Oxford and Cambridge men'. [30]

It is interesting to note how well this recruitment pattern of the Labour Party fits with Eldersveld's theory of the political party. 'The party is an open clientel-oriented structure,' he writes, 'permeable at its base as well as its apex, highly preoccupied with the recruitment of "deviant" social categories, and willing to provide mobility and access for these categories into major operational and decisional centers of the structure.' [31] In a way surprisingly similar to the local Republican and Democratic parties which Eldersveld studied, the Labour Party of the 1920s was functional to the existing political system by providing a foundation for consensus.

In contrast, the policy of the Social Democratic Party in Germany during this period was to preclude any outsider or recruit of aristocratic origins from any effective participation in the party. Three years of ordinary membership was required for nomination to party conferences and five years of organized service in the SDP was needed in order to become a parliamentary candidate. Wertheimer observed in 1929 that the continental socialist parties had 'undergone a transformation to something spiritually and psychologically in opposition to what is specifically national in their country', and was struck by how different was the Labour Party. 'Without a past that sets it in opposition to state and society, it reflects the national characteristics of the English people. . . It is more British than German social democracy is German, Polish Socialism Polish'. [32]

Of crucial importance in studying the ideology of any political party is to notice the emphasis that is given to different aspects of the ideology when the party is in office as compared with the period when it is in opposition. The 1924 and 1931 Labour governments, plagued by their minorities in Parliament, indicated that, in so far as action is determined by ideology, the *effective ideology* of the Labour Party was that which stressed the society's cohesiveness and denied its cleavages. Historians of these governments are unanimous in their verdict that Labour Ministers were motivated by a desire to pursue their national orientation and their 'responsible' intentions. Special concessions to the trade unions were refused on these very grounds and national institutions which had been condemned during the campaign were upheld and venerated. On their relationship with the monarchy, for instance, Kingsley Martin noted the readiness with which Labour Ministers fell in with court protocol. 'On the platform they had presented themselves as the pioneers of social revolution which would sweep away capitalism, class and hereditary institutions with it. Their attitude to the Monarchy, now they were in office showed they had never thought out the implications of this revolutionary talk; when it came to the pinch they would not run the risk of open class warfare.'[33]

If we are correct in our analysis, therefore, Labour's ideology in the inter-war period may be seen as accurately enunciated in the 1927 policy document *Labour and the Nation,* where it was affirmed that the party 'speaks not as the agent of this class or that, but as the political organ created to express the needs and voice the aspirations of all those who share in Labour which is the lot of mankind'. It appealed to 'men and women of good-will of all classes of the community to aid it to accomplish [its] indispensable task'.[34]

It is not argued here that this strain in the ideology was in any sense ubiquitous in the party. Opposition centred around the Independent Labour Party in the late 1920s and ran throughout the party after the 1931 debâcle. The Cook—Maxton Manifesto of 1928 symbolized this opposition by rejecting the contention 'that the party is no longer a working class party, but a party representing all sections of the Community'. It took the view that a basic principle of the labour movement was that 'only by their own efforts can the workers obtain the fullest product of their Labour'.[35] After 1931 dissension grew, despite the departure of the ILP from the party in 1932. Tawney, Laski and other left-wing intellectuals developed, under the rubric of the Socialist League, analyses which painted British society in the stark terms of the class struggle, and raised doubts about the possibility of introducing socialism without force. Attlee himself criticized the party under MacDonald for laying 'too much stress on continuity and on the fundamental unity of society to the neglect of its discordancies'.[36]

The national appeal, however, was not submerged even during the 1930s. Attlee felt that the Labour Party was 'seeking to show the people of Great Britain that the Socialism which it preaches is what the country requires in modern conditions to realize the full genius of the nation'.[37] Labour Party leaders continued to reject demands for workers' control on the grounds that if workers were to be given some control over their industries, all interests must then have equal right to representation in industry. They opted instead for Herbert Morrison's concept of the public corporaton whereby board members were appointed on the grounds of ability, not representativeness. The implications of this approach were appreciated by at least one trade-union delegate to the 1932 party conference, Henry Clay of the Transport and General Workers' Union, whose comments are worth quoting at length.

> I want to suggest that the proposal which Mr Morrison puts forward stratifies industrial society. The workers are workers, and you doom them to remain hewers of wood and drawers of water under the perpetual control of the bosses. . . There is fear, we are told, that if you open the door to labour you are opening the door to other interests. We do not accept that point of view at all, because we do not, with all respects to Mr Morrison, put labour in the industry in the same category as users . . . Mr Morrison assumes, if this argument means anything, that we are living in a Socialist society today, and we are not. This is a class society, whether we like to admit it or not, interests will be there. Every interest but that of the people who are actually doing the job.[38]

The view that all interests are equally legitimate in industry as well as in the political process—a view which denied a special role for the worker in either sphere—remained dominant in the party in the 1930s when more party theorists than at any other time accepted a class conflict view of society. The party held to an ideology which saw the answer to social problems less in a redistribution of power than in the introduction of technically competent administration. The debates over workers' control revealed, as Robert A. Dahl has observed, 'the inherent conflict between those to whom socialism is a means of economic planning and those to whom it is a means for reconstructing the position and function of the working man in industrial society'.[39] At the end of the decade the ideology is found intact in E. F. M. Durbin's *The Politics of Democratic Socialism*, the pre-war forerunner of Crosland's *The Future of Socialism*. Durbin argued that it was 'radically false . . . to suppose that the dynamic element of social life is . . . that of class struggle and class warfare'.[40] For Durbin, the most fundamental form of behaviour of the human species was that of co-operation between classes; the highest value was not the attainment of power by the working class, but the unity of the nation secured by tolerance of opposition and dissent.

The ideology we have been tracing is not only conducive to bringing various groups and classes under the aegis of one political party, although it certainly is that. It also acts as a counter to the development of a distinctive political consciousness in the working class. No doubt British political culture conditioned the development of the Labour Party; the Labour Party itself, on the other hand, has played a part in maintaining the system of values and perhaps even in creating national values foreign to the working class before it was integrated into the political system. Eric Allardt, in an examination of cleavages, ideologies and parties in Finland, has used to good effect Neil Smelser's theory of value-oriented movements to suggest that, if some ends and values in a single institutional realm has become completely dominant in a society, people are easily mobilized in terms of these values.[41] A campaign in the name of these dominant values may cause an effective mobilization regardless of previous conflict in the society. An obvious example of this occurs in times of mobilization for war. A similar process seems to operate, however, when demands of working-class organizations are termed 'sectional' and overridden with popular support, in the name of the 'national interest' and 'national unity'. The tendency of the Labour Party to shore up some of the dominant values of British society indicates that it is well suited by its past as well as its current ideology to fulfil the systemic functions postulated by the modern theory of political parties.

IV

The Labour Party is not so well suited for these functions by virtue of its special relationship with the trade unions. The strains between the 'national' values of the party and the 'sectional' basis of the unions has always appeared most clearly when the party has taken office and translated its ideas into practice. In a certain sense there seems little reason for this conflict to exist. The actual development of trade unions in Britain often limited the class struggle to fights over shares of the product, and the struggle—like the unions themselves—has been institutionalized within the borders of the capitalist domain. This institutionalization was substantially completed by the end of the Second World War, when the unions became in Churchill's phrase, 'an estate of the realm'. Participation in government bodies and agencies dates from the First World War. By the 1960s, it was more the rule than the exception. It would, therefore, appear that the trade-union organizations in Britain ought to be quite amenable to an aggregative party with a national orientation and to a government whose policies are framed 'in the national interest'. And it is true that union leaders have often been won over by an appeal to this 'higher value'.

It has frequently been noted—by Marxists as well as others—that the fundamental sociological position of the trade union is its structural connection with capitalist society, its existence as an expression of the difference between capital and labour which it cannot be expected to transcend. Perry Anderson has observed that 'trade unions are essentially a *de facto* representation of the working class at its work place. Formally they are voluntary associations, but in actual practice they are much more like institutional reflections of their environment.' And he has contrasted this with the position of a revolutionary political party, which he sees as a 'rupture with the natural environment of civil society, a voluntarist contractual collectivity, which restructures social contours.'[42]

It has just as frequently been noted, however, that trade unions play a dialectical role as both an opposition to capitalism and as a component of it. Attlee nicely handled this dichotomy. He wrote:

> The trade union movement has two aspects. It is, in the first place, an organization of wage earners working within the framework of capitalist society in order to defend its members from injustice and to gain for them advantages. On the other hand, it is also an opposition to the existing system of society which it seeks to alter. It follows from this dual function that its methods of action must be such as to satisfy these two requirements. It cannot surbordinate the immediate interest of its members entirely to the attainment of its ultimate aims or for purely political ends. On the other hand, it cannot sacrifice its ideals for society as a whole in order to obtain some transient advantages for a section of its membership, or even its entire membership.[43]

Daniel Bell also depicted the union as a revolutionary force even when it accepts capitalist society in that its aims of securing a share of power over wages, hiring, firing, etc., involve a challenge to the system. 'The worker exists in a subordinate position to the property owner and his demands involve an inherent challenge to the nature and justifications of the property system itself.'[44]

The sources of the strains between the trade unions and Labour governments, it is suggested here, may be traced to the fact that trade unions are still predominantly working-class organizations which cannot deny what their members experience at their place of work—the divisions which still exist in modern capitalist society. A major justification for the Labour Party's brand of revisionism from the early Fabians onward has been the observation that capitalist society is changing so as to undermine class divisions. This argument was presented at the beginning of this century in terms remarkably similar to those of modern social scientists we referred to at the beginning of this paper. Ironically it is *precisely* because the trade unions are the mirror image of social structure that it is difficult for them to accept a view of society that brokerage politics demands—that of many groups competing on equal terms. A political party, because it is to some extent 'a rupture with the natural environment of civil society', finds it easier to accept as its standards of social division such indices as income and consumption patterns. A trade-union organization is more firmly tied to the conception of class as determined by the authority relationships in the organization of production and is more likely to see an individual's membership of a class in terms of his lower position in the production process. As a result, it continues to perform a class function, whatever its leaders' sympathies for the values promulgated in the name of the community. It is not easy for the trade union to accommodate itself to a 'national interest' which stands for a paradigm founded on norms which reflect the same authority relations.

As a result, modern British history is full of incidents of conflict between the Labour Party or Labour governments and the trade unions. An early example occurred in 1911 when four Labour MPs tabled a bill requiring thirty days' advance notice before a strike could be called, a move roundly condemned by the 1911 TUC. As has already been indicated, the 1924 and 1929 Labour governments attempted 'to display a national consciousness by obviously disregarding their class allegiance',[45] demanded sacrifices from the unions as part of national policy and attempted to use them as agencies in implementing this policy. Despite the extensive post-war integration of union leaders into consultative bodies and governmental agencies, conflicts between the unions and Labour governments have been common, particularly as the latter have continued the practice of relying on union loyalty to introduce policies the unions would normally oppose. The controversies over incomes policy, in both the 1948–50 wage restraint period and since 1964 are particularly illustrative of this conflict, in which the rhetoric of class has figured prominently. Thus the Joint Statement of Intent of December 1964 which introduced Labour's voluntary incomes policy, was heralded by George Brown as having 'signed away the class war'. This was however less apparent to trade-union leaders—even before the 1966 freeze: John Boyd, the right-wing Amalgamated Engineering Union member of the Labour Party National Executive Committee, declared at the time of the appointment of a Tory MP to the chairmanship of the National Board for Prices and Incomes: 'Aubrey Jones is an enemy of the Party and of the working class.'[46]

Samuel Beer has traced the so-called 'transformation' of the Labour Party to the reluctance of the unions to limit their traditional functions in the wages field, which he sees as evidence of their rejection of a socialist planned economy. In the early post-war period, he argues, a change of purpose occurred in the trade-union movement due to its new position of power in national decision-making and the increased affluence of the working class which this brought about. This stance presumably drove the Labour Party from its socialist goals of economic planning and led it to embracing a mixed-market economy by 1950.[47] Union opposition to incomes policy, however, has not been based on an ideological rejection of a planned economy. Their arguments were only that wages would be 'planned' or controlled while the rest of the economy became increasingly less so as the post-war 'bonfire of controls' became a reality, and this has been substantiated to the extent that incomes policy had been used by Labour governments less for economic planning than as a short-term corrective to balance of payments crises. In a predominantly market economy where the profit motive was retained and where the nationalized industries themselves were run on the lines of efficient business management, the unions had little alternative but to maintain their market powers as well. Had the unions felt that they possessed overwhelming power in the counsels of government it would be strange indeed if they would not have accepted government wage fixing. It is instead their continued feeling that their powers in establishing government policy (as opposed to the negative powers they may have in resisting policies initiated by government and business) is in fact limited. This is the view taken by V. L. Allen on whom Beer relies extensively in his description of the new power position of the unions. Allen believes that the major advantages from the relationship between Labour governments and the unions have gone to the governments. The most effective trade-union action, he suggests, is in determining the electoral policy of the party when Labour is out of office. He see important limitations on the unions' new powers and argues that the belief in them is now a legend which diverts attention from other powerful institutions in British society. 'Unions normally react to economic movements,' he writes; 'they do not create them.'[48]

It is unclear whether the unions have spurned the idea of a centrally planned economy or are merely taking exception to the limitation of their powers in a mixed market economy, although their insistence on retaining the commitment to public ownership in the party constitution (and most of their own) suggests the former is still substantially valued. The point at issue, however, is that the unions were not faced in 1945 or in 1964 with a Labour government about to build 'a socialist commonwealth' and much less a society in which the working class had 'taken power' except in the most obtuse sense. They recognized, and probably appreciated by virtue of their close allegiance with the party, that it was an aggregative party that was driving, within a given programmatic framework, at a consensus of conflicting interests, a party which was not acting for one class, but one that admitted the legitimacy and responded to the demands of the broad range of classes and interests.[49]

The continued salience of class for British politics, emphasized by 1960s studies of working-class attitudes and voting behaviour,[50] is the foundation for the party–union conflict which serves as a structural constraint upon the ability of the Labour Party to act out its integrative role. The defeats the Labour government suffered at the 1967 and 1968 party conferences over its incomes policy (and on Vietnam), and the rejection of the unions of 'In Place of Strife' in 1969, is illustrative of the limitations of the party structure in this regard. On the one hand, the government was able to ignore these defeats and pursue its policy due to the tradition of the parliamentary party independence from conference. On the other hand, it was the Parliamentary leadership's persistent ability to control the conference that underlay this independence and, if the unions repeatedly defeat the leadership on the very issues that allows it to fulfil its integrative functions, the party may have to retreat to a more class-oriented policy, even if only marginally. It indicates at least that it will not be without continuing conflict and recriminations, as well as threats and concessions on both sides, that the Labour Party will continue to emphasize through programme and ideology that it is a national party.

It would be incorrect, however, to read too much into the disagreements between trade-union and party leaders which an integrative party ideology produces. Most union leaders themselves hardly could be associated with a conception of the working class as the agency of social change. Further research on the integrative ideology of the Labour Party, therefore, should not focus solely on the periods of conflict between the unions and the party, but also should examine the social control functions of union leaders themselves to the extent the performance of such functions are legitimized by the rejection of the class struggle, or by the acceptance of national values which the Labour Party, as an institution deeply involved in the political socialization of union leaders, may have helped to inculcate and maintain.

V

This essay has suggested that the ability of the British Labour Party to act as an integrative political party which fulfils the systemic functions of demand conversion and aggregation is affected by two variables, one ideological, the other structural. The development of the party's ideology and electoral appeal in the 1950s and 1960s must be seen in the light of the ideological history of the party, which has exhibited a belief in the fundamental unity of the society. Without this historical background or with a more superficial awareness of the party's past which concentrates mainly on the party's commitment to public ownership and neglects its attitude to the role of the working class in changing society, it is likely that political analysis will see recent social changes as causational rather than supportive of the endogenous factors which determined the party's current position. Above all, they will neglect the party's own contribution to the political socialization of the working class.

Although the party's ideological history facilitates its ability to act as an integrative party, it faces an inhibiting structural constraint in its association with trade unions. While the party ideology does not see capital and labour as permanently antagonistic forces and therefore promotes policies which integrate the demands of both these classes, the trade unions, by virtue of their very functions in industry, cannot accept this position without strain. In so far as class cleavage remains perceived by them as an important social condition, they will be less than willing to have their demands adapted by a political party which stands astride this cleavage. The result is conflict between the unions and Labour Party over the very integrative character of the party and over party policy towards the economy and industrial relations.

Most political scientists recognize that Western industrial societies, including Britain, exhibit conditions of both consensus and cleavage. We have argued that both structural and ideational factors must be explored if we are to understand the basis of these conditions. Thus the consensus which is noted in post-war Britain may be seen as a function of the role the Labour Party, along with other institutions, has historically played in inculcating the working class with national values; while causes of cleavage may be sought in structural discontinuities which reflect existing class divisions.

(1970)

Notes

1. See S. M. Lipset, 'The Changing Class Structure of Comtemporary European Politics', *Daedalus*, Winter 1964, pp. 271–303; R. Dahrendorf, 'Recent Changes in the Class Structure of European Societies', ibid., pp. 225–67; S. Beer, 'Democratic One Party Government in Britain', *Political Quarterly*, Vol. 32, no. 2 (June 1961), pp. 114–23; S. Beer, *Modern British Politics*, London 1969; L. D. Epstein, 'British Class Consciousness and the Labour Party', *Journal of British Studies*, Vol. 1 (May 1962), pp. 136–50; L. D. Epstein, *Political Parties in Western Democracies*, London 1969; Allen Potter, 'Great Britain: Opposition with a Capital "O"', in R. A. Dahl (ed.), *Political Opposition in Western Democracies*, New Haven 1966, pp. 3–33. S. M. Lipset and S. Rokkan, *Party Systems and Voter Alignments*, London 1968, especially p. 22.
2. Roy C. Macridis, 'The History, Functions and Typology of Political Parties', in Macridis (ed.), *Political Parties*, London 1967, pp. 9–23. Compare S. J. Eldersveld, *Political Parties: A Behavioral Analysis*, Chicago 1966. For an explicit set of hypotheses on the role of a party system in moderating and containing class conflict, see the reference to C. B. Macpherson in Gunnar Heckscher, *The Study of Comparative Government and Politics*, London 1957, p. 152.
3. *Political Quarterly*, vol. 29, no. 1 (January–March 1958), pp. 8–9.
4. Macridis, p. 15.
5. Beer, *Modern British Politics*, pp. 126–52.
6. This classification is used by Nigel Harris in his *Conservatism, the State and Society*, unpublished Ph.D. thesis, University of London 1963, p. 10 ff.
7. 'Ideology as a Cultural System', in David Apter (ed .), *Ideology and Discontent*, Glencoe, Illinois 1964, p. 66.
8. Beer, *Modern British Politics*, p. 389. The seminal article of the political culture literature is Gabriel Almond, 'Comparative Political Systems', *Journal of Politics*, vol. 18, August 1965, pp. 387–709. As applied to Britain, see Almond and Sidney Verba, *The Civic Culture*, Princeton 1965, and Richard Rose, *Politics in England*, London 1965.
9. Similar considerations led J. K. Galbraith to apply his concept of the 'dependence effect' to price theory in economics, in order to show how 'supply' determines 'demand' through advertising and thus undermines the theory of consumer sovereignty. *The Affluent Society*, Boston 1953, ch. 11. Beer recognizes the applicability of the dependence effect to political culture, but makes little use of it. But see Peter Nettl, *Political Mobilization*, London 1967, pp. 63, 163.
10. David Clarke, 'The Conservative Faith in a Modern Age', in Conservative Political Centre, *Conservatism 1945–50*, London 1950, pp. 13–14.
11. Robert McKenzie and Allan Silver, *Angels in Marble*, London 1968, p. 162. Martin Harrison, *Trade Unions and the Labour Party since 1945*, London 1960, p. 343.

12. Quoted in Stephen Haseler, *The Gaitskellites*, London 1969, p. 163.
13. See particularly Gaitskell's speech to the 1959 annual conference, *Report*, p. 109.
14. D. W. Rawson, 'The Frontiers of Trade Unionism', *Australian Journal of Politics and History*, vol. 1, no. 2 (May 1956), p. 18.
15. See Michael Shanks, 'Labour Philosophy and the Current Position', *Political Quarterly* vol. 31, no. 2 (July–September 1960), pp. 241–54.
16. Labour Representaton Committee, *Report of the Conference of Labour Representation*, London 1900, p. 11. A similar resolution was put and defeated at the 1901 conference, *Report of the First Annual Conference of the Labour Representation Committee*, p. 21.
17. Harold Wilson, *The Relevance of British Socialism*, London 1967, p. 1.
18. Quoted in Ralph Miliband, *Parliamentary Socialism*, London 1961, p. 98.
19. W. H. Stead, 'The Labour Party and the Books That Helped to Make It', *Review of Reviews*, vol. 33 January–June 1906, pp. 568–82. A more recent survey of a 40 per cent sample of Labour MPs shows that Shaw, Wells, Cole, Marx, Tawney and Laski are the prominent authors of influence. The Bible is mentioned less than Marx. See K. J. W. Alexander and A. Hobbs, 'What Influences Labour MPs', *New Society*, no. 11, December 1962.
20. *The Advent of the Labour Party* London 1958, p.37, n. 62. Compare Adam B. Ulam, *Philosophical Foundations of English Socialism*, New York 1964.
21. Ramsay MacDonald, *Socialism and Society*, 6th edn, London 1908, p. 114. See also *Socialism for Business Men*, ILP Pamphlet, London 1925, and Lord Elton, *The Life of James Ramsay MacDonald, 1866–1919*, London 1939.
22. Quoted in MacKenzie, *British Political Parties*, London 1963, p. 345.
23. Sidney Webb, Introduction to Bernard Shaw (ed.), *Fabian Essays, 1889*, 1920 Reprinted London 1948, p. xxvi. For assessments of Fabian influence on the party see Poirier, p. 30 ff. and A. M. McBriar, *Fabian Socialism and English Politics 1884–1918*, Cambridge 1962, especially ch. 11.
24. Sidney Webb, *Labour and the New Social Order*, p. 5.
25. Egon Wertheimer, *Portrait of the Labour Party*, London 1929, p. 55. For a similar view see G. D. H. Cole, *History of the Labour Party from 1914*, London 1948, pp. 44–64.
26. Beer, *Modern British Politics*, p. 141.
27. *166 House of Commons Debates*, 16 July 1923, pp.. 1908, 1980–81.
28. Arthur Greenwood, *The Labour Outlook*, London 1929, p. 32
29. See Catherine Ann Cline, *Recruits to Labour: The British Labour Party, 1914–1933*, Syracuse, NY 1963.
30. Wertheimer, pp. 241–2. Moseley, Kenworthy, Ponsonby, Wedgewood Benn, Sir Charles Trevelyan among others were promoted to leadership roles in the party executive and in Labour governments during this period.
31. Eldersveld, pp. 526–7.
32. Wertheimer, pp. xv, 230.
33. Kingsley Martin, *The Crown and the Establishment*, London 1965, pp. 54–5. See also Richard W. Lyman, *The First Labour Government*, London 1953, and Robert Skidelsky, *Politicians and The Labour Government of 1929–1931*, London 1967, especially pp. 122–3.
34. *Labour and the Nation*, 1928, pp. 2, 46.
35. Appendix 3 of Robert E. Dowse, *Left in the Centre: The Independent Labour Party, 1893–1940*, London 1966.
36. Clement Attlee, *The Labour Party in Perspective* (1937), London 1949, p. 55.

37. Ibid., p. 37.
38. *Labour Party Conference Report* 1932, pp. 214–16. Compare Morrison's speech, pp. 211–14, and the debate the following year, 1933, pp. 204–10.
39. 'Workers' Control of Industry and the British Labour Party', *American Political Science Review*, vol. 21, no. 5 (1947), p. 887.
40. *The Politics of Democratic Socialism*, London 1940, p. 189.
41. 'Patterns of Class Conflict and Working-Class Consciousness in Finnish Politics', in Eric Allardt and Yujo Lateman (eds.), *Ideologies and Party Systems*, Westermarck Society, vol. 10, 1964, pp. 97–131. Compare Neil Smelser, *A Theory of Collective Behaviour*, London 1964.
42. Perry Anderson, 'The Limits and Possibilities of Trade Union Action', in R. Blackburn and A. Cockburn (eds.), *The Incompatibles: Trade Union Militancy and the Consensus*, London 1967, p. 265.
43. Attlee, p. 59.
44. 'Industrial Conflict and Public Opinion', in A. Kornhauser *et al.* (eds.), *Industrial Conflict*, New York 1954, p. 242.
45. V. L. Allen, *Trade Unions and the Government*, London 1960, p. 229. See also R. Harrison, 'Labour Government Then and Now', *Political Quarterly*, vol. 41, no. 1. (January–March 1970).
46. Quoted by Ian Coulter, 'The Trade Unions' in Gerald Kaufman (ed.), *The Left*, London 1966, p. 38; and see John Hughes and Ken Alexander, *A Plan for Incomes*, Fabian Society, April 1965, p. 39.
47. Beer, *Modern British Politics*, p. 188 ff.
48. Allen, p. 313.
49. Thus when Emmanuel Shinwell said in 1948 'that those outside the reaches of organized Labour did not matter a tinker's cuss, he was corrected by Herbert Morrison who insisted that the middle classes were partners in the great social enterprise on which Labour had embarked'. Cited in Paul Derrick 'Class and the Labour Party', *Twentieth Century*, vol. 173, Spring 1965, p. 123.
50. See especially John Goldthorpe *et al.*, *The Affluent Worker: Political Attitudes and Behaviour*, Cambridge 1968. See also David Butler and Donald Stokes, *Political Change in Britain*, London 1970, and the earlier Robert Alford, *Party and Society*, London 1964, especially p. 170.

3.

Profits and Politics: Labour and the Crisis of British Capitalism

The official ideology of 'British Socialism' has always been convinced that Britain provided ideal conditions for gradual, democratic progress toward socialism—thinking primarily of parliamentarism and the avoidance of conflict which marks British public life. In fact, the British social-democratic movement has never from the day of its birth known a society in expansion, a capitalism in vigorous growth looking confidently foward to unclouded skies—and incidentally, generating the surpluses which a truly successful social-democracy demands. Instead, it has confronted an era of grudging retreat, of penny-pinching and postponement, of nostalgia and half-heartedness, of slow disintegration and sad frustration, where today is invariably sacrificed so that tomorrow can be a little more like yesterday. The Labour Party set out to build a new world in the crumbling mansions of British conservative imperial hegemony. It has ended up as a chief caretaker of the ruins. (Tom Nairn, 'The Fateful Meridian', *New Left Review*, no. 60, March–April 1970, pp. 34–5.)

We are saying, at this conference, that the crisis that we inherit when we come to power will be the occasion for fundamental change and not the excuse for postponing it. (Tony Benn, *Report of the Seventy-second Annual Conference of the Labour Party*, Blackpool 1973, p. 187.)

This essay will attempt to place an analysis of British social democracy within the context of the recent debate on the crisis of British capitalism. In concentrating attention on the political realm, it seeks to make a contribution to a debate that has been conducted primarily by economists. It also seeks to provide a counterpoint to those political analyses of social democracy in Britain that have either abstracted the study of party organization and ideology from its economic context or wrongly assumed a healthy growth-oriented capitalism as the basis for their analyses. It was precisely the failure of these analyses to understand the developing crisis of British capitalism that gave rise to such ideas as 'the end of ideology', 'embourgeoisement' and 'a decline in class politics', which have been proven so disastrously wrong in the past decade. By putting British social democracy in the context of this crisis, the tension between the Labour Party's dual role as working-class party *and* as an integrative national party is revealed, as is the continuing discrepancy between the promise and performance of Labour governments. The first main section of the essay reviews the debate on the nature of the British crisis and attempts to draw the theoretical and empirical conclusions that would be the most useful for further political analysis. The subsequent section points out the central role social democracy has come to play in the post-war system and how the class conflict endemic to the crisis is both expressed and contained within the Labour Party as revealed in tensions between the unions and the party, between conference and leadership, between the Labour left and the parliamentary party. We will conclude with a brief analysis of the apparent contradiction between the shift to the left in the party in the early 1970s and the conservative policies of the 1974–1979 Labour Government, basing our analysis on the political location of class conflict within the Labour Party itself.

I

In their *British Capitalism, Workers and the Profit Squeeze*,[1] which one critic admitted was 'the first serious empirical contribution towards an analysis of the present crisis of British capitalism',[2] Andrew Glyn and Bob Sutcliffe initiated a well sustained and theoretically rewarding debate on the nature of the modern British economy. Locating the roots of the malaise of the British economy in an accelerating decline of profitability, they attributed their findings on the declining share of profits in the national income and the declining rate of profit of domestic industry to the fact that capital has been subject to two unrelenting cross-pressures: mounting demands from the working class for a faster growth in living standards and growing competition between the capitalist countries. The first, exhibited in industrial militancy, led to rising labour costs for capital and the impetus to pass on these costs in higher prices to maintain profit margins. The second did not permit British firms to pass on these costs fully in price increases if they were to remain competitive in foreign markets. As a result, British profits were subjected to a 'squeeze', which accelerated in the context of the world-wide capitalist experience of 'stagflation' in the early and mid 1970s. The share of profits in Britain fell from 21 per cent in 1964 to 12 per cent in 1970 to 4 per cent in the second quarter of 1974; the rate of pre-tax profit fell from 14 per cent in 1964 to 10 per cent in 1970 to 5 per cent in 1974.[3]

Glyn and Sutcliffe do not maintain that British capital alone was subject to these pressures. On the contrary they argue, as have many others, that the Keynesian full-employment policies applied throughout the post-war capitalist world gave impetus to trade-union wage demands that had, since the mid 1960s at least, a profound inflationary effect and have thereby increased the vulnerability of all capitalist countries to foreign competition. But what made the pressures particularly onerous for the United Kingdom was the long-run historical decline of British capitalism relative to newer more dynamic capitalisms. The first, and the dominant, industrial nation of the nineteenth century has found itself in the twentieth century beset by a declining empire, old capital equipment and a low level of investment relative to its competitors. Indeed, except for two brief periods at the end of the 1920s and 1930s, Britain has experienced extremely low or negative investment, as well as a net capital outflow.[4] The result of this has been a slow growth in productivity, which has in turn made Britain less capable of simultaneously accommodating wage increases and sustaining its competitive position. This was the case even during the growth years of the 1950s when so many political sociologists blithely assumed that the affluent society had arrived for good. For, although the tremendous growth of the capitalist world market in the first post-war decades inevitably involved Britain to a substantial extent, the underlying position was that the rate of growth (although higher than for any sustained period since the mid nineteenth century) and the level of real wages (which increased at an unprecedented rate) were lower than in Germany, Italy or Japan.[5] The balance-of-payments crises, and the attendant 'stop—go' policies of these years, were not the product of governmental mismanagement but reflected the deeper malaise.

The one way in which the squeeze on profits could be effectively removed is at the expense of the living standards of the working class. And as we shall see in the next section, this strategy was repeatedly attempted in the post-war period—for brief periods most successfully by Labour governments. But it was precisely the strength of the British working class in the post-war period, and especially in the late 1960s and the early 1970s, that made such a solution difficult. For British governments repeatedly found that attempts to reverse the growth trend of the wage and salary component of the national income served only to enmesh British capitalism in deeper contradictions. This will be seen in the next section's consideration of incomes policies, but it can also be seen in terms of the devaluation alternative, designed to reduce export prices and increase import prices in order to cut domestic consumption, to devote more resources to exports and, consequently, to increase profits, while workers' real incomes fell as a result of the price increases engendered by devaluation.

'In practice,' Glyn and Sutcliffe point out,

> the effects of devaluation depend on the reaction of the working class. It may press successfully for higher money wages to offset price increases. If firms try to offset this by putting up prices the competitive advantage gained by the devaluation is eroded, profit margins are maintained and there is no increase in real wages; this then stimulates further increases in money wages until eventually international competition prevents further price increases. At this stage real wages do rise and profit margins fall, and so by this time the competitive advantage of the devaluation may well have been lost. Moreover, this process gives a very important boost to inflationary expectations, which will tend to be reflected in sustained higher levels of wage pressure. This makes devaluations even harder to operate. Thus the willingness of the workers to accept the initial fall in real wages determines both the success of devaluation in improving the balance of payments, and its effects in restoring profitability. Devaluation could only help British capitalism if it was accompanied by effective wage control. This was lacking after 1967 and meant that devaluation did no more than temporarily stem the fall in the share of profits.[6]

A similar contradiction can be seen in terms of the effects of government fiscal policy. There is now general consensus in the relevant literature,[7] despite some disagreements (based on different methods of calculation) as to the exact figures, that taxation had the effect of at least arresting, if not reversing, the decline in pre-tax profits in the post-war period. Tables 1 and 2 from the work of H. A. Turner and Frank Wilkinson indicate this effect.[8]

This fiscal effect is the product of a number of factors: direct state subventions to capital (exemption allowances, investment write-offs, direct grants); a greater reliance on indirect taxes (purchase tax, etc.) falling on individual consumption rather than direct taxes on corporate

Table 1
Incidence of Direct Taxation on Corporate Profits and on Employment Incomes

Corporate Profits

	Excluding Tax on Dividends	Including Tax on Dividends	Wages and Salaries
1949–52	36.5	45.6	9.8
1953–56	31.5	40.1	8.9
1957–60	25.9	35.2	10.6
1961–64	22.0	33.1	12.3
1965–68	19.0	30.9	15.5

profits; and an increase in direct taxes on employment incomes. The last factor is particularly noteworthy. As money wages increased in a nominally progressive system of direct taxation, more and more workers were brought into the tax system and more and more workers were subjected to higher rates of taxation. The total result was to shift about 5 per cent of the sum of profits and workers' incomes from wages and salaries to corporate profits between 1949 and 1968.[9] But this shift was not a stable one, for as tax increases combined with price increases to reduce the money-wage gains of workers and scuttle their expectations for a higher standard of living, workers responded with a burst of militancy in the late 1960s and early 1970s that in turn substantially increased the labour costs of corporations. And since the point of fiscal policy was to reduce consumption (the ratio of social benefits to taxes paid declined for the average working-class family throughout the 1960s), the effect of this was to add a second kind of squeeze on profits: 'The increasing incidence of direct taxation on incomes (which were also

Table 2
Total Corporate Profits as a Percentage of Aggregate Wages and Salaries

	Before Tax	After Tax (including tax on dividends)
1949–52	41.6	25.0
1953–56	39.7	26.1
1957–60	39.5	28.7
1961–64	37.6	28.6
1965–68	37.2	30.2

charges on production) meant that effective final demand was rising slower than costs, so that pre-tax profits were squeezed.'[10] The result was that the aim of government policy—to induce greater investment—was frustrated by the policy itself, or rather by the working-class response to the effects of the policy.

It is important not to leave the impression that there are no errors in the Glyn and Sutcliffe analysis. The most serious error—and one that has only rarely been mentioned in the subsequent debate—is that they tend to conflate all wage and salary earners with the working class and operate with a basic two-class model of society. This covers over the problematic class position of salaried employees, many of whom might better be classified as part of the 'new middle class'.[11] Precisely because Glyn and Sutcliffe 'see the economic sphere as a place where different classes . . . pursue their distinct interests and continually come into conflict with one another',[12] it becomes important to read carefully Britain's class structure and examine the interests and behaviour of the various classes. The different classes to which the broad range of wage and salary earners belong to may put varying pressures on profits and may respond differently to government policies such as devaluation or incomes policy.

At an empirical level, moreover, Glyn and Sutcliffe seem to have misread the post—tax profits situation during the 1964—70 period and generally underestimated the fiscal effect demonstrated by Turner and Wilkinson in the post-war period.[13] But the strength of their approach is that it can accommodate—indeed it leads one to expect—such developments. That is, rather than advance a mechanical explanation for the British crisis, cast in terms of long-run implacable economic forces leading to breakdown, they locate the crisis in the context of the class struggle and make historical developments contingent upon the strength of the parties within that struggle. Rather than reserve class struggle for revolutionary developments alone, they locate class struggle in the events of the contemporary political economy.

This kind of approach clearly has critical implications for Marxist theory, within which the analysis is broadly cast. It should be noted that Glyn and Sutcliffe do not base their analysis on Marx's famous law of the falling rate of profit. Marx contended that the 'organic composition of capital', the ratio of constant capital (raw materials and capital equipment) and variable capital (the amount of labour used in production), would rise over time as capitalists employed new methods of production to save labour costs and increase their competitiveness. The capitalist's profit, however, is based on the surplus value of the total value added by labour alone in the process of production. Hence, if constant capital rises while the rate of exploitation—the surplus value derived from variable capital or labour—remains unchanged, the capitalist's rate of profit, his return relative to his total expenditure, will tend to fall over time, although Marx was careful to point out that 'the *same* influences which produce a tendency in the general rate of profit to fall *also* call forth counter-effects.' [14] In Glyn and Sutcliffe's view, however, 'the dramatically falling rate of profit in Britain does not seem to have been caused to any significant extent by the increasing organic composition of capital, but rather by an increase in labour's share of the product (very roughly the equivalent of a decrease in the rate of exploitation)'. [15] They nevertheless maintain that their analysis is not only logically consistent with Marx's view but also derives from the basic themes running through Marx's work—that of capitalism being by definition competitive and that of class struggle.

To be sure, Marx demonstrated that if the struggle for higher wages led to a reduction in profits, as it inevitably would under competitive conditions, the result would be a crisis in which capital accumulation would fall and unemployment would rise. Two modern factors, however, have to be introduced at this point. The first is that, with the advent of monopoly capitalism, the restraints of competition in the leading sectors of the economy are felt more at the international level. While this allows for a greater degree of passing on of wage costs domestically, this cannot be infinite because of international competition and because of potential competition domestically from other monopolies already engaged in inter-industry production. It is nevertheless one basis for inflationary tendencies as capitalism develops.

A second factor is the political and economic development of the working class itself, which both led to the adoption of full employment policies in the post-war era and was in turn accelerated by those policies, as the fear of unemployment gave way to wage militancy. Although the ensuing profit squeeze does lead to pressures on the state and capital to restrict investment and increase unemployment, the outcome of these policies remains conditional upon the working-class response. For most of the post-war period the state refrained from returning to mass unemployment for fear of the political consequences. And, at least short of mass unemployment, there has been no guarantee that an increase in unemployment would itself reduce wage pressure. Indeed, continuing militancy in the face of rising unemployment was the common fate of most capitalist countries in the 1970s. This anomaly can largely be explained in terms of workers responding to cuts in social expenditures and increased taxes—designed to deflate the economy—by compensatorily increasing their wage demands. By making the working class itself a factor in the determination of crises, we can, as Geoffrey Hodgson has suggested in a critique of the 'law' of the falling rate of profit, avoid the mechanical interpretation that is sometimes given to Marx's work, whereby one proceeds

> from a pure analysis of the 'economy' and then embellishes this fabric with sociological and political 'detail'. These 'factors' cannot be mechanically isolated. The categories of Marxian political economy are at once economic, sociological and political. Consider, for example, the concept of labour power as a commodity. It invokes the existence of separate 'sociological' classes between which purchase and sale can take place, a legal framework within which a labour contract can exist, and an existence of a state which can protect capitalist social relations, as well as the more obvious 'economic' connotations. It is only within this unity of the 'political', the 'economic' and 'sociological' that we can recognize the significance and prominence of production in Marxism.[16]

Given these considerations, it is perhaps not surprising that trenchant criticism of Glyn and Sutcliffe's analysis has arisen in Marxist circles still wedded to economic determinism. Most notable in this respect is the critique by David Yaffe.[17] Yaffe affirms the significance of both the growing competition between capitalist countries and the long-run under-investment in British industry, but he emphatically rejects the notion that working-class demands may be seen as an independent variable. To see workers' expectations and demands as part of the cause of the crisis is to replace political economy with 'social psychology'. It serves, moreover, to give credence to the view propagated by the ruling class that high wage demands are the primary cause of inflation, and it thereby unwittingly underscores demands for wage restraint. Finally, by seeing wage militancy as a critical element in the class struggle it endorses trade-union economism and is therefore 'reformist'.

As opposed to Glyn and Sutcliffe, Yaffe points to the growth of state expenditure as the key factor in explaining the modern British crisis.

> State expenditure has played a significant role in maintaining social and political stability since the Second World War. State intervention proved neccessary in the reorganization and expansion of capitalist production after the war. This process could not be carried out by private capital alone and nationalizations of basic industries and government subsidies to private producers, state expenditures on military and space programmes, as well as

on welfare, education and social security, have been a necessary feature of the post-war boom and the ensuing stability. The nature and limits of this kind of expenditure, therefore is a vital question for Marxist theory. [18]

Reasserting the law of the declining rate of profit in orthodox terms, Yaffe claims: 'It is precisely the crisis of profitability that makes a growing state expenditure necessary.' This expenditure is, however, according to Yaffe, both inflationary and a drain on profits. It is directly inflationary, he argues, because it is largely financed by budget deficits and government borrowing, which leads to an increase in the money supply. It constitutes a drain on profits because state expenditure is 'unproductive' and has to be sustained from the surplus value produced in the private industrial sector of the economy. Moreover, since unproductive expenditure increases purchasing power without a simultaneous increase in profitable production, it is again inflationary, having 'the same effect as too much money chasing too few goods'. [19] The contradiction of modern capitalism, therefore, is that the very state expenditure it requires to aid profitability has the effect of bringing about inflation, thereby reducing capital's competitiveness and draining private capital accumulation. The eventual imperative of capitalist policy is to cut social expenditure and to increase directly the rate of exploitation through enforced wage restraint and planned unemployment. It is only at this point that the working class makes an entry on Yaffe's stage as an independent actor. For whether this imperative of policy can succeed is seen to 'depend on the response of the working class'. [20]

There are many problems with Yaffe's analysis. First of all, Yaffe's reiteration of the falling-rate-of-profit law is entirely cast at a formal level, without any attempt to demonstrate empirically its operation in the modern British context. Since Glyn and Sutcliffe explicitly question whether the organic composition of capital has been rising in Britain, [21] this approach is particularly dubious. At the very least it is incumbent upon anyone using the law in explaining a specific conjuncture to examine whether the tendency for countervailing effects, which Marx also identified, is relevant to the period in question. [22] The result of Yaffe's effort, particularly in light of Hodgson's and others' recent criticisms of the law, is therefore not particularly fruitful. As one critic of Yaffe has argued:

David Yaffe, by using part of Marx's substantial analysis of the essence of capitalist production, tries to present a logically ironcast case which he even donates with the vigour of algebraic presentation. But the marriage between the analytical and the formalistic part remains a rather barren one. We gain no new insight in Marx's analysis, which becomes neither less nor more convincing as a result, while the algebraic demonstration not only remains without general validity, but even in the narrow scope of a special case it produces the result of rising organic composition only tautologically. [23]

Secondly, Yaffe's categorization of all state expenditure as unproductive is at least questionable. It rests on the consideration of all state employees as unproductive on the grounds that they do not produce surplus in a unit organized for profit. But much of state employment might be regarded as part of 'collective labour', indirectly productive of surplus value. This, putatively at least, is the case with state expenditure on education and social services, which cheapens the labour costs for the employer; state provision of infrastructure (roads, research, employment services), which constitutes direct input to firms; and state financial aid to business through subsidies, capital transfers, export incentives, and so on. From this perspective, 'an increasing proportion of the total (constituting therefore a fast-growing share of GNP) are productive expenditures, producing inputs for the capitalist sector. The share of social services, infrastructure, and accumulation expenditure is growing whilst that of unproductive luxury expenditure is declining. It is quite wrong therefore to regard the growth of the state as an unproductive burden upon the capitalist sector: more and more it is a necessary precondition for private capital accumulation.' [24]

It is also highly questionable whether increased state expenditures are directly inflationary. For the most part, the rapid expansion in state expenditures in countries of the Organization for Economic Cooperation and Development (OECD) since the Second World War has not been financed out of an increase in money supply, but out of taxation. [25] And although budget deficits have been large in Britain since the early 1970s, this is more a reflection of the problems of the economy, rather than its cause. As Ian Gough pointed out with regard to the deficits of the Labour government in 1974–5:

> The basic cause is the underlying balance of class forces in Britain and the inability of the Labour Government so far decisively to challenge the trade union movement. Given the need to channel aid to the capitalist sector to prevent a total collapse of investment, to maintain public investment, to raise certain social benefits as part of the Social Contract, and to avoid any further increases in taxation for fear of their repercussions on inflation and profitability, the result is inevitably a growing gap between state expenditure and revenue. The present Budget deficit passively reflects the alignment of

class forces which have generated the current inflationary crisis: it is not itself an active cause of that crisis. [26]

Yaffe's fundamental error, finally, is to abstract the rise in state expenditures from the concrete historical forces that gave rise to them. He is by no means wrong to focus on the growing role of the state as a key factor in modern capitalism. The state socialized many of the private costs of production of monopoly capital and assumed the enormous cost of maintaining social harmony through expenditures on welfare, health, education, and so on. And in so far as he argues that state expenditures do have inflationary consequences, he does not, like the monetarist economists, quite see these expenditures as a *deus ex machina,* but as produced by the system's contradictions. Yet, all this being said, his own explanation is a grossly mechanical one, whereby the state is presented as simply and automatically responding, after the Second World War, to the private sector's need for reorganization and expansion of capitalist production. A less mechanical analysis would see the state's increased role as itself the product of class struggle, in the context of the state's relative autonomy from the capitalist class.

The increased social expenditure of the British state after the Second World War, together with the full employment commitment itself, was a *political* development, arising in response to the growing strength of the working class. [27] The Beveridge Report, which laid the programmatic foundations for the British welfare state, explicitly placed the responsibility for the avoidance of inflation on the unions, demanding a unified wage-restraint policy as a quid pro quo for full employment and social services. Only this would permit the economy to maintain the share of the national product going to the wage earner. [28] From its very inception, state social expenditure in the post-war period was introduced with the threat of wage pressure as a key element in the policy equation. This was the case moreover in other important areas of state intervention in the post-war era. It has been conclusively demonstrated that the British state's (comparatively late) adoption of formal indicative economic planning (including the creation of the tripartite National Economic Development Council itself), of which the labour movement had been the most consistent advocate, was initiated by the Conservative government in the early 1960s with the express aim in mind of thereby inducing the Trades Union Congress (TUC) to participate in an incomes policy that would reduce wage pressure. [29] And even the post-war nationalizations, on which Yaffe places much emphasis as elements of capitalist rationalization, can in no sense be abstracted from their concrete origins in the demands of the British labour movement. Thus whether we attribute inflationary pressures directly to union wage militancy, as do Glyn and Sutcliffe, or more broadly to state expenditures, as does Yaffe, we cannot avoid the conclusion that the working class is itself an underlying factor in the modern British crisis, since the working class cannot be removed as an element in our historical explanation of the increased role played by the post-war state.

In locating in this way working-class action at the origins of state expenditure, it is not intended to confuse origins and functions. The bias of the system, in that the state operates within the confines of capitalism usually ensures that the functions of state activities diverge from their historical origins. 'Social policies originally the product of class struggle will, in the absence of further struggle, be absorbed and adapted to the benefit of the interests of the dominant class', Gough writes. But even this should not be taken too far. Despite the development of full-employment and welfare policies in all liberal capitalist states, the relative strengths of the various working classes can be seen in terms of the operation of these policies. Given the relative weakness of the British economy, little else would explain why the rate of unemployment in the United States and Canada was at least double that of Britain's throughout the post-war period. As Gough goes on to suggest with regard to welfare policies, 'the strength of working-class pressure can roughly be gauged by the *comprehensiveness* and *level* of social benefits. The partial, haphazard and extremely unequal system of benefits in the United States reveals the *relative* lack of power of its labour movement (and the absence of a party based on the trade unions) as much as the Federal nature of its state.' Indeed given the centrality of the working class to his analysis of crisis, Gough suggests that we 'strictly speaking refer to a generalized recession of the international capitalist economy, but not of generalized crisis. This term should be reserved for Britain, Italy and any other country where the balance of class forces prevents the rate of exploitation being raised and the dynamics of capitalist accumulation re-established until their labour movements are first seriously weakened.' [30]

In the subseqent section, we shall question whether, according to this definition, and once the historical and contemporary association between the British working class and the Labour Party is introduced, this allusion to Britain is fully warranted. For the moment, however, it is sufficient to register agreement with the importance of assessing the balance of class forces in analysing crises. In the case of Yaffe, he recognizes the role of class struggle to the extent that it plays a part in workers' response to current capitalist solutions to the crisis, but he explicitly denies its importance as a cause of the crisis. (Ironically, by admitting that state expenditures have had the effect of maintaining social stability, Yaffe himself appears to implicitly and inadvertently reintroduce the working class as a cause of the crisis, since this implies that there must have been some threat to this stability in the first place.) In the rush to claim class struggle as the exclusive prerogative of revolutionaries, Marxists like Yaffe cannot bring themselves to see the effects that economist and reformist working-class action can have on the state and the economy. Starting from the perception that working-class struggles over distribution are not revolutionary (with which Glyn and Sutcliffe agree), Yaffe moves to the argument that such struggles do not provide contradictions for the system. [31] The result is that he sets up watertight compartments between production and distribution stuggles that are ahistorical and unwarranted. The wage militancy of British workers (distribution) cannot be mechanically separated from the shop stewards' organizations at plant level that limited managerial control over the work process as well as over pay. Capitalist production is not a thing governed by mechanical laws but is a relationship, a relationship between classes in conflict with one another. And the struggle that arises out of this relationship, in a multitude of forms and spheres, is the underlying contradiction of the system, the dynamic that governs its motion and determines its fate.

In locating, as we have, the working-class struggle as a causative element *vis-à-vis* the ills of the modern British economy, the assignment of blame is not here at issue. Those who are ideologically disposed to blaming the working class for inflation will do so with or without benefit of our analysis, while Marxists will see the crisis from the perspective of the underlying conflictual basis of the capitalist system itself. The fundamental point is that we locate class conflict not only as a potentially revolutionary force, but as the basis for understanding the past and the present.

II

Showing the class struggle as central to the analysis of the British crisis is only the starting point, however, for a full understanding of the nature and dimension of the crisis. It must be admitted that in much Marxist writing, the concept of class struggle takes on a hollow ring, proclaimed from the rooftops as the motor force of history but all too often not treated as an actual historical phenomenon, experienced and practised in social relationships in their full totality. Raymond Williams has properly warned in this regard that 'it is only by respecting the struggle as something lived and not as something assigned or assessed, that new operative theory and practice will be obtained'.[32]

When taken as a real historical phenomenon, the nature and effect of the actions of the working class in generating contradictions for British capitalism cannot be grasped in terms of industrial militancy alone. The class struggle has taken place not only at the industrial level but also in and through the dominant political institution of the British working class—the Labour Party. And it is through the interface of the industrial and political spheres that the particular nature of the struggle becomes manifest. Moreover, as Glyn and Sutcliffe repeatedly stress, the success of capitalist state policies to redress the crisis must be seen as contingent upon the response of the working class. And this response at any given moment is structured not only by historical and immediate material conditions and by trade-union and shop-floor organizations, but also by British workers' historical and contemporary association with the Labour Party. Industrial militancy, as Glyn and Sutcliffe are well aware, is not an invariant factor but a tendency that over the course of the post-war period shows greater and lesser strength. It is necessary for this reason to inquire into the way in which the Labour Party has acted to strengthen or weaken this militancy over this period and to examine its capacity to continue to act in this regard. Only when this is done can we properly assess the true dimensions of the British crisis.

Moreover, just as any analysis of the British crisis must take into account the role of the Labour Party, so also must any revolutionary proposals for the way out. For between the bridge that Glyn and Sutcliffe, and Yaffe, want to build between trade-union consciousness and revolutionary political strategy stands social democracy. This is not 1902 and this is not Russia, and a call for a return to the maxims of *What Is to Be Done?* cannot but be a hollow and shrill exercise unless it is in the context of a recognition of the historical mobilization, institutionalization, and crystallization of workers' political participation in Britain over this century through the Labour Party. The question of revolutionary strategy is therefore not one of political mobilization, but of political remobilization. This means we cannot move directly from systematic economic analysis of the crisis to a political solution, without a systematic analysis of the political structure and condition of the British working class.[33]

Any analysis attempting to place the Labour Party within the context of the economic crisis must begin by noting the apparently contradictory character of the party. It is a working-class party, and yet a national party; it is a reformist party, and yet one that seeks to stabilize the existing economic structure; it is a party whose organizational, electoral and financial strength lies on its extremely close links with the trade unions, and yet a party that has acted, with open determination, to restrain the economic demands of its trade-union base. This duality derives, I shall suggest, from Labour's location as the crucial mediating link between the British state and the working class. And it reflects many of the contradictions revealed in the economic crisis itself as these are located at the political level of British society.

It cannot be denied that the Labour Party has in many respects been the bearer and galvanizer, as well as the electoral beneficiary, of working-class strength. At the beginning of each of its post-war terms of office, in 1945, 1964 and 1974, it has introduced a number of reforms to which the labour movement has been long committed and that were themselves crucial to trade-union strength. Some of these were defensive in nature. Indeed, it is significant that virtually the first tasks undertaken by each of the Labour governments involved restoring to the trade unions rights removed under previous Conservative administrations. Thus in 1945 it repealed the restrictions imposed by the Trade Disputes and Trade Unions Act after the failure of the general strike in 1926, the consequences of which failure the unions had to bear for two decades. Similarly, in 1964 it reversed a judicial decision (*Rookes v. Barnard*) that had undermined gains won as early as 1906. And in 1974 it immediately set about the task of removing from the statute books the previous Conservative government's Industrial Relations Act. Other achievements were more positive, going beyond the restoration of the *status quo ante*. This was particularly true in the case of the 1945 government, whose commitment to full employment, nationalizations, a National Health Service and welfare reforms still stand as the beacon of succcess for the labour movement. But it was also true in a more limited sense in 1964, with social policy reforms such as the Redundancy Payments Act and the abolition of prescription charges, although these proved less stable as this Labour government later reneged on many of them under dominant-class pressures. The reform initiative was of course taken up again in 1974 through such measures as the Employment Protection Act, the maintenance of selective price controls and the repudiation of a wage-restraint policy enforced by legal penalties.

What is missed by simply listing these achievements, however, is a recognition of the role played by Labour as the guarantor of the post-war capitalist order. The logic of capitalist state interventionism, we have argued, was to defuse those militant pressures from below that threatened profitability. And Labour, unencumbered by a tradition of *laissez-faire* and an explicit bias toward business as were the Conservatives, and enjoying the loyalty of the working class, proved particularly well suited for establishing the necessary balance between capital and labour as the working-class pressures mentioned above continued to grow. Its suitability derived from its being not only a working-class party, in terms of its electoral base and its constitutional links with the unions, but one with an ideological orientation that rejects the idea and practice of class struggle and promulgates the idea and practice of 'social harmony' and class collaboration. While considerations of income and wealth redistribution and of strengthening and broadening union organization do concern the party, they are limited by a concern for national unity in which the viability of the British economy is paramount. This class-neutral definition of economic viability is shared in common with Britain's dominant classes. In other words, the party does represent immediate working-class demands but does so within the context of inculcating the working class with national values and symbols. In this light, the Labour Party restrains and reinterprets working-class demands by mediating between nation and class. By upholding the values of 'parliamentarism,' 'responsibility,' and 'economic viability' against the values of direct class action and 'irresponsible', 'sectional' wage demands, the Labour Party acts as an agency of social control against the objective expression of working-class dissent.

This ideology, never ubiquitous throughout the party but always dominant in it, was not a post-war product, as it often alleged, but was infused into the party from its very beginnings.[34] It was not something picked up in the course of post-war attempts to appeal to a growing new middle class, nor was it adopted only when the profitability problem of the economy emerged in full view. Rather its electoral strategy and its conventional response to Britain's economic difficulties derived from its long-established ideological position. It is not the crisis of accumulation that determines the Labour Party's actions when in government; it is rather the party's ideology.

To be sure, Labour's national orientation became more obvious in the post-war period, in a political and economic climate that both provided it with electoral success and gave it a direct role in administering the society. Before the war, the principle of class harmony, of co-operation with Britain's ruling classes, seemed to contradict the party's programmatic concerns—limited nationalization, welfare reforms, public control over the economy—given capital's steadfast opposition to these proposals. This left unanswered the critical question of how these might be introduced in the face of opposition from the capitalist class. (Except during the 1929 period of government when the answer was baldly given: they would not be.) After the war, however, Labour's ideology and programme became more at one with each other as a climate developed where capital accepted, if not promoted, these changes in the interests of the kind of state intervention that muted class conflict and sustained capital accumulation. Of course, Labour's own moderate critique of the capitalist system, in addition to the economic and political dangers that beset it, was a factor in the greater readiness of the capitalist class to accept state interventionism by the end of the Second World War. As such, most Labour leaders came to believe that the Fabian goal of educating the ruling class to 'socialism' had been practically achieved and that the labour movement could now deal with an efficiency-oriented managerial class for whom the national interest ultimately took precedence over profitability.[35]

The 1945 Labour government, which set the pattern for future developments, gives a good illustration of social democracy's role as a key element in modern British capitalism. In conjunction with its reform measures, it progressively dismantled the direct administrative control mechanisms introduced during the war and substituted Keynesian fiscal techniques that were consistent with private ownership and that were designed to rest on the profit motive as the dynamic of the economy. It consciously replaced command planning with what it euphemistically termed 'democratic planning'—what later came to be called 'indicative planning'—in that it allowed considerable freedom of action for private enterprise, with pressure being exerted through the market mechanism. Nationalization was mainly limited to unprofitable and failing industries; generous compensation was paid (thus freeing up capital for new, and more profitable, private investment); and the new state corporations were run, in terms of their internal authority relations, along traditional business lines. Perhaps most significantly, its initial redistributive taxation policy came to be restricted by the necessity of maintaining profits. Thus union demands for higher profits taxation and a wealth tax, consistently demanded by the Trades Union Congress since 1940, were resisted. In 1948 Stafford Cripps, then Chancellor of the Exchequer, announced at the annual TUC conference that there was no relief for wages to be had from profits and pointed out that sharing out of even one quarter of all distributed profits (retained profits had to reserved for investment, he said) would only bring four pence on the pound for each wage and salary earner.[36] This argument, that the distribution of the national wealth would not of itself yield a high standard of living for the working class, became stock in trade for subsequent Labour Chancellors. And while the point was true if simplistic, it could not of itself undermine the case for greater equality. What lay behind it was rather the necessity for inequality within a society that relies on profitability for economic growth and the constraints this imposes on a party based on the principle of co-operation with the ruling class of such a society.

What must be understood in this regard, however, is that the elaboration of social democracy's national orientation in the post-war period does not provide the programmatic and ideological foundation for Labour to become an *inter-class party*. Its very success as a national party rests on its structural integration with the working class through the trade unions, which the other major parties do not share. This is most clearly visible in the union co-operation secured by each of the post-war Labour governments for a wage-restraint policy, co-operation that no other post-war government, despite repeated attempts, has been able to secure. The importance of this aspect of social democracy's role, electorally and in terms of the Labour Party's acceptability to the dominant class, was least apparent in the 1950s when the growth of the British economy concealed its underlying problem, and this provided the economic basis for the belief, trumpeted under Hugh Gaitskell's leadership, that Labour should loosen its ties with the working class.[37] But with the urging of the Organization of Economic Cooperation and Development for an incomes policy in the United Kingdom in 1960, and with the unsuccessful attempts by the Conservatives to obtain union co-operation in the National Incomes Commission, even the Gaitskellite journal *Socialist Commentary* came to see that Labour's 'close alliance with the unions is an asset, *which it alone enjoys,* and not a liability. [Labour] must be able to show . . . that the unions will cooperate wholeheartedly only if Labour is in office.'[38]

Despite certain scepticism among social scientists as to whether incomes policies 'work', there can be no doubt of their effect in providing British capital with at least temporary respite against wage pressure. Labour's first wage policy of 1948–50 brought real wage rates, which had risen from a base rate of 100 in 1938 to 106 in 1946, back down to 101 by 1950. Similarly, the 1964 Labour government's incomes policy reduced the rate of increase in incomes by about 1 per cent per annum between 1965 and 1968, and in fact real earnings actually declined in

four of the six half-yearly periods after Labour's 1966 re-election.[39]
Indeed, when we take into account taxation as well as inflation in
computing net real income, as Turner and Wilkinson do in Table 3, a
stark contrast emerges between Labour (1948–51, 1964–70) and
Conservative (1951–64, 1970–74) periods in office.

To stop at this demonstration would be, however, to present a static
and one-sided picture of the Labour Party. It would miss, above all, the
way in which class struggle takes place at the political level within the
party itself and the conditions under which working-class ties to the
party were maintained and renewed within the limits of this struggle.
What must be noted immediately with regard to the wage-restraint
policies of both the 1945 and 1964 Labour governments is that these
policies broke down, industrially and politically, not after Conservative
governments were elected, but *before*. And in both cases the breakdown
was accompanied by significant tensions within the labour
movement—between the TUC and the Labour government, between
party conference and party leadership—and within the parliamentary
Labour Party (PLP)—between union-sponsored Members of Parliament
and the Labour left, on one hand, and the Cabinet, on the other. The
critical difference between these two periods, however, which reflected
the acceleration of a political as well as an economic crisis, was that
these tensions continued and *broadened out* to other policy issues in the

Table 3

Annual Compound Rates of Growth in Gross Money Income (%)

	Gross Money Income	Net Real Income
1948–52	6.9	0.7
1952–56	7.2	3.5
1956–60	5.0	2.1
1960–64	5.5	1.3
1964–68	6.6	0.5
1968–70	10.0	1.3
1970–73	13.1	3.5

Source: D. Jackson, H. A. Turner and F. Wilkinson, *Do Trade Unions Cause
Inflation?*, 2nd edn., Cambridge 1975, pp. xv, 66.
Note: Net real income refers to gross money income discounted by price
inflation and by the effect of direct taxation, computed for the average male
wage earner married with two children.

latter period, while they were contained in the former. The basis of the change was that (what Robert McKenzie identified as) the 'bond of mutual confidence between the parliamentary leaders and a preponderant part of the trade union leadership which is the essential key to the understanding of the functioning of the Labour Party'[40] wore down in the crisis of the late 1960s while it was maintained in the late 1940s.

The trade unions affiliated to the Labour Party formally have the vast majority of votes at party conferences, control a majority of seats on the extra-parliamentary party's administrative body, the National Executive Committee (NEC), and have substantial influence over the MPs who are electorally union-sponsored (at least one-third of the total). Nevertheless, the independence of the PLP (enshrined in the party constitution) to decide policy priorities, the operation of Michelsian oligarchic factors to the benefit of the party leadership and the bond of trust between most of the union and party leaderships, have traditionally given the parliamentary leadership preeminent control over the PLP, the NEC and the party conference.[41]

The particular importance of the union leadership in sustaining this control was especially seen during 1948–50. There was a barrage of constituency and dissident union resolutions at party conferences proposing that wage restraint be made conditional upon the introduction of a directive economic plan, extended price controls, statutory profit controls, a wealth tax and the maintenance of wartime price subsidies on essential goods (which were being phased out). In general, union leaders supported these demands, but they removed the conditional element from official resolutions and proceeded to speak to the resolutions in terms of a straightforward defence of the wages policy and the government. In this way, union leadership was able to deflect the consequences of dissent for the government, while continuing to look—in terms of the wording of resolutions—as though they were pursuing their members' interests. The union leadership itself, however, increasingly came under heavy pressure from their members as the effects of the policy were felt. This was evidenced in a decline in union membership, an increase in unofficial strikes and, finally, in the defeat of the TUC General Council itself on the issue of wage restraint at the 1950 congress. This led to the collapse of the policy (despite government attempts to revive it), but it did not signal a change in the party's direction. This was because the union leaders recognized the common grievances being voiced by the dissidents in the party and by their own militants against a leadership in both wings of the movement that shared a common ideology of growing conservatism in social and economic policy and a commitment to American hegemony and anti-Communism. In these conditions, the party leadership could keep dissent in the party quite effectively bottled up, especially during its years in opposition. Except for one minor vote in 1950, not a single conference vote went against the party leadership until the unilateral nuclear disarmament defeat of 1960, and even that was reversed in the following year.

The 1960 conference defeats for the leadership on foreign policy and clause four (the commitment to a publicly owned economy in the party constitution) were harbingers of the changes in union—party relations that came to plague the next Labour government. These changes were, however, slow in coming, despite the election of Frank Cousins as a leftwing leader of Britain's largest union, that of the transport workers. Cousins patched up his differences with party leadership on earlier issues, supported the party—union agreement on incomes policy in 1963 and joined the new Labour cabinet as the key government link with the union movement. In the early years of the government, the unions showed remarkable loyalty despite the very rapid abandonment by the government—in face of the balance-of-payments crisis it inherited upon taking office—of the economic growth, social expenditure and planning policies upon which it had been elected and upon which it had secured union co-operation in incomes policy. This loyalty extended to tacit support for the introduction of a statutory incomes policy (involving criminal penalties on trade unionists who did not support the policy), which the government turned to in 1965–6 under pressure from the American Treasury.[42] And it even extended—in effective and concrete terms as well as in party votes—to the wage freeze and massive deflation of 1966.

But the cement could not hold. Cousins himself resigned from the government on the statutory-incomes policy issue, and in any case he had not mobilized union support for the government, being opposed in Cabinet to the direction of policy generally and supportive of his own union's early opposition to the incomes policy. By the end of a year of wage freeze, other unions began to follow the transport workers lead in droves. On one hand, there was a tremendous increase in rank-and-file militancy, which the union bureaucracy either had to lead or lose control of and, on the other hand, there was a decline in union membership in 1966 and 1967 of unprecedented post-war proportions. (This was marked by the largest fall in individual trade unionists paying the unions' 'political levy' to the Labour party since 1927.) The 1967 congress came out against the incomes policy, and this was followed by the TUC initiation of its own annual economic policy document. The election of Hugh Scanlon to the leadership of the Engineering Union later in 1967, by a left-Labour and Communist alliance in the union, put the largest unions into the hands of a left-wing leadership. Cousins was succeeded in 1968 by Jack Jones, who was directly associated with the left-wing Tribune Group in the PLP. These were union leaders who, together with the leadership of the white-collar Supervisory, Staff and Technicians Union (a fast-growing union in Britain) and some new leaders in the mineworkers' union, were less inclined than their predecessors to protect party leadership from conference or to expect union MPs and the party executive to act as 'instruments of the government'.

A number of deeper structural changes in the unions explain this reaction. The sustained period of high labour demand under full employment had created favourable conditions for local shop-floor bargaining, led by militant shop stewards close to the rank and file and ready to lead unofficial strikes (often as much against a conservative union hierarchy as against the bosses). It was this development that came to form the backbone of working-class industrial strength in the 1960s. The election of new leadership in the unions was often a product of this development and, although they were not always at one with the shop-floor militants, there was an initial readiness to open the unions out to rank-and-file pressures. Another important structural change was rooted in the growth of white-collar employment, which provided the main avenue for union growth and gave rise to a number of new TUC affiliates. A number of these were organized and led by people on the left of the Labour Party and sometimes outside of the Labour Party on the left. Although their membership was the least likely to be affiliated to the Labour Party, the very fact that they did not have to take account of the strong appeal to loyalty exercised by a Labour government over the members of manual unions gave these leaders a high degree of independence in expressing political dissent against government policies.

The effects of these shifts on the party were considerable, although on the critical question of incomes policy they took some time to work their way through. At the 1966 Labour Party conference the platform was defeated on three major issues, but the wage freeze was sustained. At the 1967 conference, the leadership again were defeated three times.[43] But despite the TUC's vote against the government's incomes policy a month earlier, the party leadership was able to sustain its policy at the conference by a narrow vote of 3,212,000 to 3,091,000. In 1968, however, the roof fell in. With Frank Cousins announcing that the Labour Party was 'almost getting to the state of accepting that the workers are on one side and the Government is on the other side', the leadership suffered five major defeats, including a resolution against the statutory incomes policy by a five-to-one majority. A resolution moved by Scanlon pledging support for the government 'subject to the reservations passed in the policy decisions of the TUC' was also passed. Indeed a measure of the breadth of the conflict was given when a radical constituency party resolution, entirely out of spirit with the dominant ideology of the party, was defeated by only 3,282,000 to 2,921,000 votes. It declared 'that the policies of the Government have been and are dictated by the monopolies and the big financial interests . . . only by taking into public ownership the 500 monopolies, private banks, finance houses and insurance companies now dominating the economy . . . can the Government effectively develop the resources of our country for the benefit of the people'. [44]

These defeats did not change the direction of the government. But when in the following year it attempted to forestall the coming wave of industrial militancy by legislating penalties against unofficial strikers, the dissent that had come to pit the labour movement against the Labour government finally broke through to Westminster. Unable to carry the vast majority of Labour MPs with it, the government was forced to abandon its 'In Place of Strife' legislation. Until this point most MPs, including the vast majority of the Trade Union Group, had sustained the government through thick and thin—mostly thin. Yet certain changes in the PLP were notable. Most scholars have pointed to the continuously growing proportion of Labour MPs from middle-class (that is professional) occupational backgrounds, while the proportion of workers has continuously declined. Between the 1951 and October 1974 elections, which elected respectively 305 and 319 Labour MPs, those with professional backgrounds grew from 31.5 per cent to 49 per cent, while the number of ex-workers (skilled and unskilled manual, clerks, and miscellaneous white collar) had declined from 42.9 per cent to 31.9 per cent. [45] There is scant evidence, however, that this has materially affected the ideological direction of the party, particularly since the largest increase by far occurred among teaches and lecturers, who have a relatively high degree of ideological autonomy from the class structure. More significant, and not revealed by statistical calculations, has been the entry of a new type of union MP since 1964, with considerable direct experience of and personal sympathy for industrial militancy. In the 1964–70 parliaments these MPs made up about half of the Tribune Group's approximately thirty hard-core members and changed the character of the PLP left by giving it a stronger base in the union movement.

The Tribune Group conducted a series of (what one Tribune MP called) 'regretful revolts' in the Commons, primarily designed to register protest rather than defeat the government on the issues. Nevertheless, these MPs acted as the 'official opposition' of the labour movement inside the House of Commons and maintained particularly close ties with leftist union leaders. And by 1968 they began to gain more committed adherents. On an amendment to delete statutory wage controls from the 1968 Prices and Incomes Bill (thereby removing the guts from the legislation), twenty-three MPs actually voted against the government and twenty more abstained. The government was saved only by a last-minute deal with the Liberals.[46] It was, however, a harbinger of the following year's events around 'In Place of Strife', when the Labour government attempted to restrict severely the legality of unofficial strikes and to undermine thereby the key base of union militancy.

It should be pointed out that despite these open conflicts there was very little danger in fact that the party would break up under the pressures of the 1964–70 Labour government's actions in defence of British capitalism. Even during the 'In Place of Strife' controversy, the attitude of the vast majority of MPs was conditioned by the concern to preserve the alliance with the unions and, if the TUC had been prepared to 'do a deal' with the government on the legislation, the PLP would have accepted this with alacrity. The union leadership itself was far from anxious to bring down a Labour government and despite the victory they secured by defeating the 'In Place of Strife' proposals, they refrained from carrying this forward, at least during the remaining life of the government, to a challenge to the party leadership itself or to the fundamental ideology of the party. The bond of trust had stretched, strained, creaked and groaned, but it had not broken.

It is in this context that the shift to the left of the Labour Party during its years in opposition from 1970 to 1974 must be understood. That a shift took place cannot be denied, but it took place within the rubric of Labour's dominant ideology and without a marked change in party leadership. The policy changes were indeed substantial. Spurred on by the tremendous industrial militancy of the early 1970s and by a degree of industrial and political class conflict (mainly around the Conservatives' Industrial Relations Act) unseen in Britain since the mid

1920s, party conferences recommitted Labour to extensive public ownership and price control, massive redistributive policies and non-interference by the state in collective bargaining by statutory means. The radicalism at the base of the party was seen not only in constituency party and union resolutions, but in candidate selection, as when twenty-eight of the fifty new Labour MPs elected in February 1974 immediately joined the Tribune Group (bringing its number to 68).[47] The sentiments quoted by Tony Benn at the beginning of this paper were shared by a very broad section indeed of the labour movement.

But the idea of 'fundamental change' can be interpreted in various ways. The word *revolution* has become commonplace enough in the advertising industry to make one aware of the difference between form and substance. One main test of the difference lay in the failure—based on the union leadership's unwillingness—to change the party leadership or even the party structure so that the leadership was subject to conference control. The key to the question of the future direction of British social democracy, however, continued to lie in its attitude to the industrial militancy that is the contemporary source of the British crisis. For the essential question was whether Labour would lead this industrial class conflict into political channels or seek to contain and restrain it as required by British capitalism. The answer was largely provided by the urgings of the party leadership against the overtly political strikes that rendered the Conservative Industrial Relations Act inoperative and that eventually defeated the government. It was provided more explicitly by Harold Wilson's own attitude to the class conflict engendered by the Act, when he complained of inadvertent fostering of revolutionary tendencies in the working class: 'the growth of shop floor power, industrial militancy, part of it spontaneous and part of it capable of being created by unscrupulous unofficial leaders . . . is the central fact of the 1970s . . . Faced with this new and dangerous development . . . the court of the right hon. Gentlemen opposite shows as much understanding in the revolutionary situation as the court of Louis XVI or Nicholas II or King Farouk.'[48]

This is not to say that the leadership's attitude on the question of industrial militancy did not change. It did. But it did in the sense of a pragmatic recognition that direct statutory state control over the union movement was as dangerous economically and politically as a decision to reject the Keynesian alternative would have been in 1945. The British trade-union leadership's opposition to statutory interference in collective bargaining rests on the desire for maximum freedom of action in their bargaining activities, but it has gone beyond this and become a cornerstone of their ideology. Their immediate and genuine response to legislation in this field is that it is as dangerous to democracy as it is to freedom of the press, speech or assembly. Of course, this doctrine is not the only aspect of the ideology and can be—and was—overcome at times either by appeals to patriotism and party loyalty or by threat of mass unemployment; but it is abandoned only reluctantly and usually only temporarily.

It was in terms of the decision to work with, rather than against, this central element in the union ideology that Labour leadership set about re-knitting the 'bond of mutual confidence' that it had so disastrously allowed to decay to the detriment of Labour's capacity to perform its critical role in British capitalism. A crucial element in this process was the absorption into the leadership of Michael Foot, who, in terms of the close relationship established between the Tribune Group and left-wing union leaders, was cast in an important mediatory role. In January 1972 a liaison committee was established between the PLP, the TUC and the party NEC to frame what came to be known as the social contract, which laid the basis for a voluntary incomes policy in combination with statutory price control, large scale income redistribution, new elements of state intervention and industrial democracy, and the long-elusive wealth tax.

The 1964 Labour government inherited a balance of payments deficit of £800 million per annum and an inflation rate of 3 per cent. The 1974 Labour government inherited a balance-of-payment deficit of £4,000 million per annum and an inflation rate of 19 per cent. That with this kind of acceleration in the crisis of British capitalism a Labour government, ostensibly commited to the kind of programme outlined in the social contract, should have been elected at all was a significant measure of the balance of class forces in British society. But it was an event full of contradictions for the British working class. The repeal of the Industrial Relations Act, the abolition of the Conservatives' Pay Board (together with the temporary maintenance of price-related threshold wage agreements that allowed workers to keep pace with rampant inflation in 1974) and the reintroduction of food subsidies all represented important gains. But that the union leadership so quickly—and effectively—joined the government in a wage-restraint policy was no less significant. In the summer of 1974 the TUC agreed to a zero real income growth, and the following summer to a £6 pay limit. The effect of the success of these policies reduced workers' real incomes, and this was followed by a TUC-government agreement on a

4.5 per cent ceiling on wage increases plus modest tax cuts for 1976–77, which as estimated by *The Economist,* was designed to produce a 2.75 per cent reduction in real wages. Not surprisingly *The Economist* also crowed that 'if the pay deal sticks, there is no escaping the conclusion that companies are in for a bonanza'.[49]

Given the government's explicit commitment to 'a private sector which is vigorous, alert, imaginative—and profitable',[50] the actual introduction of the redistributive programme envisioned in the social contract was quickly placed outside the bounds of 'serious' consideration by the Labour government in the condition British capitalism found itself. Yet the £6 pay limit of 1975–6 was endorsed by the General Council, and subsequently by the annual TUC congress and party conference. And the 1976–7 wage-restraint policy received increased majority support from each of these bodies. That the Labour government was able to secure this kind of support in the absence of its meeting most of the conditions of the social contract, and in the context of over a million unemployed, signalled for all to see the effective re-establishment of the 'bond of mutual trust' between party and union leaders. To be sure the tensions that ran so high before did not disappear. In March 1976 the government suffered a major defeat on its White Paper on social expenditure cuts when some forty MPs (over half of them trade-union-sponsored) abstained on the commons vote.[51] But the immediate negative response to this by Jack Jones and Hugh Scanlon was an indication of growing isolation between the Labour left and the union leadership. There was also, however, significant evidence of the latter's own growing isolation from the militant rank and file. Scanlon's inability in March 1977 to secure a prompt return to work on the part of his members at British Leyland, who were striking against the continuation of the wage-restraint policy, indeed the hostility with which his appeal to them was greeted ('go home, bum'),[52] was but the most visible manifestation of the tensions at work.

Nevertheless, the ability of the Labour Party to act again as a key agent of social control over trade-union militancy in the mid 1970s stands as an imposing attestation to the independent effect of political structures in any current reading of the British crisis. The sheer depth of emotional commitment of the union leadership to the party, as well as their pragmatic calculation of Conservative intentions; their long-standing acceptance of parliamentary modes of political action, with its implications for the independence of Labour leaders from party conference control; the structural limitations of trade unionism itself, confined to bargaining rewards within capitalism and thus denied a role as direct agents of revolutionary change; the ideological hegemony of

Labourism over the British working class (especially its direct and enormous role as an agency of political socialization for working-class activists), which has consigned Marxism to the margins of the history of socialism in this society: all these factors serve to give the British Labour Party a relative autonomy from the economic strength and industrial militancy of the working class and a continuing role as a national integrative force over and against that strength and militancy. The reassertion of social democracy's political hegemony over the British working class to defuse class conflict, however temporarily, stands as yet another warning against theories of crisis that embellish economic 'laws' with mere political 'detail'. It may serve as a reminder of 'one of the basic axioms of historical materialism: that secular struggle between classes is ultimately resolved at the *political*—not the economic or cultural—level of society'.[53]

(1976)

Notes

1. Andrew Glyn and Bob Sutcliffe, *British Capitalism, Workers and the Profit Squeeze*, London 1972.

2. David Yaffe, 'The Crisis of Profitability: A Critique of the Glyn-Sutcliffe Thesis' *New Left Review*, no. 80, July–August 1973, p. 45. Although I mainly concentrate here on the early contributions that established the main limits of the debate, the debate has continued and extended into an intensive re-examination of Marxist economic theory, primarily in the pages of the *Bulletin of the Conference of Socialist Economists* (hereafter referred to as CSE Bulletin). A comprehensive bibliography is to be found in Ben Fine and Laurence Harris, 'Controversial Issues in Marxist Economic Theory', in R. Miliband and J. Saville (eds.) *The Socialist Register 1976* London 1976, pp. 141–78. Two important American contributions to the debate are Peter F. Bell, 'Marxist Theory, Class Struggle, and the Crisis of Capitalism', and Erik Olin Wright, 'Alternative Perspectives in the Marxist Theory of Accumulation and Crisis' in Jesse Schwarts (ed.) *The Subtle Anatomy of Capitalism*, Santa Monica 1977, pp. 170–94 and 195–231.

3. See A. Glyn, 'Notes on the Profit Squeeze', *Bulletin of the Conference of Socialist Economists*, February 1975. It should be pointed out that the share of profits in the national income and the rate of profit are conceptually distinct calculations, nor do they necessarily move in a parallel direction. The share of profits may decline, but if the overall rate of growth is large the rate of profits may increase.

4. In a particularly incisive analysis, Glyn and Sutcliffe identify one of the primary factors in this to be the lack of integration between the industrial and financial fractions of the capitalist class relative to Germany, France and the United States (although similar to Canada, we might note). Because of the rivalry rather than the integration of these fractions, Britain's industry has had to rely more heavily on generating investment from its own resources. This rivalry can be seen in the City of London's commitment (until 1967 at least) to a high exchange rate when industry

106

needed devaluation, in the City's pressure for high interest rates to attract foreign funds while industry has wanted low interest rates to cheapen its investment, and in the City's consistent opposition to increases in government expenditure when industry needed higher levels of demand for its products. In general, the financial sector tended not to involve itself directly in domestic industry in the expectation of larger, or more stable, profits abroad. And it is very likely that, as Glyn and Sutcliffe suggest, 'one of the underlying reasons for this was the realization that the growing strength of the working class would make the profitability of industrial investment at home increasingly precarious'. Glyn and Sutcliffe, *British Capitalism*, p. 43. For an excellent discussion of the political effects of this lack of integration between financial and industrial capital, particularly during the 1931 and 1966 crises, see Royden Harrison, 'Labour Government: Then and Now', *Political Quarterly*, vol. 41, no. 1 (January–March 1970).

5.   Glyn and Sutcliffe, *British Capitalism*, pp. 38–9
6.   Ibid., pp. 167–8.
7.   For a good review of the literature, see G. J. Burgess and A. J. Webb, 'The Profits of British Industry', *Lloyds Bank Review*, April 1974, pp. 1–18.
8.   'The Wage-Tax Spiral and Labour Militancy', in D. Jackson *et al.* (eds.) *Do Trade Unions Cause Inflation?*, 2nd edn., Cambridge 1975, pp. 80–81, tables 10, 11.
9.   Ibid., p. 80.
10. Ibid., p. 85.
11. Michael Brady, of the Amalgamated Union of Engineering Workers Research Department, noted this failing in a letter to the *New Statesman*, 22 December 1972, p. 944. Unfortunately his own approach, which was to identify only wage workers with the working class and all salary earners with the middle class, was no less problematic, if not more so. For an outstanding theoretical examination of this question, see G. Carchedi, 'On the Economic Identification of the New Middle Class', *Economy and Society*, vol. 4, no. 4. (November 1975).
12. Glyn and Sutcliffe, *British Capitalism*, p. 9
13. Ibid., pp. 67–8. But also Glyn, 'Notes on the Profit Squeeze' (for a more recent consideration).
14. Quoted in Fine and Harris, 'Controversial Issues', p. 162.
15. Glyn and Sutcliffe, *British Capitalism*, p. 231.
16. 'The Theory of the Falling Rate of Profit, *New Left Review*, no. 84 (March–April 1974) p. 78.
17. Yaffe, 'The Crisis of Profitability', pp. 45–62. See G. Hodgson, *Trotsky and Fatalistic Marxism*, Nottingham 1975, for a critical attempt to place Yaffe within the Trotskyist tradition. Although Yaffe's article will be strongly criticized here, its seriousness should be compared with the trivial and blatantly ideological critique offered by the social democratic economist Wilfred Beckerman, who does in fact draw the conclusion from Glyn and Sutcliffe that Yaffe warns of, that is, that 'never before has the need for restraint been so vital'. See Beckerman, 'Inflation and the Class Struggle', *New Statesman*, 8 December 1972, pp. 856–8, and the reply by Glyn and Sutcliffe, *New Statesman*, 15 December 1972, p. 900.
18. Yaffe, *'Crisis of Profitability'*, p. 51. Yaffe's argument here draws on his earlier article 'The Marxian Theory of Crisis, Capital and the State', *CSE Bulletin*, Winter 1972, pp. 5–50 (republished in *Economy and Society*, vol. 2, no. 2).
19. Yaffe, 'Crisis of Profitability', p. 52.
20. Ibid., p. 59.
21. Glyn and Sutcliffe, *British Capitalism*, p. 321. Compare A. Glyn, 'Capitalist Crisis and Organic Compositions', CSE Bulletin, Winter 1972, pp. 93–103.

22. See Fine and Harris, 'Controversial Issues,' pp. 159–67; Compare E. Mandel, *Late Capitalism*, Atlantic Highlands, NJ 1975, pp. 149–51.
23. G. Catephores, 'Some Remarks on the Falling Rate of Profit', CSE Bulletin, Spring 1973, p. 42.
24. Ian Gough, 'State Expenditure in Advanced Capitalism', *New Left Review*, no. 92, July–August 1975, p. 80. Cf. G. Carchedi, 'The Economic Identification of State Employers', *Social Praxis 3*, nos. 1–2, (1975); pp. 93–121, and J. O'Connor, *The Fiscal Crisis of the State*, New York 1973, especially chap. 4.
25. Ibid., p. 51. The main exception is the United States.
26. Ibid., pp. 90–91.
27. For an elaboration of this argument, see 'The Development of Corporatism in Liberal Democracies', ch. 5 below.
28. See Sir William Beveridge, *Full Employment in a Free Society'. A Report*, London 1945, especially p. 200.
29. See Leo Panitch, *Social Democracy and Industrial Militancy*, Cambridge 1976, pp. 47–52, and Gerald Dorfman, *Wage Politics in Britain*, Ames, Iowa 1973, pp. 98–106.
30. Gough, 'State Expenditure', pp. 75, 77, 88.
31. 'It is not the antagonism for the share of the net product that underlies the contradictions of capitalist production, as the radical Ricardians would have it. It is the constant requirement to increase the exploitation of labour as investment takes place in order that sufficient profits can be produced to compensate for the tendency of the rate of profit to fall.' Moreover, 'the contradictions of state intervention have to be located at the point of production of surplus value and not in the distribution of national income'. Yaffe, 'Crisis of Profitability', pp. 49, 51.
32. Raymond Williams, 'Notes on Marxism in Britain since 1945', *New Left Review*, no. 100, November 1976–January 1977, p. 93.
33. Glyn and Sutcliffe are of course well aware of the important role of this political dimension and deal with it in their work. They do so, however, more *en passant* than in a systematic fashion.
34. The critical question of how the British working class came to be mobilized by such a party in the first place is usefully examined in Perry Anderson, 'Origins of the Present Crisis', and Tom Nairn, in 'The Nature of the Labour Party', Anderson and R. Blackburn (eds.) *Towards Socialism*, London 1965.
35. For an early and incisive examination of the Labour leadership's acceptance of the 'managerial' thesis by the late 1940s, se R. A. Brady, *Crisis in Britain*, London 1950, p. 563.
36. 1948 TUC *Report*, p. 861–2. For the government's distinction between 'totalitarian' and 'democratic' planning, see *Economic Survey for 1947*, Cmd. 7046, and *White Paper on European Co-operation*, Cmd. 7572, 1948.
37. See especially Stephen Haseler, *The Gaitskellites*, London 1969.
38. 'Election Agenda', *Socialist Commentary*, May 1962, p. 5.
39. For the full statistics see Panitch, *Social Democracy*, pp. 26, 159 and appendix 3.
40. *British Political Parties*, 2nd edn, London 1963, p. 505.
41. For a good review of Labour and union organization, see Lewis Minkin, 'The British Labour Party and the Trade Unions: Crisis and Compact', *Industrial and Labour Relations Review*, vol. 28, no. 1 (October 1974, pp. 7–37).
42. On this pressure, see Henry Brandon, *In the Red: The Struggle for Sterling*, London 1966, pp. 85 ff; Harold Wilson, *The Labour Government, 1964–70*, London 1971, pp. 131–2; and Panitch, *Social Democracy*, p. 87 ff.
43. See Minkin, *British Labour Party*, p. 24.

44. *Report of the Sixty-Seventh Annual Conference of the Labour Party,* 1968, p. 123.

45. Derived from tabular data in W. L. Guttsman, 'Elite Recruitment and Political Leadership in Britain and Germany since 1950: A Comparative Study of MPs and Cabinets' in Ivor Crewe (ed.) *British Political Sociology Yearbook 1,* London 1974, p. 105; and D. Butler and D. Kavanagh, *The British General Election of October 1974,* London 1975, p. 215. It should be noted that the definition of worker employed here differs from that of both authors. Their complete listing of occupational categories, however, has made my more accurate (I believe) recalculation possible. In any case, the trend remains unchanged by the recalculation.

46. See Panitch, *Social Democracy,* pp. 155–9.

47. Butler and Kavanagh, *British General Election,* p. 216.

48. 808 *House of Commons Debates,* 15 December 1970, cc. 1233–5.

49. *The Economist,* 8 May 1976, p. 82.

50. Denis Healey, quoted in *Daily Telegraph,* 17 May 1974.

51. The calculations were based on the division lists in Hansard for 10, 11 March 1976 on the White Paper and the subsequent confidence motion and then checked against MPs biographies to determine union sponsorship.

52. James Lewis, 'Scanlon: The Emperor Has No Clothes', *Manchester Guardian Weekly,* 20 March 1977, p. 3.

53. Perry Anderson, *Lineages of the Absolutist State,* London 1974, p. 11.

4.
Socialists and the Labour Party:
A Reappraisal

In the 1973 *Socialist Register*, Ken Coates produced a timely and brilliant defence of socialists working within the Labour Party. The argument was largely cast in terms of the absence of any alternative agency capable of maintaining a full-scale political presence outside the Labour Party. But at the same time Ken Coates provide a positive case for working within the party, stressing the critical role it plays in defensive struggles, the importance of parliamentary activity and the possibilities for change in the party contained in the radicalization of the unions in the late 1960s and early 1970s. The article was notably free of illusions on radicalization of the parliamentary leadership of the party, but it contended that the 'cardinal tenets of late fabianism have been refuted by events' and therefore that the ideas of the leadership could no longer dominate the labour movement, 'since the integrating force of their dogma has rotted away'. The changing balance of forces in the movement would come to be reflected in its political councils: the parliamentary party would have to elect a new leader acceptable to the unions or face a 'shattering rift', indeed, 'a candidate with the insight and skill to present a platform of socialist change [was] very likely to win'. The idea that the *status quo* pragmatism of Wilsonism 'might be botched along for another parliamentary term [was] not completely absurd', but the consequences of this for Labour would be immense:

> Another Wilsonite government would split the labour movement into irreconcilable camps, the vastly larger of which would be in sharp opposition to it. . . If this scenario is plausible, where must the socialists engage

themselves? There can hardly be a moment's doubt. Another Labour Government offers socialists the chance to do well the work they botched up last time: to force the imposition of socialist policies, or to isolate and defeat those who oppose them. While external critics might aid in this process in its essentials it will either be an inside job or it won't get done. [1]

The challenge Coates presented to socialists outside the Labour Party has not stood alone. Despite the actual emergence of another 'Wilsonite' government, similar arguments directed to, or at least against, the extra-Labour left have continued to be advanced, most notably by Geoff Hodgson, Peter Jenkins and Frank Ward. [2] And most recently, Lewis Minkin's monumental study, *The Labour Party Conference,* while meticulously uncovering the organizational bases of leadership control over the party, has also sought to challenge the orthodox view that intra-party democracy is ineffectual or inconsistent with parliamentary government and to show that the unions' policy commitment to extensive public ownership never waned, but was only temporarily concealed by the party leadership. On both counts he clearly identifies the Labour left of the 1970s with the forces 'which party tradition nourishes' and contends, albeit more circumspectly than Ken Coates, that the alignment between the left and the unions on the floor of the party conference which emerged in the late 1960s was 'bound to have long-term consequences for the distribution of power in the party as a whole'. [3]

Taken as a whole, these writing may be seen as a regeneration in the 1970s of what Ralph Miliband has called 'the belief in the effective transformation of the Labour Party into an instrument of socialist policies [which] is the most crippling of illusions to which socialists in Britain have been prone'. [4] It is the purpose of this article to reassess the case for working within the Labour Party not only in the light of the record of the 1974–9 Labour government, but of the behaviour of the trade unions and the Labour left since the late 1960s. As the labour movement moves into a period of opposition against a clearly reactionary Tory government, as the actions of the Labour Party leadership against the working class recede from centre stage, as the appeal for defensive solidarity re-emerges with urgency and cogency, the pull to join the Labour Party will gain renewed strength. And with it the illusion that Labour can be transformed will cast its shadow over many dedicated socialists. As it does, the argument that there is no viable alternative to the Labour Party is liable to take on the hue of a self-fulfilling prophesy.

I

It has always been its unique relationship with trade unions that has drawn socialists to the Labour Party. To a large extent this has simply reflected the perception that it is necessary to locate one's political work on that terrain where the working class is itself engaged. But more than this is involved. Precisely because the Labour Party is *part* of the labour movement, this means that the development of class struggle, even if not initiated by the party, is bound to affect it considerably from *within*. The great paradox of the Labour Party, and the source of the continued renewal of the belief that it can be changed, lies in this fact. The 'class harmony' ideology, which has dominated the thinking of the leadership since the founding conventions rejected the concept of class struggle, is consistently challenged not merely by external events and by socialist currents in the party, but by the direct expression of working-class struggle within the party, above all on those occasions when the trade unions act as immediate agencies of working-class defence against the actions of Labour governments.

The central factor underlying the belief in the 1970s that the Labour Party was ripe for socialist change may be located in the specific manifestation of this contradiction in the late 1960s. The broadening and deepening of militancy at the base and the increasing decentralization of collective bargaining began to come to fruition in the mid 1960s and resulted in a greater radicalization of union conferences and delegations to Trade Union Congress congresses and Labour Party conferences, and in the election of left-wing leaders in some major unions. After the enormous political loyalty and material sacrifice shown by the union movement from 1965 to 1967, and as a direct reaction against it, there ensued a period of sustained conflict within the Labour Party which was unparalleled in the party's history. To Minkin these developments proved that 'the bond of mutual confidence between the parliamentary and union leadership' was 'a contingent and not an endemic feature of the pattern of power within the party.'[6] Coates was more emphatic:

> Wilson injected an unprecedented scepticism about Labour politicians into nearly all the unions, which serum took effect from top to bottom. At the same time, the reaction produced a notable democratization of the main unions, which process has adamantly resisted the Industrial Relations Act, and shows not the slightest sign of recession. No new leader of the party can avoid coming to terms with this profound development, which already carries

the problem of accommodation far beyond the scope of the kind of bureaucratic intrigue which was open to leaders of the Gaitskell era. Unlike Lawther and Williamson, whose capacity to uphold conservative policies rested on widespread mass lethargy, Jones and Scanlon can only lend their weight to policies which carry support in an active and self-assertive rank and file. Of course, they could always theoretically abandon the rank and file; but if they ever did, they would be of little value to the establishment without it. All this means, quite plainly, that the unions will not be easily diverted from the pursuit of serious social change.[7]

Indeed, in the 1970–74 'interregnum' the unions supported policies which, while not amounting to a socialist programme, certainly went as far in proposing to test the limits of reforms within capitalism as any in Labour Party history. Suffused in the spirit of the greatest period of class confrontation in Britain for fifty years and encouraged by the alliance between the Transport and General Worker's Union and Amalgamated Union of Engineering Workers and the Labour left forged in the late 1960s, party conferences breathed the rhetorical fire of socialism with uncharacteristically little intake of the reformist smoke that is inevitably present on these occasions. The National Executive Committee's 1973 Programme, while going nowhere near as far as some successful conference resolutions of 1971 and 1972, nevertheless promised a major extension of public ownership and control, above all through the proposed National Enterprise Board's acquisition of 'some twenty-five of our largest manufacturers', and through a system of planning agreements with the top hundred companies, both backed up by extensive compulsory powers in a new Industry Act.[8] When combined with the commitments established in the TUC–Labour Party Liaison Committee's 'Social Contract' on repealing the Industrial Realations Act, 'real moves' towards industrial democracy, extensive wealth and income redistribution, and statutory price controls, socialists in the party could with justification claim to have made major gains. It was all summed up in Coates's challenge to sceptics: 'If the unions decide to support real socialist options, why should the socialists need to split away?'[9]

Yet if the events of 1968–74 were indicative of the extent to which the party is internally affected by major periods of class struggle, they by no means disposed of the question of whether the Labour Party can actually be transformed into a socialist party by struggles on its own terrain. On the contrary, the intra-party conflicts of this period were subject to specific limitations which considerably undermined their potential for change. In the first place, the shift to the left in the unions was not nearly as pronounced as was sometimes imagined. As Minkin himself has shown, 'in spite of the move to the left evident in the resolutions submitted and votes cast there was no major change in the leadership of the largest unions between 1970 and 1973. Those changes which did take place in fact reinforced the position of the right . . . thus it was still the case in 1975 that most of the senior officials of the ten largest unions were to the right of the party's political centre of gravity.'[10] Secondly, the extent of the rift between the left-wing union leadership and the party leadership was often exaggerated. Both the left-wing union leaders and the parliamentary left had a consistently great regard for Harold Wilson's 'tolerance' of minority opinion in the party and a marked tendency to put real stock in the (re)conversions of their erstwhile Bevanite colleagues. This did not apply to the Jenkinsites, both because they showed less tolerance and less readiness to employ socialist rhetoric to conceal their orthodoxy and because they never fully appreciated as did Wilson (and Callaghan) that without the unions the party would be 'uneasily poised between the Liberals and the Bow Group' without a mass base.[11] To be sure, the establishment of the Liaison Committee and the absorption of Michael Foot into the leadership specifically to act as what Tony Benn called 'the link and buckle with the industrial wing of the movement'[12] greatly facilitated the accommodation between Jones and Scanlon and the leadership. But apart from the stipulation that a Labour government never again impose statutory penalties on collective bargaining, this accommodation was much more 'endemic' and much less 'conditional' than Coates or Minkin allowed.

Thirdly, the force of union solidarity and tradition, which had been a source of the cleavage regarding the issue of state intervention in collective bargaining, was at the same time a source of continuity and conservatism in terms of maintaining the dominance of the party leadership. Again as Minkin admirably has shown, even the left-wing unions continued to cast their votes for the Conference Arrangements Committee and the NEC largely on the basis of traditional arrangements and understanding, leaving right-wing sitting tenants in place. Although these committees were more responsive to delegate pressures in the early 1970s, it was significant that Constituency Labour Party resolutions which would have required MPs to abide by conference decisions were either kept off the agenda or remitted to the executive. Similarly left-wing union leaders refused to countenance the idea of instructing their union's sponsored MPs on how to vote. The party leadership were still able to draw substantially on the union leadership's feeling, gained from experience in managing their own union conferences, that a 'good conference' was one that did not go too far towards divisiveness and their sensitivity that unions should not be seen to be 'running' the party. All this was reflective of the 'typically limited role' which Ralph Miliband identified the union leaders as playing in the party, whereby they see themselves as 'representatives of organized labour, involved in a bargaining relationship, notably over industrial and economic issues with their political colleagues in the Labour Party, and not in the lead as political rivals intending to capture control of the party for purposes radically different from those of the men who now control it'. [13] This is not so much a matter, as Ken Coates seemed to think in challenging this view in his 1973 article, of union leaders failing to put themselves forward from time to time as political leaders or even acting as policy initiators; it is rather the unions' maintenance of traditional practices *vis-à-vis* the party leadership which inhibits them from throwing the full weight of their organizational strength in the party behind the forces for change, even when their differences with the leadership on major policy issues is significant.

But far the most important factor prohibiting change in the party, which in fact reproduces the unions' 'limited role', is the very commitment of the unions to maintaining the Labour Party as a 'viable' political force, both out of immediate defensive and electoral considerations and out of overwhelming loyalty to the party as an institution. The very process that suggested to Coates that the party 'might possibly recover from a whole succession of Wilsons'—the threat of a Conservative government to the interests of the working class and the lack of any ready alternative to Labour's political machine—is the same process which all but guarantees that the party *will* actually have to face a whole succession of Wilsons, however 'implausible' Coates finds this prospect. For to carry intra-party conflict to the point of forcing the imposition of socialist policies, or isolating and defeating those who oppose them, entails too great a risk to party unity in terms of the primacy of immediate electoral and defensive campaigns. It is party unity, not change, which is ultimately paramount from the unions' perspective when intra-party conflict emerges. There may be some good defensive reasons for this, but it is not the basis for the kind of transformation entailed in changing the Labour Party.

What Coates called the 'barely concealed civil war' between the party and union leadership in 1968 and 1969 is particularly illustrative in this regard. The 'Solemn and Binding Agreement' between the TUC and the government, which resolved the immediate controversy over 'In Place of

Strife', may be seen from one perspective as a sterling victory by the labour movement over a Labour government. But from another perspective, the long and abrasive negotiations between Wilson, Barbara Castle and the General Council was not only about avoiding the proposed legislation, but about avoiding an actual 'civil war' in the party. The union leadership, no less than the party leadership, were reaching for some political formula to heal the immediate scission and were for that reason anxious that 'extraneous' issues (such as those which were at the source of the division) should not be raised. What stood out about the victory over 'In Place of Strife' was its purely defensive character: it involved neither a change in party leadership nor ideology, indeed it did not even address the question of the government's continuing commitment to a statutory incomes policy. Although it did not by any means re-establish a consensus between the unions and the government, it certainly left the latter in a much stronger position *vis-à-vis* the Labour Party than it had been a year earlier. Whereas the leadership had been defeated in five major policy issues at the 1968 conference, the 1969 conference left the Transport and General Workers Union and Amalgamated Engineering Union in virtual isolation amongst the unions in opposing the leadership on incomes policy, and the delegates were treated to the sight of Hugh Scanlon moving fulsome support for the government, without the reservations he had insisted on (and obtained) a year earlier.

It can, of course, be said of 1968 (as Coates said of 1973—and is being said of 1979) that the 'battle-lines are just beginning to form.' But in the 1970—73 period again the very factors that Coates identified as ensuring that 'the whole alliance did not fall apart'—the common struggle against the Tory government and the necessity of maintaining Labour as a viable political force to fight the next election—also ensured that the battle would not go so far as to risk party unity. This was most critically evident with regard to Harold Wilson's successful opposition to the NEC's 'twenty-five companies' proposal. As Minkin has put it, the 'triumvirate' of Foot, Jones and Wilson 'acted as a reconciling force between the party's factions and a restraint upon the leftism in the programme. Thus in 1973, the advantages of this link went to the party leadership as both large union delegations responded to the call for moderation and pre-election unity: there was no concerted attempt to push the more radical interpretation of the role of the National Enterprise Board.'[14] In these circumstances, Harold Wilson did not actually have to use his threatened 'veto' by the Shadow Cabinet against including this proposal in the manifesto. But his view that 'it was inconceivable that the party would go into general election on this proposal, nor could any incoming Labour Government be so committed'[15] was overwhelmingly confirmed by the 1973 conference.

The result was that the Labour Party emerged out of its period of opposition with a most ambiguous programme. The NEC's Programme itself had already exhibited considerable ambiguity by noting that the proposed Planning Agreements System had 'developed from those already in operation in France, Belgium and Italy', thus inviting the question of whether this was in fact to be the centrepiece of a socialist economic strategy or of a modernized state capitalism. Similar questions could have been raised about the resemblance between the NEB and Italian state holding companies. Precisely because it could have been argued, however, that the way that these new policies would be used by a Labour government would depend on the balance of forces in the party and the state, Wilson's pre-election victory on this question was so significant. For it indicated how easily openings for change in the party are closed in the face of immediate pressures of party unity. In so far as the unions were concerned in 1973, the battle-lines for change were hardly being drawn. On the contrary, the hatchet was being buried.

II

The limitations which the requirements of defensive and electoral unity place upon changing the Labour Party entail consequences which by no means can simply be measured in terms of the ambiguity of Labour's election manifestos or even the failure of Labour governments to implement those reforms which the manifestos do explicitly promise. For the problem with the Labour Party is not simply that in the absence of a better alternative, the working class has to make do with a reformist rather than a revolutionary party. It is that the party itself plays an active role as an agency of social control *over* the working class. Ken Coates was indeed right to explain the importance of parliamentary politics and the stability of the Labour Party on the grounds that no alternative socialist grouping can become an alternative vehicle 'for the development of the outlook of a whole social class until they can be seen to have the potential to enable that class to speak for itself at every political level on which its interests are the object of contention. Even the corporate interests of the subordinate class cannot be safeguarded without organization on this scale.' But when he immediately went on to maintain that 'it is manifestly silly to speak about "hegemonic aspirations" developing within such a class unless it has safely passed the point at which its self-defence is relatively assured', [16] it was he who was being unrealistic. This is not only because self-defence entails a constant struggle and is never 'assured'; but more importantly because continued subordination may be inscribed within the very process of self-defence. In the case of the Labour Party, self-defence takes place *at the expense* of the hegemonic development of the working class.

This is not just a matter of Labour governments introducing reforms which are specifically structured to integrate the working class in the existing social order, reforms which constitute real gains for the class—but are designed to close rather than open room for further struggle. [17] Nor is it just a matter of leaving a party leadership in place which proclaims and maintains those 'national' values which *prescribe* subordination of the working class and which treat the *whole class* as a mere *sectional* group in the society. (In periods of mass quiescence this may not entail misrepresentation; but it certainly will greatly reinforce the quiescence.) It is also a matter of Labour governments employing the loyalty and solidarity inherent in the movement actually to *demobilize* the working class at critical junctures in its development and to secure real material sacrifices from the working class at those very moments when economic militancy threatens profitability. The very self-confidence and self-awareness of an active working class, which is the force behind the election of Labour governments, becomes the very *object* of the attempt to subdue and extirpate this energy. Although these attempts are only partially and temporarily successful, they nevertheless mean that it is never quite a matter of just picking up where one left off when class conflict re-emerges again.

The 1974–9 Labour government has to be seen precisely in this light. It was composed of a party leadership which, in Coates's words, 'inspires no sacrifice, blazes no trails, bodes no fundamental changes, and meets no spiritual needs'. But this is too negative a view. It was a leadership which continued to see itself playing, and did play, an active and indispensable role in the British political system—above all the role of tempering, containing and channelling into 'responsible' outlets the industrial militancy of its time. The Labour leadership's part in the defensive campaign against the Industrial Relations Bill was not merely that of fighting the battle in Parliament, but of urging the unions not to take the very industrial-cum-political action which in the end scuppered the Act. A prime basis of Wilson's opposition to the Act was that it fostered revolutionary tendencies in the working class, that it was a 'militants' charter', that it treated industrial relations as part of 'a wider political conflict'. Throughout its years in opposition the Labour leadership remained committed, moreover, to one fixed ideal—resurrecting union agreement to wage restraint. Wilson and Callaghan did come to appreciate that a statutory incomes policy was unacceptable to the unions; indeed, this was the one genuine 'conversion' they experienced while in opposition, the one real lesson they learned from Michael Foot and Jack Jones. But this did not dampen their enthusiasm for wage restraint. On the contrary, they continued to hold to the view, first elaborated in the early 1960s, that the Labour Party's ability to promise this was its major electoral asset. Although they could not obtain from the unions the kind of fulsome commitment to incomes policy than they had engineered in 1963, they continued to press for it via the Liaison Committee and in the drawing up of the manifesto, right through the industrial crisis of December 1973 and January 1974. The Labour left were able to convince themselves, as they had done from 1959 to 1964, that what was involved was a 'socialist incomes policy', in which wage restraint was not the object of the exercise but an inevitable part of socialist planning. The Labour leadership, however, clearly accepted the more radical elements of the Social Contract only to the extent that unions insisted that, as the February election manifesto put it, 'only deeds can persuade . . . that an incomes policy is not some kind of trick to force [the worker] . . . to bear the brunt of the national burden'. If it turned out that such persuasion was possible without too many such deeds, so much the better.

And what happened? Within a year of the February 1974 election, incomes policy became the centrepiece of the social contract and the unions responded with an exercise in voluntary wage restraint unparalleled in modern British history. Increases in gross money earnings for the average worker fell from 25.5 per cent in 1974–5 to 12.4 per cent in 1975–6 to 8.8 per cent in 1976–7. As the rate of inflation fell more slowly (from 25 per cent to 14 per cent over the three years) real wages fell considerably. Even taking into account the compensatory tax concessions offered by the government, real wages fell by 5.5 per cent, 1.6 per cent and almost 1 per cent in the three respective years. [18] The real weekly net income of the average male worker, married with two children, if calculated in terms of October 1978 prices, had stood at £68.90 in September 1970, risen to £74.50 in September 1972 and maintained that level until September 1974; it fell by September 1977 to £68.10—that is over £6 per week. In 1977–8, with a less restrictive pay norm, a rate of inflation of 8 per cent, additional tax concessions and the first instances of breakdown of union co-operation, real net earnings recovered substantially (increasing by 9 per cent). But this still left the average worker with a real weekly take-home pay in September 1978 which was £3.50 less than in 1974 and almost £1 a week less in terms of real net weekly income (that is, taking account of increased transfer payments of 1977–8). [19]

It would of course be absurd to attribute these losses to the Labour government's wage restraint policies alone in abstraction from the economic crisis. But the sacrifice entailed in wage restraint would have been one thing had it been inspired on the basis of Tony Benn's promise to the 1973 conference (broadly incorporated into the 1974 manifesto) that 'the crisis we inherit when we come to power will be the occasion for fundamental change and not the excuse for postponing it'. [20] Instead the crisis became the basis for maintaining the existing balance of wealth and power in British society by increasing the exploitation of the working class. Wage restraint was secured and maintained: while the statutory price controls and food subsidies introduced in 1974 were weakened and phased out, in the context of massively deflationary budgets and an increase in the unemployed, once school leavers were included, by almost one million; and while public expenditure programmes were cut and subjected to cash limits so that instead of the promised 13 per cent growth there was no growth at all in real terms from 1974 to 1978. As Stuart Holland put it in commenting on the Thatcher government's budget of 1979: 'Certainly, the edge of Mrs Thatcher's axe was first ground and then fell under successive Healey budgets.' [21]

As for the industrial strategy, the true basis of the case for a 'socialist incomes policy', the wage restraint programme was launched *after* Tony Benn had been dismissed from the Department of Industry, an act which Jack Jones, speaking for the TUC as a whole, warned at the time would constitute 'a grave affront to the trade-union movement'. [22] The Industry Bill was shorn of its compulsory dimensions and the singular Planning Agreement entered into with a private company occurred in the context of the government sanctifying in this way the bail-out of Chrysler. As for the National Enterprise Board, it was largely absorbed into the role of traditional state fire-fighting on closures and in any case operated, as its intellectual progenitor put it with great dismay, 'purely on commercial, rather than public, or social criteria'. [23] In these circumstances, the locus of the Industrial Strategy shifted back to the National Economic Development Council and the tripartite sectoral working parties established under its auspices in 1975. It was all summed up in 1977 by Jack Jones: 'Somehow, somewhere, the government's objectives seem to have been hijacked off course, and I mean "hijacked" . . . an industrial strategy which relies only on the deliberations of sectoral working parties, on polite talks with industrialists and trade associations . . . is not a strategy at all, but an excuse for one.'[24]

Why then did the unions display such loyalty? One explanation, which is fairly common on the Labour left, was expressed in Ian Mikardo's early admission to the 1975 conference: 'We were all conned'[25]—with the implication that the unions were simply conned for a longer period. This is an attractive explanation for the Labour left for it carries within it the premise that you can't fool all the people all the time and that at some point the party will rise up against the charlatans. But this will not do as an explanation of the unions' loyalty. Jack Jones's own account of the government's behaviour, that they were 'hijacked', already indicates a very different perspective: the government were themselves unsuspecting 'victims' of the 'hijack'. This was indeed the dominant view among the union leadership and was reflective of the strength of the 'bond of confidence' established in the pre-1974 period.

This bond was in fact *strengthened* by the precarious parliamentary position of the government and the constant spectre of another Tory government (which would have of course acted as even less of a buffer against the worst effects of the crisis than Labour was doing). And no less important was the fact that this government, far more than had been the case in 1964–70, showed a sanguine understanding of the unions' own priorities—that when push came to shove, the unions would insist on those policies in the Social Contract that pertained directly to industrial relations and would exert less pressure when it came to the economic strategy. This order of priorities stemmed not only from narrow organizational interests, but also from the unions' own fears and frustration with the effects of economic militancy and high inflation on real wages and employment. It also stemmed from the union leadership's own lack of confidence in the alternative economic strategy they and the Labour left advanced in the face of the harsh 'economic realities' put forward by the government, the Treasury and foreign 'experts' from the International Monetary Fund. The fact that Michael Foot allowed the TUC to write its own ticket on industrial relations legislation served, in terms of the unions' own priorities, to cement the ties between the unions and the government at the same time as reactionary economic policies were pursued. Moreover, the government proved amenable to introducing wage restraint in the form advanced by Jack Jones, that is, the £6 across-the-board norm so that the low paid would suffer less. And the very fact that the government was seen to be resisting strong Treasury pressures to institute a statutory policy[26] confirmed the unions' resolve to meet their 'obligations' to the government.

The *defensive* priorities of the union movement in the context of the crisis were secured, in other words, at the *expense* of insisting on alternative, let alone socialist, economic policies. The question remains, however, of whether the defensive gains were so great as to be worth the sacrifice. The egalitarian thrust of the £6 norm, such as it was, certainly struck a responsive chord in the labour movement, at least temporarily. But this cannot obscure the fact that it mainly concerned redistribution within the working class (involving Labourism's new twist on socialism—what I have called before its 'socialism in one class'[27]) in a context of a policy which reduced the proportion of the national income going to the class as a whole. Much more of a case can be made for the industrial relations legislation of 1974–6. Yet it is certainly questionable how much the unions have benefited from this in concrete terms. The Tory Industrial Relations Act had before its repeal been rendered more or less impotent by the unions. The role that the Advisory, Conciliation and Arbitration Service has been able to play in extending union recognition under the legislation has been very limited, particularly when conciliation has failed. As a number of long and futile recognition strikes have shown, moreover, employer intransigence and an anti-union judiciary are able to render the new procedures useless. In other areas—disclosure of information, job security, equal pay for women—the laws are not only deficient in certain respects, but are only effective when unions are already strong enough to advance their members' interests beyond minimum legal guarantees. Above all, there is a real danger, that litigation of issues (for example unfair dismissal) undermines shop-floor struggle and saps the time and energy of officials who become embroiled in the legalistic procedures. In two internal TUC reassessments of the legislation at the end of 1978, all this was being admitted, although little was said publicly lest it be used by the Conservatives to remove the advantages the laws do give. But this should not conceal what the TUC's own counsel, Lord Wedderburn, has called the unions' own

self-doubt as to the degree to which the trade union movement should in future come to rely upon machinery provided by the State to achieve that which in the past it has collectively won largely without the help of—often despite—the State's laws. Already the movement has been disillusioned by the operation of some of 'its' laws and has realised afresh the limitations that inevitably fall upon trade unions who trust in the regulation of industrial relations by the law. Even the floor of *individual* laws is often found to be ineffective without industrial strength to support them, especially in the case of equal pay for women. What the law gives the law can take away. [28]

The point to be drawn from this, however, is that the Labour leadership can hardly be accused of 'conning' the unions on this question—they were fulfilling 'their side' of the social contract. Indeed what Ken Coates did not foresee in predicting the scission that another Wilsonite government would produce in the movement was that this was another Wilsonite government with one major difference from the last one—it was bent on ensuring that it was not the Labour leadership that would become isolated from the union leadership, but the Labour left (as indeed occurred over public expenditure cuts and wage restraints in 1976). To this end, the government even maintained the form of the rest of the Social Contract while violating its spirit in most respects. Unlike the 1964–70 government's abandonment of the Economic Plan, this government never rejected the Industrial Strategy. All its constitutive elements—the Industry Act, statutory price controls, the NEB, even the concept of Planning Agreements were retained. Even the public expenditure cuts were defended, both by Labour and union leaders, [29] in terms of the industrial strategy, as freeing resources for investment in manufacturing industry. Even while union leaders recognized that the brunt of policy was in the opposite direction from what they had intended, the fact that the formal structures were in place (as was also the case with the Royal Commission on Income and Wealth and the Bullock Inquiry on Industrial Democracy) allowed them to expect that a new spirit might be injected into them once the immediate crisis passed. Above all the government did maintain close consultation with the union leadership. The accommodation between them, which Ken Coates believed could be secured only on the basis of socialist policies, was in fact reached on the basis of corporatist ones. Only occasionally did a union leader admit the reality of the situation to the movement, as did Alan Fisher at the time of the TUC's twenty-to-one endorsement of wage restraint in 1976:

we in the movement should understand the nature of bargaining at the national level between the TUC and the government . . . it is possible that we will become mesmerized by the process itself rather than considering the results that it achieves . . . capital will not hold back from using its power to influence these negotiations. One example we have is by pushing down the value of the pound. In that context, it is dangerous for the movement to accept incorporation in the apparatus of the State, articulated through what may be a loyalty to a Labour government and the test for the trade union movement is to develop effective bargaining power at this level, if necessary through new procedures and new institutions, and not to regard the State as in some mysterious way a neutral body. It never has been and never will be. [30]

The big question, of course, remains why the rank and file went along with the leadership. Coates's confidence rested after all on the 'active and self-assertive rank and file' without whose continuing support Jones's and Scanlon's 'theoretically possible' about-face would be of little worth to the establishment. It was in fact worth a great deal. As Steve Jeffries has pointed out, ' "left" union leaders either led or were prominently placed in four of the five most strikeprone industries. Despite the fact that the five only employed 6 per cent of the total labour force, they accounted for 47 per cent of the working days lost in 1969–74; by 1975–6 this figure had declined to 22 per cent, in a period of falling strike statistics.' [31] The level of resistance to phases one and two of the social contract was simply minimal. Both the deep reserves of loyalty to a Labour government among activists and the same fears and frustrations that beset the union leadership must surely have been factors in this. Just as there was a mistaken tendency among some of the Trotskyist left in the early 1970s to assume that the shop stewards of today are the revolutionary vanguard of tomorrow, so it must be said that many on the Labour left vastly overestimated the staying power of economic militancy and the political effects which an 'active and self-asserting rank and file' would have as a force for change within the Labour Party. In order to forestall criticisms for being wise after the fact, it might be permissible in this instance to quote something I wrote in 1974:

> It is true that industrial militancy does have a clear political character. The dissatisfaction with existing social relations is inherent in wage claims of 25, 30 or 40 per cent; in the expectation by dockers or car workers or miners that they be paid as much or more than groups high above them in the status hierarchy; in occupations of factories shut down in accordance with the law of profit; in the large number of strikes challenging managerial prerogatives. But this militancy retains a non-political veneer by virtue of the fact that it arises from separate segments of the working class at different times, and arises moreover in the absence of a generalized and explicit rejection of the economic and political structures in which these social relations are embedded. This is indeed an inherent limitation of trade unionism; demands for a 40 per cent increase in the income of the working class as a whole, and

for workers' control over production, cannot be effectively expressed industrially but only politically, and although we have seen in recent years a number of overt and official political strikes for the first time since the TUC left Trafalgar Square for Whitehall in the aftermath of the General Strike, these actions have been hesitant, sporadic and defensive. Without a political party which would maintain and give focus to industrial militancy, it is not unlikely to be dissipated in yet another phase of quasi-corporatist policies, or, if not, to be met by a more fully authoritarian challenge than the British labour movement has yet faced.[32]

That this militancy was indeed dissipated from 1975 to 1977 has a great deal to do with the inability of the Labour left, *no less than the various socialist groupings outside of it,* to capture the political imagination of rank-and-file activists. The fact that the Labour vote continued to drop in 1974 despite Labour's more radical programme was proof of this and suggested that the 'unprecedented scepticism about Labour politicians' which Coates identified was by no means highly discriminating between right and left and not necessarily an entirely positive force for social change. Steve Jeffries's admission, from an International Socialist/Socialist Workers' Party perspective, that 'in the face of the crisis there appeared to be no "practical" alternative' as far as most workers were concerned, and that 'when the general conviction was that there was little you could do, you just had to put up with the government's pay policy; then this is what the shop stewards generally felt as well'[33] is a damning testament to the ineffectiveness of the IS/SWP in the previous period. It is even more damning testament to the failure of the Labour left, whose alternative might be thought more 'practical', to touch the roots of the movement for all its visibility at the national level in the 1970s.

Of course the forces that originally produced this militancy were not themselves dissipated during this period and, as had been the case with the wage restraint policies of both the 1945 and 1966 Labour governments, the breakdown of restraints occurred not *after* Labour was defeated at the polls, but *before*. This indicated once again that while Labour remains able to foreclose class struggle for a certain period, it is unable to quash for too long the class antagonisms of British society. Callaghan's cynical manipulation of the 1978 congress, encouraging it to pronounce its opposition to the 5 per cent guidelines only in faint whispers by giving it the impression that a general election was imminent, may have looked like a brilliant political manoeuvre at the time, but it proved to be a major blunder. For the union leadership by this stage could simply not hold back the rising tide of economic militancy that had begun to surface spontaneously as early as a year before. (Indeed to some extent they may have encouraged it, despite their effective co-operation in wage restraint until 1978, by their verbal recommitment to full collective bargaining and by their more open criticisms of the government's policies from 1977 onwards.) As a result the class collaboration dogma of social democracy faltered again on its own terms: Labour's claim that it was the governing party of 'consensus' while the Tories were the party of 'confrontation' lost a good deal of its electoral credibility.

The resurgence of economic militancy in the winter of 1978–9 certainly reflects the resilience of the working class and its continuing ability to impose severe barriers to the strategic options of capital and the state. But in terms of the question of changing the Labour Party there is little comfort to be drawn from it. It most certainly does not conform to Coates's scenario of an irreconcilable split between the vast proportion of the labour movement and the Labour leadership. There has been renewed friction, but what is remarkable is how the conflicts within the movement were politically contained in the last years of the government. Both the NEC and the party conference were certainly much less the mouthpieces of the leadership throughout this government, but their ability to control or even influence its actions showed no marked increase. On the contrary, the existence of the Liaison Committee has allowed the leadership to by-pass conference resolutions without openly flouting them by promising to work out policy disagreements at a higher level. The Liaison Committee's policy statements have invariably turned out to be much less radical than those of the NEC or than conference resolutions. And even when conflict with unions broke into the open, as they did on the first day of the 1978 conference when the unions defeated the leadership on both the 5 per cent guidelines and economic policy as a whole, the unions refused to widen the conflict. On the very next day, enough union votes were available—including the TGWU's—to defeat the constitutional amendment for an electoral college, encompassing both the extra-parliamentary and parliamentary party, to elect the leader. The fact that this was combined with the defeat, on the basis of Hugh Scanlon miscasting the AUEW vote, of mandatory reselection of MPs, made Coates's burial of 'bureaucratic intrigue' in the party look very premature indeed.

Nor did matters change as the industrial conflict of the winter gained momentum. In order to protect the government as far as they could from the electoral consequences of the media rampage against its 'weakness' in the face of anarchy, the General Council was drawn into producing, with indecent haste, a new Solemn and Binding Agreement, the so-called 'Concordat', in which they agreed to undertake voluntary control on picketing, the closed shop, inter-union disputes and (eventually) wage demands. Even seen as a symbolic electoral exercise pure and simple, it was nevertheless significant how purely *defensive* a document it was. It was accompanied moreover by a policy statement by 'moderate' union leaders which endorsed the economic policies of the leadership. With no little justification, and in the midst of the winter's industrial strife, Shirley Williams could observe that the unions were 'moving clearly back to the centre' and scorn earlier suggestions that the social democrats in the party were politically 'dead'.[34] Not surprisingly, the hopes of the Labour left in the fall of 1978 that the postponement of the election would give them the chance to avoid the election manifesto 'watering down' the NEC's 1976 programme were entirely frustrated.[35]

To be sure, the battle is not over. It is in the nature of the Labour Party that the battle-lines will continue to be drawn up to and including the Day of Judgement. But given the experience of the last dozen years, what foundation remains for the argument that the party can be changed? The NEC has once again put the issues of election of the leader and mandatory reselection on the agenda of the 1979 party conference and, despite considerable noise from 'moderate' union leaders against friction in the party, it is by no means certain that these proposals will be defeated. But even if these proposals were carried, would they constitute an effective basis for changing the party? It was certainly clear from Callaghan's election that a leader who is 'acceptable to the unions' is not necessarily one who is committed to socialist policies. And if a Michael Foot or even a Tony Benn were elected, and setting aside all doubts as to their socialist 'credentials', how fundamentally different a tack could they take, given the fine array of upstanding gentlemen that numerically dominate the PLP?

The mandatory selection procedure is presumably designed to obviate this problem. But the parliamentary left is itself divided on this issue; the unions are concerned about its effects on sponsorship; and it is unlikely that those constituency parties that are presently moribund will suddenly spring to life just to turn out a sitting MP. As a theory of an inevitable fall from grace of socialist parties, the 'iron law of oligarchy' may have little to recommend it. But as an account of how MPs will be able to use considerable organizational and psychological resources to maintain their position *vis-à-vis* their constituency parties, mandatory reselection or not, it is discounted only by the naive.

But what about 'forcing the imposition of socialist policies'? This, as Coates made clear, will depend on the unions. Minkin's identification of a steady undercurrent of union support for public ownership, despite the revisionist machinations of the party leadership, says nothing about the efforts they will make to force its imposition on the Labour leadership. If anything, the 1970s provided rather strong evidence that too much stock should not be put in union conference resolutions on public ownership.

This may be especially seen with regard to the union's reaction to the NEC's 1976 statement on 'Banking and Finance', which proposed taking over the biggest four clearing banks, a merchant bank and the top seven insurance companies. Like all NEC proposals of this kind, it was primarily defended as a means of facilitating investment in manufacturing industry and specifically drew its inspiration from the publicly owned financial institutions of Britain's capitalist competitor countries (in this case, France, Japan and Italy). Nevertheless for the Labour Party it was a very radical proposal indeed. Although it drew screams of anguish from the City and strong public opposition from Callaghan and other Labour Ministers, it did not come out of the blue (having stemmed from a conference resolution passed in 1971 and revived in 1975). Nor was it without apparent support from the unions directly involved—at least those affiliated to the Labour Party. The Union of Shop, Distributive and Allied Workers' annual conference, which Minkin describes as 'that weathercock of the British trade union movement', passed resolutions in 1973 and 1974 proposing to 'eliminate the capitalist system' and specifically endorsing the takeover of the banks, the Stock Exchange and the insurance companies.[37] But while the 1976 party conference endorsed the statement by an overwhelming majority of 3,314,000 to 526,000, it turned out the unions weren't too keen on the idea. The total votes cast already indicated a substantial number of abstentions; the TGWU had reservations about 'timing'; and the unions in the field of banking and insurance demanded 'further consultation'. When nine relevant TUC unions were consulted by a NEC working party, they were found to be 'to varying degrees, hostile to the proposals on nationalization'. Fears of redundancy and loss of overseas earnings were apparently involved but most interesting was the fact that both USDAW and the Association of Scientific, Technical and Managerial Staffs, while agreeing that 'some reform was necessary . . . questioned the conclusion that ownership was the best means of exercising contol'.[38] Despite the conference decision, it was clear that the issue was now a dead letter. The 1978 Liaison

Committee statement, 'Into the Eighties', and the 1979 election manifesto made this abundantly clear. It will be less easily resurrected than mandatory reselection.

This critical episode suggests that a concerted push by the unions *against* the party leadership on socialist policies is less of a possibility than the Labour left would like to think. There remains, however, one other prospect suggested by Coates (although he was none too keen on the idea): that if the party could not be won over, it might be divided with the left retaining a considerable hold over 'the apparatus . . . necessary to meet the demands of full participation in political life'.[39] Yet the likelihood of such a division being initiated by either of the major groupings on the right or the left must be counted as remote in the extreme. The leadership as a whole understands only too well the importance of retaining their hold over this apparatus; a Prentice or a Taverne may go from time to time, but attrition at this rate is not going to matter much. A resurrection of 1931 is perhaps more likely, but this would leave the party composed of much the same forces as before. One would still have to ask whether, apart from a temporary hiccup, the party could be changed against 'those who helped to sustain MacDonald's supremacy and Snowden's economics to the eleventh hour of the last day',[40] but who had the sagacity to stay.

As for the Labour left, it must surely be recognized that whatever else it is about, it is not about dividing the Labour Party. Precisely because it identifies itself with party tradition, the thought of dividing the party is particularly abhorrent to it. (It must be said that to the extent it makes this identification unambiguously, it is either hypocritical or mistaken. In terms of the class harmony ideology, the policies effectively pursued and the absence of mass socialist education via the party at the base, the task of changing the Labour Party surely involves wrenching it *out* of its tradition.) The left has always taken the burden of party unity on its shoulders and has been far more ready than the right to compromise its principles to this end.

What then *is* the alternative for socialists? In a number of respects Coates cannot be faulted. The issue is not about 'parliamentarianism versus insurrectionism'. The question of whether Parliament can be the effective vehicle for implementing a socialist programme will indeed 'only be answered when it has been tried' (which it never has in Britain or any other major capitalist country), and tried, moreover, on the basis of the crystallization of the kind of socialist consciousness 'in the whole active part of the subordinate class' which Coates envisages.[41] The point about the Labour Party is that it has always been dominated by a leadership which, with the support of most of the movement, has not only been unable or unwilling to develop a coherent socialist programme, but has not seen its task as one of instilling such a consciousness. It has lived off the existing consciousness of the working class, it has even represented it, but rather than attempting the difficult task of securing working-class support by undermining those values of national unity and moderation which encapsulate class subordination, it has chosen the easier route of engaging working-class allegiance by associating itself with those values. The problem with the Labour Party is not that it has sought to bring the working class to power by peaceful means. Rather the fact that it has not seen its task as bringing the working class to power has determined the *kind* of parliamentarianism which it practises.

Coates was also right in his assessment that existing revolutionary groups will not stand serious scrutiny as viable alternatives to the Labour Party, not least because of their doctrinaire refusal to allow any 'equivocation' on a parliamentary strategy.[42] And however one might applaud certain changes in the Communist Party, the vast historical weight under which it staggers, no less than the transparency of its illusion that the Labour Party might be remotely interested in an alliance with it, suggests that it will continue to fail to make much progress as a viable alternative.

To sum up: the Labour Party will not conveniently fall apart; a good measure of parliamentary success is indeed essential; the present alternatives hold out little hope. It is scarcely surprising that many socialists cling to the illusion that the Labour Party can be changed, although one might expect from them greater candour about the costs involved—that is, that by continuing to work within the Labour Party they necessarily do their bit to sustain Labourism's strangling hegemony over the politically active working class. But given the Sisyphus-like task they appear to be engaged in, it is by no means inappropriate to ask whether it is not indeed worth the candle for socialists in Britain to come together to 'try again' in the 1980s: to make a start at building a mass socialist party. Certainly such a party would have to detach many activists, and perhaps eventually some major unions, from the Labour Party. But it need not inherit by this token the same structure or all the burdens that come with the Labour Party tradition. With different leaders, a different ethos and with a positive attitude to Marxism, these elements would necessarily combine in a different way. Even if a federated structure were adopted, it need not carry with it the same separation between parliamentary and extra-parliamentary activity and the same division of labour between industrial and political leadership. One important reason for making the attempt is that even a remotely viable alternative would act as pole of attraction for those socialist elements within the Labour Party to break out of the vicious circle of both trying to change the party *and* maintain its defensive unity, and put their energy, their talents and the respect and legitimacy they enjoy in the eyes of many trade unionists to more positive use.   The fact that what is entailed in creating a mass socialist party today is not the political mobilization of the working class, but its *remobilization,* is indeed what makes such an attempt seem so Herculean. That there is little historical evidence for such a successful remobilization is true. But where are the examples of a transformed social democratic party? With no less justification, indeed with rather more in light of the experience of the past six years, one might indeed launch such an attempt at remobilization by quoting Coates's own concluding call to arms: 'The work will be arduous and intricate, daunting indeed. It will need all the socialist forces we can muster and, indeed, it needs them now.'[43]

(1979)

Notes

1. Ken Coates, 'Socialists and the Labour Party', *The Socialist Register 1973*, London 1973, p. 174.
2. Geoff Hodgson, *Socialism and Parliamentary Democracy*, Nottingham 1977; Peter Jenkins, 'The Labour Party and the Politics of Transition', *The Socialist Register 1977*, London 1977; Frank Ward, *In Defence of Democratic Socialism*, London 1978.
3. Lewis Minkin, *The Labour Party Conference*, Harmondsworth 1978, p. 322.
4. Ralph Miliband, 'Moving On', *The Socialist Register 1976*, London 1976, p. 128.
5. Robert McKenzie, *British Political Parties*, London 1963, p. 505.
6. Minkin, p. 321.
7. Coates, pp. 176–7.
8. See *Labour Programme 1973*, especially pp. 13–39.
9. Coates, p. 176.
10. Minkin, p. 344.
11. Harold Wilson, quoted in *Financial Times*, 16 and 31 May 1968.
12. Tony Benn, *A New Course for Labour*, London 1976, p. 10.
13. Ralph Miliband, *Parliamentary Socialism*, London 1972, p. 375.
14. Minkin, p. 344.
15. Quote in Michael Hatfield, *The House the Left Built*, London 1978, p. 199.
16. Coates, p. 156.
17. When Hodgson (pp. 60–61, 129) and Jenkins (pp. 21–2) use the examples of the New Deal to argue that legislative reforms are possible even in a period of capitalist crisis and can have a 'galvanizing effect on large numbers of workers', they ignore

the longer-term role that industrial relations legislation has played in the United States in containing, juridifying and deadening autonomous working-class struggle. The 'right to belong to a union' sanctioned by the state against the wishes of the employers in the 1930s was by no means an entirely unmixed blessing given the package it became enveloped in.

18. See Ralph Tarling and Frank Wilkinson, 'The Social Contract: Post-war Incomes Policies and Their Inflationary Impact', *Cambridge Journal of Economics*, vol. 1, no. 4 (December 1977). The figures for each year have kindly been supplied by the authors in personal communication.

19. The quarterly figures for real weekly income from 1970 to 1978 at October 1978 prices are presented in tabular form in 'Written Answers by Robert Sheldon' in *House of Commons Debates*, vol. 960, 15 December 1978 and 19 January 1979, cc. 519–20 and cc. 969–70.

20. *Labour Party Annual Conference Report (LPACR)* 1973, p. 187.

21. 'Budget That Sells Seed Grain for a Decade', *Guardian*, 18 June 1979.

22. Quoted in Hatfield, pp. 148–9.

23. Stuart Holland, 'Planning Agreements: A Case Study of Industrial Suicide', *Tribune*, 19 September 1978, p. 3.

24. TUC, *The Trade Union Role in Industrial Policy*, report of a conference of affiliated unions, 31 October 1977, p. 33.

25. *LPACR*, 1975, p. 323.

26. See Joe Haines, *The Politics of Power*, London 1977, ch. 3.

27. See my *Social Democracy and Industrial Militancy*, Cambridge 1976, p. 124.

28. Lord Wedderburn 'The New Structure of Labour Law in Britain', *Israel Law Review*, vol. 13, no. 4 (October 1978), p. 457.

29. See Scanlon's speech in *LPACR* 1976, p. 167.

30. TUC, *The Social Contract 1976–77*, report of the Special Congress, 19 June 1976, p. 39.

31. Steve Jeffries, 'Striking into the Eighties', *International Socialism*, series 2, no. 5, Summer 1979, p. 33.

32. *Social Democracy and Industrial Militancy*, p. 253.

33. Jeffries, pp. 33, 35.

34. *Financial Times*, 21 February 1979.

35. See Eric Heffer, 'Conference Gives Labour the Lead on the Election Manifesto', *Tribune*, 29 September 1978, p. 5.

36. The Labour Party, *Banking and Finance*, 1976.

37. Minkin, p. 325.

38. *LPACR* 1978, Appendix 2, pp. 450, 453.

39. Coates, p. 171.

40. Michael Foot, *Aneurin Bevan*, vol. I, London 1975, p. 136.

41. Coates, p. 158.

42. See Duncan Hallas's reproach to Ralph Miliband in 'How Can We Move On?', *The Socialist Register 1977*, London 1977, p. 10.

43. Coates, p. 177.

5.
The Development of Corporatism in Liberal Democracies

I

Corporatism as an ideology has a long history. It finds its modern roots in those versions of nineteenth-century social and political thought which reacted against the individualism and competition which characterized the emerging dominance of the capitalist mode of production, and against the industrial and political conflict between classes which was the ineluctable product of this development. Although the varieties of corporatist theory are many, the common premise was that class harmony and organic unity were essential to society and could be secured if the various functional groups, and especially the organizations of capital and labour, were imbued with a conception of mutual rights and obligations somewhat similar to that presumed to have united the medieval estates in a stable society. Accordingly, corporatist programmes advocated a universal scheme of vocational, industrial or sectoral organization, whereby the constituent units would have the right of representation in national decision-making and a high degree of functional autonomy, but would have the duty of maintaining the social hierarchy and discipline consistent with the needs of the nation-state as a whole. A limited organizational pluralism, generally operating under the aegis of the state as the supreme collective community, would guarantee the major value of corporatism—social harmony. [1]

When we turn to actual corporatist structures, the most famous—or rather infamous—instances of corporatism in practice, that of the fascist states, gave a rude answer to the question of how the social harmony trumpeted in theory would in fact come to replace the competition and class conflict of capitalist society. Corporatism was introduced concomitantly with the abrogation of liberal democracy and the smashing of the indigenous organizations of the working class to the end of repressing both political and industrial class conflict. Nigel Harris has observed of this experience:

> The relationship between forces and the appearance of unanimity is not settled in the modern, any more than in the earlier corporatist writings: it is assumed. Yet as Pirou notes in relationship to Italian Fascism and Neumann with reference to the Nazis, corporatism in these countries was not, and could not be, much more than a decorative façade for force. For the harmony which it is assumed is intrinsic to society—if the squabbling cabals can be swept away—can in practice only be reproduced by the use of force. And the use of force directly contradicts the assumption of intrinsic harmony. In Vichy France and in Salazar's Portugal, overtly corporatist societies, the same comment is appropriate. Corporatism assumes what it is designed to create, and destroys what it seeks to create by pursuing the only practicable means available: coercion. [2]

But the historical experience with corporatism in this century has not been confined to fascist states. In liberal democracies implicit tendencies toward corporatist structures developed both before and concurrently with the emergence of fascism. [3] One British Cabinet member contended in the 1930s: 'it seems to me to be courting failure to tell people that they have first to dress themselves in black shirts and throw their opponents downstairs in order to get the corporative state. . . . This new economic order has already developed further in England than is generally recognized.' [4] Bowen observed more generally of the pre-Second World War period:

> In countries where liberal-democratic political institutions continued to function, these authoritarian versions of 'corporatism' were generally repudiated with some vehemence. At the same time, however, there appeared signs of a growing awareness that in modern industrial society certain fundamental tendencies which might be described as 'corporative' had for some time been at work. Economists and historians found one such tendency to be the decline of atomistic competition in economic life, a sphere in the 'free play of individual forces' was increasingly being superseded by the operation of collective agreements concluded among solidly organized 'communities of interest.' Jurists and political scientists observed a parallel decline of atomistic individualism in politics, noting that private bodies

claiming to represent the group interests of labour, of employers, of farmers, of consumers, of particular branches of industry and of other economic and social groups tended to become more inclusive and more highly integrated with a view to increasing their direct influence upon governmental policies. In some democratic countries, notably in pre-Nazi Germany, in France and in Czechoslovakia, groups of this kind were given a degree of official recognition when they were allowed representation in National Economic Councils created to serve as advisory 'parliaments of industry.'[5]

In the late 1930s, during the Second World War, and especially in the post-war period, these tendencies toward corporatist structures accelerated and became more systematically developed in liberal democratic societies. They were particularly associated with the increased state involvement in managing the advanced capitalist economy and centred on the integration of central trade-union and business organizations in national economic planning and incomes-policy programmes and bodies. This development took place within the framework of the maintenance of liberal political freedoms, entailed the integration of indigenous class organizations for the most part, and state coercion played a secondary, or at least a sporadic and indirect, role in the process. For the most part, however, this development rarely, or at least only in very specific contexts, was announced or even acknowledged as corporatist by politicians, group leaders of bureaucrats, or was described as such in even the 'serious' press. Corporatism, not surprisingly, had become a term of denigration in the course of the anti-fascist war throughout liberal capitalist societies and especially among Western labour movements whose participation in the new structures was the *sine qua non* of their development. Indeed, in so far as the term was used—outside of intellectual or academic circles—it was used by labour leaders or left-wing social democrats and Marxists as a means of opposing trade-union integration in these structures.[6]

Among scholars, however, and especially among social scientists interested in questions of interest-group representation and economic planning in liberal capitalist societies, the term corporatism, usually prefixed by 'neo' or 'quasi', or qualified by the adjective 'liberal', has become increasingly common. In the mid 1960s, Samuel Beer identified a 'new group politics' in Britain, a 'system of quasi-corporation bringing government and producers' groups into intimate and continuous relationship' in framing, applying and legitimating state policies.[7] 'The welfare state and especially the managed economy of recent decades,' Beer contended, 'simply could not operate without the advice and cooperation of the great organized producer groups of business, labour and agriculture. And the history of these groups displays the powerful influence of government in calling them into existence, shaping their goals and endowing them with effective power.'[8] More generally, Shonfield's influential *Modern Capitalism* explicitly argued: 'The term "corporatist" is not to be understood in a pejorative sense. All planning of the modern capitalist type implies the acceptance of some measure of corporatism in political organization: that follows from basing the conduct of economic affairs on the deliberate decisions of organized groups of producers, instead of leaving the outcome to the clash between individual competitors in the market.'[9] More recently, Lehmbruch has defined 'liberal corporatism' as 'a special type of participation of large economic social groups in public, especially economic policy-making. Consultation and cooperation among administrations and organized interests is of course common in all constitutional democracies with a highly developed capitalist economy. But the distinguishing trait of "liberal corporatism" is a high degree of cooperation among those groups themselves in the shaping of public policy.' Significantly, Lehmbruch carefully warned that 'Liberal corporatism must be distinguished from the traditional corporatism of pre-industrial Europe on the one hand, from authoritarian corporatism of the fascist type on the other. Its essential feature is the large measure of constitutional autonomy of the groups involved, hence the voluntary character of institutionalized integration of conflicting social groups.'[10]

The most rigorous contemporary specification of the corporatist concept in ideal-typical, but nevertheless in empirically-bounded structural and behavioural terms has been provided in an outstanding article by Philippe Schmitter. His definition is purposefully constructed to cover both authoritarian and liberal democratic corporatism, but Schmitter goes on immediately to distinguish between 'societal' and 'state' subtypes. The distinguishing structural and behavioural differences between the two are seen to depend on whether the nature of the constituent units, in terms of their limited numbers, singularity, compulsory character and monopolistic representation of functional groups is a product more of general socio-economic developments and voluntarist arrangements than of state imposition, and whether the state's controls on their leadership selection and interest articulation is a product of 'reciprocal consensus on procedure and/or goals, or of an asymmetric imposition by the "organized monopolists of legitimate violence" '.[11]

The foregoing examples of the employment of the concept of corporatism in the liberal democratic context are presented not merely as indicators of its growing acceptance in social science, but because, more as a corpus than individually, they capture the essence of the 'neo-' 'quasi-' 'liberal-' 'societal-' corporatist paradigm. Whereas many mainstream social scientists have joined the company of corporatist apologists and have seen the above developments as constituting 'a distinct form of economic structure', [12] an alternative or sequel to capitalism, even of the mixed economy variety, corporatism as used in this essay is a *political structure* that attends, if is not actually produced by, the emergence of the *advanced capitalist economy*. Whereas some scholars have carelessly characterized virtually any and all intimate interest group-state relations which have become accepted as legitimate in the political culture as corporatist, [13] corporatism as used here stresses the centrality of the large socio-economic groups' relationship to the state and the co-operative interaction among them as essential to the paradigm. Whereas some scholars have attempted to conflate consociationalism and corporatism, so that religious and ideological pillarization and elite accommodation are characterized as corporatism, [14] the concept as used here maintains a distinction between the two, stressing the centrality of *functional representation* in socio-economic policy-making. Finally, whereas many scholars have used the term one-dimensionally to apply only to interest group *representation*, corporatism as used here focuses as well on the state's *reciprocal* influence on interest groups and their consequent employment as agencies of mobilization and social control for the state *vis-à-vis* their members.

The corporatist paradigm as understood to connote *a political structure within advanced capitalism which integrates organized socio-economic producer groups through a system of representation and co-operative mutual interaction at the leadership level and of mobilization and social control at the mass level* can be a heuristic tool for appropriating the political reality of many Western liberal democracies. As a working model in political analysis, it has manifest advantages over pluralist theory unencumbered as it is by the latter's unwieldy assumptions of extensive group multiplicity, passive state behaviour, and stability as a product of overlapping membership and the unseen hand of group competition. [15]

Nevertheless, even considering the more careful and rigorous practitioners of the corporatist paradigm, one cannot but come away from a reading of the literature with a profound sense of unease. Schmitter, in assessing the use to be made of 'state corporatist' theorists in constructing an operational paradigm of the beast, decries their lack of candour, indeed their apologetics, about 'corporatism's relation to capitalism and specific class interests', as well as the role of state coercion in the implementation of corporatism 'as an instrument for rescuing and consolidating capitalism rather than replacing it'. The unanimous emphasis they place on functional interdependence, he suggests, leads them to ignore factors of class conflict, status antagonism and centre–periphery tension that state corporatism is designed to suppress. Schmitter finds the record of societal corporatist theorists, especially Shonfield, better, suggesting they have set us off to an 'impressive, if still speculative, start' in our understanding of this animal.[16] But if the theory of corporatism within liberal democracies is better, that does not make it good. For there is also a pronounced–indeed, unmistakable–tendency in most instances to ignore the question of which class interests liberal corporatism serves. This tendency is the product of the widespread assumption that liberal capitalist societies, while subject to tension and strain, are no longer subject to contradiction with the coming of the welfare state and state economic planning. It is assumed, rather than demonstrated, in other words, that there is in fact an underlying social harmony in modern capitalist societies and that in the circumstances the concept of national or public interest is an unproblematic one. Characteristic in this regard is Shonfield's assertion that French planning is a 'conspiracy in the public interest between big business and big officialdom'.[17] As Watson has pointed out, 'whether and why it is in the public interest, he seems to take for granted.'[18]

There are three specific, although highly interrelated, areas in which the liberal corporatist paradigm may be judged deficient. There is, first of all, a critical lack of a rigorous theory of the state in advanced capitalist society, despite the large, important, even determining role that is assigned to the state in the corporatist framework. There appears to be a theoretical closure to the question of whether the increased role and changing functions of the state is not a product of the changing needs of the capitalist class in terms of maintaining its political, economic and ideological dominance. That is not to say that instances of bias are not discerned (although it is usually assumed that the state's role has been to reduce power differentials between the classes), but that the question of a *systematic* bias toward capitalist class dominance on the part of the state is not addressed.

Second, there is an assumption that the functional representation in economic decision-making of trade unions and business organizations takes place within the framework of an equivalence of power and influence between the two. This assumption is one that derives from traditional liberal theory. It is based on the view that if producers' organizations voluntarily enter into a 'social contract', they must do so on the basis of equality, just as liberal economic theory assumes with regard to individuals in the market. As Macpherson has pointed out, liberal freedoms allowed capitalism to appear 'as the system in which production is carried on without authoritarian allocation of work or rewards, but by contractual relations between free individuals (each possessing some resources be it only his labour-power) who calculate their most profitable course of action and employ their resources as that calculation dictates'. But at the same time, 'the market economy, with its concentration of capital ownership and its distribution of rewards in accordance with the marginal productivity of each of the contributors to the product, maintained a massive inequality between owners and workers'. [19] The importance of liberal democracy for capitalism lies in the guarantee of individual legal and political equality which makes the wage contract *appear* as an exchange between equals in a massively unequal society. The importance of liberal democracy for corporatism in such a society is that the guarantee of legal and political equality for functional groups makes the 'social contract' appear as an exchange between equals, despite vast inequalities between the groups in power and distributional terms. The assumption of equivalence within the liberal corporatist paradigm has led to the valid concern that 'it may be that corporatism obscures as much about different configurations of power as the notion of pluralism has'. [20]

Finally, there has been a tendency to ignore the high degree of instability that marks corporatist structures within liberal democracy. This has been particularly evident in the crucial area of incomes policy, where tripartite structures have proved difficult to establish in the first place and much more difficult to protect from breakdown once established. But it extends to economic planning structures as well, or at least to the instability of co-operative group behaviour within them. The tendency to ignore, or at least the inability to explain, this instability is largely a product of the above-mentioned defects—the assumptions of underlying social harmony, state neutrality *vis-à-vis* the groups and power equivalence between them. In the absence of underlying social harmony between classes, and in the face of policy outputs which reflect capitalist class dominance *vis-à-vis* the state and trade unions, the latter have often had to opt out of corporatist structures, or at least abstain from accommodative behaviour if they were not to be repudiated by their rank-and-file membership. This very instability brings us directly back to the question raised at the beginning, that is, whether state coercion, at least in the form of repressing rank-and-file actions and insulating union leadership from its effects, is not a *sine qua non* of establishing stable corporatist structures. And this raises in turn the fundamental question of the contradiction between corporatism and political freedom.

It has not been our intention to suggest that these concerns have been entirely overlooked among students of corporatism within liberal democracy. Lehmbruch addresses the question of instability in the face of class conflict; Schmitter explicitly raises the element of class dominance; and all the above concerns are central to Harris's study of modern British Conservatism and my own study of modern British Labour. But these contributions have been made by a minority of students of liberal corporatism and have yet to be systematically developed. In the pages that follow we shall attempt to make a further contribution toward that development.

II

In his seminal essay, Schmitter suggests that students of corporatism avoid the tempting game of finding fascism under the bed of every tripartite stucture in liberal democracies and, more generally, that we avoid tying it to any particular ideology or political movement. The advice is well taken. But it does not mean that we should ignore the question of the similarities between fascist and liberal corporatism in terms of origin, structure, behaviour or internal contradiction. And Schmitter himself places fascist and liberal corporatism under the same definitional and historical rubric, while discerning the important differences between them. Bowen, writing shortly after the end of the Second World War, insightfully noted:

> Italian Fascism and German Nazism lie in ruins, but many of the economic and cultural forces that brought them into existence have not ceased to operate . . . Unless Germany's social structure should be completely revolutionized in the near future, important sections of the community may well continue to see in some kind of non-Marxian, non-liberal social ideal the promise of class harmony, national solidarity and economic stability.[21]

Before turning to an examination of the structural factors which may be seen to account for the development of corporatism within liberal democracies, therefore, a short discussion on the admittedly less crucial ideological influences is necessary. What is most important to note, at the ideological level, is the common affinity of the three major governing ideologies in European liberal democracies—Catholicism, liberal-conservatism, and social democracy—to corporatist thought. Indeed, the common affinity is striking enough upon examination to have led one student of the Netherlands to suggest that consociationalism is less a product of ideological cleavage than of ideological congruence between 'pillars' influenced by the common corporatist goal and that this congruence has been mobilized to 'moderate, retard or even prevent the development in salience of other identification criteria which have greater potential for leading to social instability' (that is, revolutionary socialism). [22]

The corporatism of modern Catholic thought has been stressed enough to need no repetition here. What has been less noticed is the affinity between aspects of fascist corporatism and modern conservatism, at least in terms of their analysis of society's ills. [23] This may be illustrated by comparing the following two quotations. The Italian Fascist Confederation of Industrialists, in a 1939 publication, stressed the necessity

> of correcting and neutralizing a condition brought about by the industrial revolution of the nineteenth century which associated capital and labour in industry, giving rise on the one hand to a capitalist class of employers of labour and on the other to a great propertyless class, the industrial proletariat. The juxtaposition of these classes inevitably led to the clash of their opposing interests. [24]

The British Conservative industrialist, politician, and theorist, Aubrey Jones, a prime mover of corporatist structures under both Conservative and Labour governments, similarly contended in 1950:

> The greatest evil of all wrought by individualist capitalism was the division it drove between the two classes . . . status had been replaced by contract, and the labourer, preoccupied with the day, was left bargaining helplessly against an employer secure in the present and uncertain only about the future . . . The classic remedy for labour's plight, trade unionism, in fact solves only part of his troubles . . . [It] was never calculated to bridge the gap that had grown between employers and employed; it served rather to widen it and to exacerbate the strife between the two sides. For trade unionism itself became infested with the doctrine that the struggle of the classes was something inevitable; this struggle was looked upon as scrawling itself across the whole of history; and the more inevitable it is accepted to be, the more implacable and the more permanent does it become. [25]

But if the analysis of the problem was common, the proposed remedy differed in important respects (although both, of course, addressed themselves to the need to eliminate conflict within capitalism, rather than capitalism itself).

The Fascist answer is by organizing the people in groups according to their respective activities, groups which through their leaders . . . rise by stages as in a pyramid, at the base of which are the masses and at the apex the state. No group outside the state, no group against the state, all groups within the state . . . which . . . is the nation itself rendered articulate. [26]

Jones, while a major Conservative spokesman for state intervention in the economy and a subsequent architect of a tripartite incomes policy enforced with the state's coercive powers, looked, on the other hand, to a more reformist, integrative solution:

Conflict follows only because labour is an outsider in industry . . . the bigness or smallness of the common pool of profits means nothing to it; it is intent only on the size of its own share; and so it is tempted to act irresponsibly. It is so acting today. This irresponsibility can be overcome if only labour is made to feel that it has the same purpose as capital, and that while they remain rivals, their rivalry is subordinate to a unity. That, after all, is the first condition of a healthy society. [27]

To this end, Jones recommended that the consultative system of voluntary joint union–employer production committees, which had evolved during the Second World War, be promoted: '*Authority remains with the employer, it is he who still controls. But those who are controlled are taken into his confidence; their views are solicited; and so the control, by becoming less of an imposition, is made to operate more effectively.*'[28] A more candid view of the liberal–conservative corporatist position is hard to come by.

The ideological affinities of social democracy and corporatism are less readily apparent. Certainly the movements that have evolved under their respective banners differ enough in social base as well as philosophy and practice to render ludicrous any attempt to revive the ill-conceived and tragic (in its consequences) strategy of the Communists in the late 1920s of attacking social democracy as social fascism. To be sure, the more stable tripartite arrangements in Europe have been established or at least sustained by social democratic parties, and it is a telling sign that social democracy has been reduced in some eyes to tripartism itself.[29] But social democracy, for all its gradualism and promotion of class co-operation, has always entailed more than a call for tripartism within capitalism. This is because its strategy did involve at least reducing the capitalist class's power through some public ownership and because it was a political movement with a predominantly working-class base.

How, then, is the social democratic proclivity toward corporatist structures to be explained? Although the major factors are structural, set in the historical context of the timing of the ascension to office of social democratic parties, an important facilitating factor has been that dominant ideological strain within social democracy which rejects the notion of the class struggle as the dynamic of social change. Those who would search for the corporatist roots of social democracy will find them less in its explicit programmatic links with guild socialism as a left-wing variant of corporatism or even with the Fabian or Bernsteinian dislike for the 'class war' methods of industrial bargaining, and more in the fundamental differences between social democracy and Marxism. A succinct expression of the difference is to be found in Durbin's *The Politics of Democratic Socialism:*

> if there is a principle of living more fundamental than another, of the human species—and therefore of history—it is the principle and practice of cooperation.
> It is radically false, therefore, to suppose that the dynamic element in social life is solely that of warfare and struggle—especially that of class struggle and class warfare.
> There is no end to the sectoral disputes of free people . . . how are these disputes to be resolved? . . . the only solution that is compatible with the maintenance of social peace and the growth of mutual respect between contending groups is that of open and honest compromise.
> When individuals or groups disagree—including nations and classes and Parties within the state—the most important question is not what they disagree about, but the method by which their disputes are to be resolved. [30]

This ideological linchpin of social democracy fits well with liberal corporatism, which, as Lehmbrunch points out, also 'rests on the theoretical premise that there exists strong interdependence among the interests of conflicting social groups in a capitalist economy. This "interdependence of interests" image of society is clearly opposed to the "conflict of interests" image which (as in the Marxist concept of class conflict) stresses the ultimate incompatibility of antagonistic group interests.'[31]

The importance of this ideological factor is to be seen in terms of the fact that corporatist structures and practices have developed more fully in the post-war period in those countries where confessional and social democratic unions have dominated the labour movement, including in the three countries which we examine in some detail in the following sections: the Netherlands, Sweden and Britain. Where a large communist movement has existed, on the other hand, the establishment of corporatist stuctures and practices has been much less marked. Post-war Italy and even post-war France, despite the major role played by the state in their post-war economies, have furnished far fewer examples of tripartism. Heisler's contention that societies that approximate his corporative 'European polity model' exhibit a high level of development to co-opt groups 'virtually without regard to their supportive or opposing orientations to the regime and its norms'[32] cannot be supported. If the communist movements of Italy and France are being 'co-opted' at present, it is far more due to their participation in the parliamentary institutions of liberal democracy than in the corporatist ones.[33]

But if ideology is an important factor, it is primarily a facilitating one rather than a creative one. To understand how and why ideology becomes operative, we have to understand the deeper structural factors that have impelled corporatist developments in liberal democracies. The example of Canada is instructive in this regard. Despite a strong Catholic corporatist tradition in Quebec (including the establishment of a Catholic trade-union confederation), an English-speaking trade-union leadership which was predominantly social democratic, and a powerful Liberal prime minister for almost a quarter of a century who explicitly ascribed to corporatist principles as early as 1918 and consistently held to them throughout his career, Canada has seen very little of liberal corporatist developments. Why? Because the petty bourgeoisie remained the largest subordinate class in Canada until the Second World War; because, even subsequently, labour has rarely posed a *centralized* threat politically or industrially with which the state has been forced to deal; and because the Canadian economy has had so little autonomy from the American (the problem of incorporating multinational corporations in national economic planning is particularly marked in Canada's 'branch-plant' industry).[34] Ideas, if they are socially disembodied in the sense of not correlating with the major socioeconomic forces in a society, can themselves have little impact.

III

As we suggested earlier, although corporatist tendencies in liberal democracies may be traced as far back as the First World War, the introduction of corporatism as a widespread systematic process, with corporatist structures playing a significant political and economic role, is more properly traced (as it is by most scholars) to the Second World War period. The crucial factor, and the fact that allows us to locate its development in a country like Sweden, or Norway, *before* the war, is the state's commitment to full employment. This provided the material basis for industrial militancy in the post-war period and for the reactive (in some cases preventative) introduction of incomes policies and social welfare measures designed to coerce or induce wage restraint on the part of trade unions.[35] In virtually every liberal democratic country in which corporatist structures became at all important an incomes policy designed to abate the wage pressure of trade unions was the frontispiece of corporatist development.

The full employment commitment, and the consequences it had for greater state involvement in the economy and corporatism, was a product of *political* forces. It is often presented as a technical achievement, based on the Keynesian discovery of the budgetary deficit as a solution to the disease of underconsumption and the attendant depressionary symptoms of the capitalist economy, and on the administrative planning experience and political confidence acquired by the state in the war economy. Yet not only had the experience of the war economy existed before (and in any case the kind of planning adopted during the Second World War was largely abandoned afterwards), but the Keynesian 'discovery' (as advocated by Keynes as well as other economists) had been available for well over a decade before its widespread acceptance. Governments in capitalist democracies, with the main exceptions of Sweden and Norway, had explicitly rejected a policy of increasing employment through budgetary deficits during the depression. As the economist Kalecki pointed out in a brilliant article in 1943, the reason for this rejection largely lay in the negative attitude of big business. This attitude was based on a number of concerns. First, the desire to maintain the powerful controlling device over governments which the need to sustain 'business confidence' entailed in a *laissez-faire* economy governed by the principles of 'sound finance'; second, the suspicion of government spending, particularly of the kind of spending necessary to maintain effective demand in the Keynesian context, that is, public investment and the subsidizing of mass consumption (the former constituting a potential competition to private investment, the latter undermining the fundamentals of capitalist ethics—as Kalecki puts it: 'You shall earn your bread in sweat—unless you happen to have private means'). The main concern, however, was that

> under a regime of full employment, 'the sack' would cease to play its role as a disciplinary measure. The social position of the boss would be undermined and the self assurance and class consciousness of the working class would grow, strikes for wage increases and improvements in conditions of work would create political tension. It is true that profits would be higher under a regime of full employment than they are on the average under 'laissez-faire' and even the rise in wage rates resulting from the stronger bargaining power of the workers is less likely to reduce profits than to increase prices, and to affect adversely only the rentier interests. But 'discipline in the factories' and 'political stability' are more appreciated by the business leaders than profits. Their class instinct tells them that lasting full employment is unsound from their point of view and that unemployment is an integral part of the normal capitalist system.[36]

As Kalecki pointed out, business leaders in the Allied countries had come during the Second World War to agree that 'something must be done during a slump', but the conflict continued as to the direction of government intervention and as to whether it should be used merely to alleviate slumps or to secure sustained full employment. But, although the outcome was still indeterminate at the time Kalecki wrote, he recognized the possibility that continuing opposition to full employment might at least temporarily be overcome 'under the pressure of the masses'. It was precisely this pressure that did turn the tide, as the political dangers of not introducing full employment loomed far larger and far more immediate than the political danger of introducing it. The necessity of sustaining trade-union co-operation during the course of the war with the promise of continued prominence in decision-making after the war and a commitment not to return to pre-war conditions; the recognition that the experience of full employment and comprehensive planning had led to rising expectations of a post-war rise in living standards and security on the part of the working class; the example of the Soviet economy (much played up during the wartime alliance) and the concern regarding its effect on the working class in the post-war period; and, finally, the mass radicalism that exhibited itself in the electoral success of working-class parties in the immediate post-war years—these were elements in the final decision.

It was the changing balance of class forces which attended the commitment to full employment and the consequent development of economic planning to deal with its consequences that lay at the heart of corporatist developments. The point has been made by Warren: 'Full employment policy . . . was a product of the fear of the *political* repercussions of a repetition of the mass unemployment of the 1930s. Capitalist planning was, on the contrary, designed to deal with the economic, as much as the political, consequences of full employment policies.'[37] The consequence of full employment was that trade unions were in a much stronger position than heretofore to raise money wages. If these increases were passed on in price increases, however, this had the effect, given the growth rate of productivity, of affecting a country's foreign competitiveness. If the increases were not passed on in an inflationary spiral, on the other hand, the motor force of the capitalist economy—profits—tended to be squeezed. It was this problem that provided the spur to state economic planning in the post-war era, directed both at raising productivity (and hence economic growth) and inducing trade unions to co-operate in an incomes policy which would restrain money-wage demands.

Although specific factors have affected the character and timing of developments in each country, corporatist structures have been most pronounced precisely in those countries where incomes policy has been at the heart of economic planning. Although the operative details of the various systems cannot be adumbrated here, Sweden and the Netherlands may be taken as two major examples of post-war economic planning being secondary or at least facilitative to the early establishment of incomes policy as the central focus of economic policy, although direct state intervention in the wage bargaining process differs markedly in the two systems.[38] Britain, on the other hand, provides a prime example of tripartite economic planning structures being developed in the first place with the primary aim of inducing the trade unions to co-operate in the incomes policy.[39] However, where a tripartite incomes policy has not been central to economic planning, as in France, planning has been a much more closed exercise, largely confined to senior civil servants and big business, with 'functional representation', including that of organized labour, largely passed by. When emphasis has been given to achieving tripartite consensus in the context of French planning, wage restraint via an incomes policy has provided the motivation for, and the central content of, discussions.[40]

It would be wrong, of course, to tie corporatist developments solely to incomes policy. For instance, the specific geopolitical location of Austria and West Germany in the post-war balance of international forces may be seen as a particularly powerful factor in cementing an institutionalized alliance between capital and social democratic-led labour. Moreover, even within the economic policy framework, the transition to advanced capitalism required much more state involvement in the economy than was directly necessitated by the full employment commitment or the formalized process of indicative planning. To facilitate capital accumulation under monopoly capitalism (as well as to the end of securing the economic growth and higher productivity to accommodate consumer demand and increased wage costs), the state promoted the tendency toward even greater industrial concentration, undertook to socialize the risks of private production through subsidies, tax write-offs, building infrastructure, manpower training and so on, and sought to integrate private and public investment and planning decisions. To the end of legitimating this increased state-business interface, as well as to facilitate labour co-operation at the level of individual industries, joint consultative structures, works councils, and the like were often promoted. Moreover, access to the state was made relatively easy for groups other than business. But in so far as this entailed the *offer* of an effective say for labour in national economic policy (rather than a formalized, legitimating process such as the annual presentation of views to the Cabinet), the topic of the unions administering a wage restraint policy to their members or at least moving toward centralized wage bargaining (to contain as much as possible wage drift) never lagged far behind.

The reason that incomes policy generally lies at the heart of corporatist developments is that, far more than is the case in other fields of state intervention in the economy, it requires the direct co-operation of the trade unions. Unions might be induced to legitimate other policies, such as taxation policy, automation, man-power policy, and so on, but the administrative arm remains the state or the corporation. The union is the direct object of an incomes policy, however, for it is its behaviour the policy is designed to affect, and it must be the vehicle for administering the policy to the rank and file. And because business groups must in turn agree to at least nominal state supervision of prices, profits and dividends, the stage is set for that co-operative behaviour between the groups themselves in the framing and administering of public policy that is the 'distinguishing trait' of liberal corporatism. Moreover, the establishment of a wage norm inevitably involves the unions in discussions of what fiscal, monetary and even private and public investment policies are consistent with the norm. With a social democratic party in office, the prospect of union influence on decision-making and of state control over profits and prices and thus the distribution of incomes becomes a tempting inducement to union co-operation in wage restraint.

The process we have been describing can be theoretically explicated by employing a theory of the state along the lines suggested both by Miliband and Poulantzas. [41] If we employ a theory of the state which permits it to respond *only* to the needs and demands of the capitalist class, our location of the origin of corporatist planning and incomes-policy developments in the victory of the working class on the full time employment issue makes little sense. If we employ a theory of the state, on the other hand, which sees the state as relatively autonomous from this class, acting on its behalf but not necessarily at its behest, we can discern how the state responds directly to various class pressures. As Miliband has pointed out with regard to Marx's famous formulation that 'the executive of the modern state is but a committee for managing the common affairs of the whole bourgeoisie': 'The notion of common affairs assumes the existence of particular ones; and the notion of the whole bourgeoisie implies the existence of separate elements which make up that whole. This being the case, there is an obvious need for an institution of the kind [Marx and Engels] refer to, namely the state, and the state *cannot* meet this end without enjoying a certain degree of autonomy. In other words, that nature of autonomy is embedded in the definition itself, is an intrinsic part of it.'[42] Precisely because of this relative autonomy, the actions of the state have to be 'situated within the field of the class struggle'.[43] At times, the state will intervene against the short-term interest of the capitalist class as a whole, or even against the long-term interests of a fraction of that class to the end of engaging in compromises and sacrifices which will maintain the long-term interests of the whole class. This was precisely the basis of the introduction of successful reforms in the post-war era; they were reforms in the true sense—that is, they left untouched the fundamental structure of capitalist society, but nevertheless constituted material economic and social gains for the working class.

The shift in the balance of class forces after the Second World War (and before it in Sweden and Norway) has been widely recognized by most students of advanced capitalism. Unfortunately, however, it has been usually correspondingly assumed that at this time the state shed its systematic relationship with the class structure and emerged as Brenner puts it, as 'the political arm of the community'.[44] But the autonomy evidenced in the state's interventionism and the access given to non-capitalist groups do not entail state independence from the system of class domination.

This can be seen from the conclusions to the major survey of planning in the liberal democratic state which re-examined the field after Shonfield's study.

> The nature of planning is to be judged in the first place by its works. Such a balance sheet shows that the social reforming potential, which has not lacked government sponsors, has proved largely illusory, dominated by the preoccupation with management of the economic system of modern capitalism. This establishes the real sense in which planning is compatible with the mixed economy, in so far as it works for the maintenance of the social and political structure associated with it rather than for its change.[45]

The outcome in terms of the distribution of resources may be seen by taking what is generally judged to be the strongest case of corporatist planning with a social purpose—that of Sweden. Despite the widespread myth with regard to the income redistribution effects of Swedish policy, a report submitted to the Landsorganisationen (LO; the Swedish confederation of trade unions) shortly before the strike explosion of the late 1960s which shook the corporatist system found that not only had there been no marked change in income distribution since 1948, but that the fraction of persons with 40 per cent or less of mean income had considerably increased, while the group with 'normal' income decreased and the proportion with high incomes increased. This was matched by a growing concentration of wealth in Sweden.[46]

This kind of outcome may be attributed partly to the imbalance between the groups in corporatist arrangements. In characterizing the post-war British system as 'quasi-corporatist', Beer identified the source for the power of functional organizations in the state's need for the expert advice in the formation of policy, for their acquiescence or voluntary agreement to administer state policies and for their approval and legitimation of state policy in the eyes of their members. It was particularly the state's need of these things from the unions, according to Beer, which accounted for their 'unrecognizably transformed power position'.[47] My own study of economic policy-making in Britain in the post-war period has shown, however, that government policies were repeatedly formed either without first securing the advice of the unions, or after having explicitly rejected their advice.[48] It was not their advice but their acquiescence and approval which were studiously courted, usually *after* policy decisions were reached. The advice on which the 1966 Labour government acted in introducing massive deflation and a statutory wage freeze and abandoning the economic plan was that of the Confederation of British Industry, the City of London, and Britain's foreign creditors, in the light of the latter's immediate concern to protect the pound against devaluation. Indeed, even when this advice proved faulty in the extreme, as devaluation was eventually forced on the government, Labour had to continue to promote private business incentive to foster economic growth. For in so far as the logic of class co-operation ruled out command reformist planning, it also ruled out a redistributive fiscal policy.

Watson has put the point more generally, summing up the planning experience of France, Italy and Britain:

> Notwithstanding the participation of a variety of interests, an established hierarchy has existed on the effectiveness of their contributions. A *de facto* convergence between planners, officials and industrial management has dominated the process . . . Undoubtedly some planners and officials have regretted the extent of this alignment, but seen it as virtually inevitable, given the lack of trade-union expertise. Notwithstanding the great improvement that has occurred in national accounts and statistics, information from industry remains crucial for the planners designs, especially when they are seeking to deal directly with specific problems which the strategic, operational orientation of planning involves. Yet the reluctance of industrialists to disclose information, particularly to the unions, has not diminished. Here planning has singularly failed to bring about explicitness in decision-making.[49]

That a similar situation existed in Sweden, despite the vaunted 'partnership' between the LO and the central employers' federation, can be seen in the LO's demand in the early 1970s after the system was shaken by rank-and-file unrest, that the unions be provided information by employers on their recruitment policy and labour-force planning. Without direct access to managerial information, and with a staff of 90 at the LO headquarters, for the requisite 'expertise' the LO had to develop for corporatist policy-making it was obviously highly dependent on its 'partner'.

What this suggests is that the bias of the system is less attributable to direct pressure from business than to the logic entailed in state planning in a capitalist economy. To quote Watson again:

> The expertise on which planning has been based requires that there be definite constants in the economic process, above all its authority structure. Social science solutions rely on people behaving as their assigned role requires. Insofar as planning has been the medium for propagating the reasoning underpinning such solutions, the circle involved has remained the very restricted one of those having a direct relationship to the management

function, whether at the micro or macro level, since they are the ones on which successful steering is taken essentially to depend. The system is viewed as structured to permit management a discrete, specialized, and hierarchical function.[50]

The consequence of this is that planning's success rests on the participants' speaking the same language as management, given the state's prior acceptance of the prevailing authority structures in industry. Indeed, one of corporatism's main functions appears to be a matter of diffusing this language among the union leadership, who have often been willing apprentices since without it their concerns appear to be irrelevant, if not hostile, to the planning exercise. It is in this manner, as much as through the overt pressure of particular capitalist interests, that corporatism within liberal democracies has become a powerful vehicle for reinforcing class dominance.

But it is also in this light that the instability of corporatism within liberal democracies must be understood. For in accepting the one-dimensional rationality entailed in its decision-making, trade-union leaders become unable to promote the interests of their membership. Moreover, since their primary involvement in the system relates to the economy's problem with wage pressure, rather than to a mere legitimizing role they might play, they are forced to carry this rationality back to their members in the concrete, if unpalatable, form of wage restraint. Not surprisingly, in the absence of effective union input in economic decision-making and in the absence of extensive price and profit controls and a redistributive fiscal policy, union leaders eventually come under heavy pressure from their membership to withdraw from the incomes-policy structures and abstain from co-operative behaviour in broader economic planning structures. The legitimation and union which the state needs, in other words, delegitimizes the union leadership in the eyes of their base.

IV

The foremost example of corporatism's instability is that of Britain. The Trades Union Congress (TUC) was first forced to withdraw from the tripartite wages policy in which it had co-operated for two years when the General Council suffered a rare defeat at the 1950 congress on the issue. Having been once burned, and without the pull of loyalty to the Labour Party, the TUC refused participation when the question was broached by the Conservatives in the 1950s, and although they joined the tripartite National Economic Development Council when it was established to induce them to co-operate in an incomes policy in the early 1960s, they refused to co-operate with the Conservative government's pay pause or National Incomes Commission. When the latter was swept away after Labour's 1964 victory, the unions joined in a voluntary tripartite policy on the promise of full employment, a national economic plan and extensive trade union input in decision-making. But under the impact of the introduction of statutory backing (only three months after the policy was inaugurated, at the insistence of Britain's foreign creditors and the domestic financial community), the abandonment of planning and full employment, and price control of a mainly symbolic nature, the unions, after three years of extensive co-operation, were forced by the defeat of right-wing union leaders, and rank-and-file dissent which culminated in the wage and strike explosion of 1969, to withdraw their co-operation. Since then we have seen the Heath government's unsuccessful attempt to re-establish corporatist arrangements through its incomes policy of 1972–4 and the eventual breakdown of the more successful social contract at the end of the 1974–9 Labour government's term of office.

It is mainly those union leaderships which are highly insulated from membership pressures at the plant level which can sustain participation in corporatist arrangements for any considerable period of time. It is no coincidence that those societies most commonly listed as corporatist—Austria, Norway, Sweden and the Netherlands—contain the most highly centralized union confederations in the Western world.[51] This insulation may be provided by central bargaining and control over strike funds, the purposive atrophy of union locals and the underrepresentation of oppositional elements at the central level, as well as by the state's use of its coercive powers to prohibit unofficial strikes and provide a statutory framework for collective bargaining and incomes policy with severe penalties against their breach.

Under many of these conditions, the corporatist arrangements of Sweden proved more stable than the British. But what is striking as one examines this system more closely is that this stability was rather precarious while it lasted. The voluntaristic incomes policy contained in the Swedish annual central negotiations was effectively established during the 1950s only after the unions had opted out of a state-imposed wages policy similar to the British in the late 1940s.[52] And even this system, sustained as it was by an active manpower policy pursued by the government, was far more subject to disruptive influences than is generally recognized or admitted by the central actors. As has been recently demonstrated unofficial strikes have been fairly common in Swedish industry at the plant level throughout the post-war period, although 'the myth of labour peace and the focus of interest on the institutional structure have long obscured this fact.'[53] It is this shop-floor power which has provided the basis for the extensive wage drift which occurs outside the central wage agreement. This suggests that

> in the Swedish case more and more open conflict appears as one descends from the central level of organizational interaction to the shop-floor. The pattern of this conflict and its similarity with that of other industrial societies suggest that whatever the institutional superstructure, the economic and technological substructures tend to impose their own pattern.[54]

To those less subject to accept the LO's explanation of employer-union peace in terms of 'we has a meeting'[55] then, the explosion of industrial strife in the late 1960s and early 1970s was likely to come as less of a surprise. The industrial unrest of this period weakened the power of the central union organization and, following the 1974 settlement, a new wave of unofficial strikes hit the economy.

In the Dutch case, the débâcle came earlier, as should perhaps be expected from a policy that was much more obviously one of wage restraint and one in which the state was much more directly involved. The policy for years held back the Netherlands' real wages to a level below that of other European countries and it would have been impossible to sustain but for the coercive powers that backed it up and the extremely high degree of central union bureaucratic independence from rank and file. By the late 1950s, rank-and-file pressure (including the formation of independent unions outside the recognized structure) led to a reorientation of the policy (significantly, after the socialists left the governing coalition, thus weakening the pull of loyalty on the socialist union leadership). The unofficial strikes and wage explosion of 1963 finally convinced the union leadership that they could not hold the line and led to their subsequent rejection of central wage controls. The strikes of the following decade, and the union decentralization that accompanied them, indicated that the system could not easily be put together again.[56]

The manifest instability of corporatist arrangements in liberal democracies by the late 1960s and early 1970s led in most cases to a state response of a coercive kind. In Sweden this was seen in the government taking the unprecedented step of suspending the right to strike for public employees in 1971. In the Netherlands, it was seen in the Law of Wage Formation (submitted to Parliament in 1968 and passed in 1970) which permitted the government to invalidate wage contracts which were considered detrimental to the national economy. It must be noted again that in neither of these countries was this coercive intrusion entirely new. Since 1928, unofficial strikes in Sweden (more particularly strikes and related actions during the period of an agreement) have been prohibited by the law. The famous 1938 Basic Agreement between the LO and the employers' federation, the linchpin of the post-war incomes policy, was itself struck under an immediate government threat of legislation. In the 'guided wage policy' of the Netherlands, statutory powers played a major role. These older coercive elements already tainted the much-vaunted voluntarist nature of liberal corporatism. The new controls did even more so.

The shift toward coercion was more striking in Britain because of the previous absence of statutory interference in collective bargaining. It began with the statutory incomes policy of 1965 (which required unions to refrain from pursuing any agreement referred to the Prices and Incomes Board for a four-month period) and was maintained in the face of union opposition throughout the life of the Labour government. It took on new dimensions in 1968–9 when the government attempted to impose a compulsory cooling-off period on unofficial strikes. This development had indeed been foreseen as necessary inside the government as early as 1965, when the incomes policy was inaugurated. The Ministry of Labour had seen 'one obvious general problem' with the new tripartite arrangements: 'If trade-union leaders accept these wide responsibilities there is a risk they will cease to be regarded as representative of their members interests and their influence and authority may be transferred to unofficial leaders.'[57]

The proposed legislation was withdrawn when the furor it produced in the labour movement led to the revolt of the party caucus, but not before the government attempted to get the TUC to rewrite its constitution to expel unions which failed to apply sanctions against unofficial strikers. The effort failed in the face of pressure on the union leadership from the rank and file. This was followed, after the Labour government's defeat in 1970, by the Conservatives' Industrial Relations Act, which reserved the very term 'trade union' only for those organizations that registered under the act and which undertook to discipline unofficial strikers, whose actions were in any case now made illegal by the act.

The primary aim of these coercive measures was not to destroy trade unions, as was often alleged in the course of the labour movement's struggle against them, but rather to define, codify and back by state sanctions the obligations of unions to employers and the state in a way consistent with securing a stable corporatism. The philosophy behind them was perhaps best expressed, in explicitly corporatist terms, by none other than Shonfield as a member of the Royal Commission on Trade Unions and Employers' Associations:

> The distinction between labour organizations which explicitly accept certain responsibilities towards society as a whole, as well as toward their members, and those which refuse to do so needs to be pressed further. This should be done by demanding of trade unions the fulfilment of certain minimum standards of behaviour . . . notably those which express the duty of trade unions to conduct their industrial relations in such a way as not to hold back improvements in the standard of living of the community as a whole.[58]

If trade unions as voluntary democratic organizations were not going to adopt a corporatist conception of the national interest, then state coercive force was necessary to make them do so.

But the line between authoritarian and liberal corporatism is not as thin as this would suggest. For what has been remarkable about the recent development of the state's coercive force over labour is its ineffectiveness. The inability of the Swedish labour courts to stop the dockers' strike of May 1970, despite its application of maximum fines on seventy-eight workers, was symptomatic of the problem, and in most cases the unofficial strikes did not lead to prosecution.[59] The Law of Wage Formation in the Netherlands was met with implacable union opposition and led to the withdrawal of the two largest of the three labour centres from the preparation of the semi-annual economic reports in the Social and Economic Council, 'an act of key significance, an open show of non-cooperation, which ruptured the established system of industrial relations'.[60] This action, together with the mobilization surrounding the one-hour general strike of December 1970 and the setbacks suffered by the Christian parties in the 1971 elections, led to the emasculation of the law by the new government. In Britain, the Industrial Relations Act was rendered inoperative within three months of its implementation by the refusal of most trade unions to register under it, and more significantly by the real threat of a general strike in the face of the imprisonment of five unofficial dock leaders.

The reason behind the ineffectiveness of the new state coercive measures in this period is to be found in the contradictions they posed to liberal democracy itself. To meet the challenge of a working class united against the operation of laws that contradict the freedoms of their indigenous class organizations, coercive measures have to go far beyond the immediate field of industrial relations. To have made these laws operable, the extensive use of police powers would likely have been necessary, and probably would have involved limiting the rights to mobilize opposition through free speech and assembly. It could have entailed, in other words, the abrogation of liberal democracy itself. It should be pointed out that even under fascism industrial class struggle continued to take place in the form of indiscipline, abstentions from work and even sectional wage demands.[61] What kept the conflict closed (it was never healed) was the iron fist of the state preventing the working class from mobilizing and unifying itself industrially or politically. That the advanced capitalist state has backed off from such a venture may be attributed partly to the self-identification of political leaders and the capitalist class itself with the principles of liberal democracy. More important still, however, must be the risks it would entail for a capitalist society with a large working class prepared to defend its indigenous organizations and itself highly conscious of the value of political freedom.

The foregoing does not suggest by any means that we have seen the end of corporatist developments in advanced capitalist liberal democracies. On the contrary, in the absence of much evidence of the immediate emergence of a political movement (with the possible exception of Italy and France) which would merge with and go beyond the massive industrial militancy of the last decade, and particularly in countries with social democratic governments, we are likely to see a further cycle of the establishment, breakdown and reestablishment of corporatist structures. To be sure, it is unlikely that these cycles can be continued indefinitely and, in the face of the inability of the working class to effect its own resolution to capitalism's contradictions, the dynamics of these repeated cycles will eventually lead to a fully authoritarian response by the state. In any event, it is certainly clear that the much-vaunted view of corporatism as representing a new avenue of democratic stability for advanced capitalism contains no fewer contradictions than the traditional corporatist theory itself.

(1976)

Notes

1. For useful discussions, in English, of European corporatist theory, see especially R. H. Bowen, *German Theories of the Corporatist State*, New York 1947; M. H. Elbow, *French Corporative Theory 1784–1948*, New York 1966; and N. Harris, *Competition and the Corporate Society*, London 1972. P. Schmitter's 'Still the Century of Corporatism?', *Review of Politics*, no. 36, January 1974, provides an outstanding bibliography and introduction to the range of corporatist thinkers.
2. Harris, p. 72.
3. The early American experience is covered in H. Draper, 'Neo-corporatism and neo-reformers', *New Politics*, no. 1, June 1961, and in J. Weinstein, *The Corporate Ideal in the Liberal State, 1900–1918*, Boston 1968, although both are too ready to identify as corporatism any form of class collaboration.
4. Quoted in Harris, p. 55.
5. Bowen, pp. 3–4.
6. For examples of this form of use of the terms, see L. Panitch, *Social Democracy and Industrial Militancy*, Cambridge 1976. In the mid 1970s it became more commonly employed, at least in the Canadian and British press, as a descriptive term (with only continuing nuances of opprobrium) for Trudeau's 'New Society' and Wilson's 'Social Contract' programmes of wage restraint. And the Executive Council of the Canadian Labour Congress went so far in the 'Manifesto' presented to the May 1976 convention as to condemn Trudeau's 'New Society' proposals as 'liberal corporatism' (where 'tripartism would mean that the institutions of organized labour would function to ensure the acquiescence of workers to decisions in which their representatives have no real power'), but to advocate a system of 'social corporatism' where labour would be an 'equal partner' in economic decision-making with business and government. The use of the term in a positive sense produced widespread outrage at the convention, however, and the leadership amended the document, perhaps tellingly, to read 'social democracy' rather than 'social corporatism'. See Canadian Labour Congress, *Labour's Manifesto for Canada*, Ottawa 1976.
7. S. Beer, *Modern British Politics*, London 1969, p. 419.
8. Ibid., p. 395.
9. A. Shonfield, *Modern Capitalism*, London, 1965, p. 161.
10. G. Lehmbruch, 'Consociational Democracy, Class Conflict and the New Corporatism'. Paper presented to the IPSA Round Table on Political Integration, Jerusalem 1974, pp. 1–2.
11. Schmitter, pp. 93–4, 105, 103–4.
12. The phrase is from R. E. Pahl and J. T. Winkler, 'The Coming Corporatism', *Challenge*, March–April 1975. This widely read article, by two British sociologists, is not without its insights, but stands as a prime contemporary example of the lack of definitional rigour and loose thinking in much theorizing about corporatism.
13. See for example T. Lowi, *The End of Liberalism*, New York 1969; R. Presthus, *Elite Accommodation in Canadian Politics*, Toronto 1973.
14. Apart from Presthus's utter confusion between the two, M. Heisler (ed.), *Politics in Europe*, New York 1974, pp. 42ff, 88, also tends towards a conflation of corporatism and consociationalism.
15. Both M. J. Brenner, 'Functional Representation and Interest Group Theory', *Comparative Politics*, no. 2, October 1969, and Schmitter provide useful contrasts between the pluralist and corporatist paradigms.
16. Schmitter, pp. 115–6.

17. Shonfield, p. 128.
18. M. Watson, 'Planning in the Liberal Democratic State', in J. Hayward and M. Watson (eds.), *Planning, Politics and Public Policy*, Cambridge 1975, p. 461.
19. C. B. Macpherson, *Democratic Theory*, Oxford 1973, pp. 180–1.
20. A. Martin, 'Is Democratic Control of Capitalist Economies Possible?', in L. Lindberg et al. (eds.), *Stress and Contradiction in Modern Capitalism*, Lexington, Mass. p. 56, n. 19.
21. Bowen, pp. 5–6.
22. I. Scholten, 'The Netherlands: The Development of Pluralist Corporatism in a Multicultural Society', (unpublished), Rotterdam 1976, p. 2.
23. But see Harris and L. P. Carpenter, 'Corporatism in Britain, 1930–45', *Journal of Contemporary History*, no. 11, 1976.
24. Quoted in H. Arendt, *The Origins of Totalitarianism*, London 1967, p. 258, n. 94.
25. A. Jones, *Industrial Order*, London 1950, pp. 24–7.
26. Quoted in Arendt, p. 258, n. 95.
27. Jones, pp. 28–9
28. Ibid., p. 31 (emphasis added).
29. See note 5.
30. E. F. M. Durbin, *The Politics of Democratic Socialism*, London 1940, pp. 186, 189, 264, 271.
31. Lehmbruch, p. 3.
32. Heisler, p. 57.
33. Heisler, p.87, does not explicitly consider Italy as approximating this model, but he does France.
34. See W. L. M. King, *Industry and Humanity*, Toronto 1973 (1918). The consistency with which the views expressed in this book were held over time may be seen from an entry to the *King Diaries* on 29 June 1937. On a visit to Germany at the time, King had been impressed, above all, with the corporative element in German fascism, almost to the total neglect of its effects on working-class institutions and the freedom of the working people. 'They are truly establishing an industrial commonwealth, and other nations would be wise to evolve rapidly on similar lines of giving to labour its place in the control of the industry.' For a fuller discussion of this see L. Panitch, *The Canadian State, Political Economy and Political Power*, Toronto 1977, pp. 202, and Panitch, 'Corporatism in Canada', *Studies in Political Economy*, no. 1, Spring 1979.
35. The widely influential Beveridge report, W. Beveridge, *Full Employment in a Free Society*, London 1945, which laid the programmatic foundations for the British welfare state and, it might be argued, for the post-war capitalist state generally, explicitly placed the responsibility for the avoidance of inflation on the unions, demanding a unified wage restraint policy as a *quid pro quo* for full employment and social services.
36. M. Kalecki, *Selected Essays on the Dynamics of the Capitalist Economy*, Cambridge 1971, pp. 140–41.
37. B. Warren, 'The State and Capitalist Planning', *New Left Review*, no. 72, March–April 1972, pp. 3–4.
38. On Sweden see Shonfield, pp. 196, 189–211; A. Martin, 'Labour Movement Parties and Inflation: Contrasting Responses in Britain and Sweden', *Polity*, no. 7, Summer 1975; C. Van Otter, 'Sweden: Labour Reformism Reshapes the System', in S. Barkin (ed.), *Worker Militancy and Its Consequences 1965–1975*, New York 1975; S. Sunesson. 'Does Sweden Show the Way?', *International Socialist Journal* no. 3,

December 1966. On the Netherlands see Shonfield, pp. 211–20; B. Peper, 'The Netherlands: from an Ordered Harmonic to a Bargaining Relationship', in Barkin; M. Edelman and R. W. Fleming, *The Politics of Wage-Price Decisions*, Urbana 1965.

39. See Panitch, *Social Democracy*; J. Corina, 'Planning and the British labour market', in Hayward and Watson (eds.); G. A. Dorfman, *Wage Politics in Britain 1945–1967*, Ames 1973.

40. See Shonfield, pp. 130–31, 143; J. E. S. Hayward, 'Interest Groups and Incomes Policy in France', *British Journal of Industrial Relations*, no. 4, July 1966; J. E. S. Hayward, 'State Intervention in France: The Changing Style of Government Industry Relations', *Political Studies* no. 20, 1972.

41. R. Miliband, *The State in Capitalist Society*, London 1969; N. Poulantzas, *Political Power and Social Classes*, London 1973.

42. R. Miliband, 'Poulantzas and the Capitalist State', *New Left Review*, no. 82. November–December 1973, p. 85, n. 4.

43. I. Gough, 'State Expenditure in Advanced Capitalism', *New Left Review*, no. 92, July–August 1975, p. 64.

44. Brenner, p. 119.

45. Watson, p. 447.

46. S. D. Anderman (ed.), *Trade Unions and Technological Change*, London, 1967, p. 111. Anderman's conclusions are drawn from the findings of the 1964 Swedish Royal Commission on Taxation. On the regressivity of the Swedish tax system see Van Otter, pp. 222–3. For similar findings in Britain see R. J. Nicholson, 'The Distribution of Personal Incomes', *Lloyd's Bank Review* no. 83, January 1967, and R. Blackburn, 'The Unequal Society', in R. Blackburn and A. Cockburn, *The Incompatibles*, London 1967.

47. Beer, p. 211.

48. Panitch, *Social Democracy and Industrial Militancy*.

49. Watson, p. 468.

50. Ibid., p. 458.

51. For an index of union centralization see B. Headey, 'Trade Unions and National Wage Policies', *Journal of Politics*, no. 32, 1970, table.5, pp. 433–4. On the index, the confederations of the countries mentioned score from 25 to 35 in centralization – as compared with those of France, Britain, the United States, and Italy, which score 0 to 5.

52. Martin, 'Labour Movements Parties and Inflation', pp. 429–32.

53. J. Fulcher, 'Class Conflict in Sweden', *Sociology*, no.7, January 1973, p. 52.

54. Ibid., p. 54.

55. Shonfield, p. 119.

56. See Peper; E. Marx and W. Kendall, *Unions in Europe*, Sussex, 1971; H. A. Turner and D. A. S. Jackson, 'On the Stability of Wage Differences and Productivity-based Wage Policies: An International Analysis', *British Journal of Industrial Relations*, no. 7, March 1969.

57. Ministry of Labour, *Written Evidence of the Ministry of Labour to the Royal Commission on Trade Unions and Employers' Associations*, London 1965, p. 3.

58. A. Shonfield, 'Note of reservation by Mr Andrew Shonfield', in *Royal Commission on Trade Unions and Employers' Associations 1965–1968*, London 1968, p. 284.

59. Fulcher, pp. 54–5.

60. Peper, pp. 132–3.

61. T. W. Mason, 'Labour in the Third Reich', *Past and Present*, no. 33, April 1966.

6.
Theories of Corporatism:
Reflections on a Growth Industry

I

Until recently, corporatism was a term either largely restricted to the study of the history of ideologies and/or fascist regimes, or a popular (especially in the labour movement) term of denigration of trade-union co-operation in state incomes policy or economic planning structures. As a social scientific term applied to certain developments or arrangements in contemporary advanced capitalist societies corporatism was employed by a notably limited number of scholars. Only in the 1970s did we witness a veritable explosion of social scientific production which employs the term corporatism in the latter sense. This has occurred to such an extent that it is hardly incorrect to speak of corporatism as a major 'field of study' itself, with a spillover of usage of the term in the media and among political actors. Yet the first thing that strikes one as one reads through the recent literature on modern corporatism is the profound lack of agreement on what the concept actually refers to. It is obvious that considerable confusion must attend a field in which the central concept is variously understood to connote a distinct economic system or mode of production (feudalism, capitalism, socialism, . . . corporatism) a state form (parliamentarism, fascism . . . corporatism), and a system of interest intermediation (pluralism, syndicalism, monism . . . corporatism). This confusion must be compounded when, for instance, within the interest intermediation approach alone, one finds a range of theoretical and research practices which are at odds with one another, 'with respect to conceptual usage, substantive funding, causal reference or normative preference'.[1] The view that the recent appearance of corporatism on the terminological stage of political science makes it 'somewhat premature to take its meaning for granted', [2] may in this light be seen as both understatement and false optimism. For as the quantity of work on corporatism has expanded, it has been difficult to discern whether definitional convergence has really tended to outpace definitional refraction.

Given this situation, there appears to be little basis for the belief that positive foundations have in fact been established for considering corporatism as an alternative *problematique* to pluralism[3] or indeed anything else. This is not necessarily to be lamented. As Meier has written, 'there is no need of pressing different approaches into one common framework. However, it appears reasonable to me to try to be as explicit as possible concerning the basic underlying problem definitions and assumptions; only then can we hope to become aware of conceptual research progress, material implications of different investigations, and remaining points of theoretical and factual controversy worthwhile debating.'[4] It is in this spirit that this paper is written. It seeks to cast a critical eye on this new field, to point out inconsistent definitions and usages and, in particular, to focus on certain tendencies among the various recent theorizations which may impede fruitful study and foster illusions about corporatism. It is not intended to be a catalogue or a summary of the recent literature, but rather a reflection on central theoretical problems which appear to be at the core of the confusion that presently marks the field.[5]

In my own work, I have tended to employ the term corporatism descriptively and narrowly, reserving it to demarcate a set of specific and partial political structures, such as the tripartite economic planning and incomes policy bodies which have emerged in a good number of advanced capitalist liberal democracies. The corporatist political structure is *specific* in the sense that it involves: a linkage between the state and functional groups constituted by institutionalized representation in public policy making; interaction among the groups themselves in this process (in contrast with the one-to-one relationship between interest groups and the state normally constitutive of pressure group politics); and an element of state control over the groups whereby their autonomy is limited and they are employed as agencies of mobilization or administration for state policy. The corporatist political structure is *partial* in the sense that it does not displace parliamentary representation, bureaucratic administration and interest group lobbying, but exists alongside them and is in many ways interwoven with them. Moreover, corporatist political structures do not appear to extend to all interest group-state relations. Their establishment and functioning mainly pertains to economic policy-making and it is those associations which are based directly on the social division of labour that are drawn into such structures. More specifically, it is the interest associations of business and labour, representing directly the central actors in the balance of class forces in advanced capitalist societies, which are the constituent elements, alongside the state, of corporatist political structures.

On the basis of this kind of approach, corporatism in the modern context can be seen as a specific form of state-induced class collaboration. Such an approach to modern corporatism can be justified on etymological, descriptive, analytic and explanatory grounds. *Etymologically,* it reflects the original meaning of corporatism as it emerged in European social thought, the similarities with which is presumably the reason these new structures are called corporatist at all. (It does this in two senses: it is consistent with the original view of the constituent units of society as functional producer groups; and it is consistent with the original significance of corporatism as an ideology designed to secure class harmony in the face of class conflict.) *Descriptively,* this approach to modern corporatism is consistent with the empirical evidence of most students in the field, which is markedly concentrated on the corporatization of trade unions and employers' associations, and particularly the former. *Analytically,* it facilitates comparison between the consultation and co-operation characteristic of state-interest group relations in all liberal democracies and the interaction among the groups themselves as well as with the state which is distinctive of corporatism. And this approach to corporatism can be justified on *explanatory* grounds in that it can be linked with a class-theoretical historical materialist framework, to which a great many, if not most, of the recent theorists of corporatism are self-avowedly partial.

In so far as students of corporatism concentrated on examining the origins, dynamics, limitations and contradictions of particular corporatist structures with advanced capitalist liberal democratic societies, there was much to be learned from their work. There has been an increasingly common tendency, however, to see these particular corporatist structures, not as representing new *partial* elements *within* the existing economic and political system, but as corporatist ideology once claimed they would be, new political and/or economic systems *in their own right.* It shall be the central argument of this paper that at the root of much of the confusion which presently marks the study of modern corporatism, lies the tendency to offer paradigmatic definitions of corporatism in ideal-typical terms, and at the level of total systems. These systems have never existed as described, but are logical constructs created to stand as alternatives to capitalism or pluralism or parliamentarism. This is a very different form of abstraction than that of abstracting the basic properties of a given existing structure, removing the historical and extraneous to get at the basic relationship which may be said to define the structure. Instead, we have seen with regard to corporatism a form of 'abstraction' which proceeds by expansion rather than contraction, that is, that on the basis of particular structures creates a definition for a whole system, whether of interest inter-mediation or state form or mode of production. Although it is usually immediately admitted that a full corporatist system nowhere exists, and that one is dealing with questions of more or less, mixtures or articulations with other systems, there is nevertheless the presumption—rooted in the definition itself—that corporatism has it within its nature to become a full system. In order to demonstrate this one would need a dynamic historical theory which would establish the conditions for the spread of corporatist structures throughout the whole system. Such a theory has not been offered. The result of this 'Macro-Gestalt' of corporatism, [6] however, is that research is oriented away from the questions of why corporatism has developed in particular sectors and amongst particular groups, or classes, the role it plays and the contradictions it introduces *as such* in maintaining the existing system of interest mediation, state form or mode of production.

II

The grandest, and the weakest, of approaches to corporatism as a total system is that which understands by the term an alternative economic system to capitalism and socialism. This approach is most conspicuously espoused in the corporatism field by Jack Winkler, who defines corporatism 'as an economic system in which the state directs and controls predominately privately-owned business according to four principles; unity, order, nationalism and success . . . stripped to its essentials, corporatism is principally defined by one particularly important qualitative change, the shift from a supportive to a directive role for the state in the economy'. [7] The key factor underlying a transition from capitalism to corporatism is industrial concentration which 'makes the notion of a "market" and of "competition" within that market unreal'. Given this development, since deconcentration is 'unlikely' and corporate self-regulation 'untenable', state control of profit becomes inevitable. 'For the state to tolerate (and in some cases to sponsor) concentration to this level and still allow profit maximization would be to license corporate plunder, to issue a permit to hold the nation to ransom. This is an intolerable situation, not just in political terms, but economically to the other consumer and supplies firms of the dominants . . . The choice is state control of profit.'[8]

It will be seen immediately that there are certain problems here. First of all, it is clear that the conception of capitalism involved is one derived from neo-classical economics, entailing not only an image of the *laissez faire* state (amended to speak of a supportive role for the state rather than a non-existent one), but also of perfect inter-firm competition with unrestricted access within each particular market. As Clifton has shown, the theory of imperfect competition is based on using perfect competition as a benchmark, 'a standard of competition against which all other varieties of capitalist economy that arise in the course of history are measured . . . As a result the development and continued growth of large firms in the economy are necessarily interpreted as a progressive deviation away from competitive conditions.'[9] Apart from the untenable assumption that capitalism exists in the purest form at its earliest stage, rather like any mode of production unfolding over time (as is appreciated by the theories of organized capitalism and state monopoly capitalism), this conception of capitalism also involves a restricted definition of competition which organized capitalism and state monopoly theories also share. If the idea of competition as being restricted to price competition amongst a multitude of firms within an industry is abandoned, we can see that modern capitalism on the basis of large corporations remains competitive in the sense of competition among corporate giants over rates of profit in an era of finance capital when *capital mobility*, internationally and inter-industry, is greater than ever before. As Clifton puts it:

> The structural condition of free capital mobility renders competition among firms in the dominant corporate sector more abstract, since it is more general or economy-wide in nature. The abstract character is evident in the fact that it is now direct competition among cohesive sums of self-expanding finance that dominates the economic process, rather than competition among producers of soap on the one hand and producers of books on the other.

Because production for each firm is general, firms are directly competing with a much larger number of firms than those in any one of its operating divisions. Further, the tremendous number of commodities produced by each firm and the dominant strategy of growth through product innovation add enormous complexity and changeability to the competitive interrelationships among firms. [10]

If Winkler's theory of the operative dynamics of modern capitalism is faulty, we find as regards the corporatist economic system that is allegedly replacing it, we have not a faulty theory but none at all. It is not the economic rules of operation of the corporatist system that provide the basis for Winkler's definition, but rather state intervention into a capitalist economy according to certain policy goals established by the state itself. It is this autonomous role for the state that makes this corporatism 'fascism with a human face'. Apart from the fact that this revives the erroneous notion of fascism as an economic system, rather than a particular kind of capitalist state form, it also entails a view of the state as a neutral and independent subject, 'an anthropomorphic superperson'[11] ultimately free of class determination or even determination by the mode of production in which it operates. In any case, Winkler fails completely to establish that the state intervention that is constitutive of his corporatist model takes place on the basis of economic criteria that are distinctive from those of capitalism. As John Westergaard has pointed out in an outstanding critique:

> The four guiding 'principles' of corporatist policy set no prescriptions for allocation of resources. They are empty vessels into which this, that or another formula for investment and production may be poured. The formula could well be that characteristic of capitalism, under which resources are allocated in general to achieve long-run profit maximization: corporatist concerns for 'unity' and 'order', 'nation' and 'success' need in no significant way clash with the general use of profit yardsticks.

As for the principles of distribution in Winkler's model, they too 'merely echo those at work in the capitalist system which corporatism is supposed to be replacing'. [12] The most significant passage in Winkler's work, the one on which his definition of corporatism would ultimately have to rest or fall, is to be found in a footnote[13] where he tells us that 'surplus-value, exchange value and accumulation would not be significantly altered by a move toward corporatism. The law of value, commodity production, appropriation, entrepreneurship and freedom of contact would.' Unfortunately, we are not offered definitions of these terms and, on the basis of currently accepted ones, it is difficult, to say the least, to see how one can have surplus value without the law of value, exchange value without commodity production, accumulation without appropriation.

Winkler does not claim that his ideal-typical model is a description of any concrete society, but is rather 'a mechanism for generating predictions about future developments'. [14] But in so far as the ideal type is generated in large part on the basis of his reading of developments in the real world, its validity as a predictive model must depend on historical and contemporary evidence of accumulating trends. And when we come to examine the empirical evidence of corporatism that Winkler offers, we can see the particular weakness of his argument. This evidence is drawn exclusively from the British context, and the two main illustrations of directive state contol over privately owned business adduced are profit and price controls associated with incomes policy and the system of planning agreement instituted by the Labour Government of 1974. Yet, as Winkler himself demonstrates, the Planning Agreements System was 'severely emasculated' shortly after Labour took power. (The one agreement in the private sector merely legitimated subsidization of a firm unable to compete – Chrysler.) As for the selective profit and price controls associated with incomes policy, the vast weight of evidence on the largely symbolic attributes of these controls as *quid pro quo* for effective wage restraint [15] makes their characterization, without detailed evidence, as controls which change the nature of the economic system clearly untenable. And even if these controls were effective, to generalize from the relatively few dominant corporations they touch to the entire economics system is 'definition by expansion' carried to the extreme. In so far as one can find effective directive state control in Winkler's own evidence, it is the context of his footnoted evidence that while the 'planning agreement system has been considerably weakened, wage controls have been rather promptly and easily reinstituted' under the Labour government. [16]

As a basis for prediction then, Winkler's own evidence would seem to suggest above all the distinct limits to state control on profits even under an avowedly interventionist government. Winkler seems, at least implicitly, to be aware of the quantitative aspect of these limits, that is, that the expansion of state ownership of the economy, however necessary a large public sector may be for modern capitalism, cannot go so far as to *displace* private ownership without a substantial political fissure induced by the active resistance of the bourgeoisie. But Winkler fails to recognize that there are also qualitative limits to state intervention.

State economic planning in capitalist societies, with or without planning agreements, is primarily a forecasting exercise. Selective interventions of a more positive kind, which actually affect the structure of capital in particular sectors (although mainly through financial inducements rather than directive controls) are, as Poulantzas put it, 'constituted as ad-hoc tinkering with conditions already laid down by the process of valorization of capital', while the 'hard core of capitalist relations of production' remain subject either to the process of 'non-decision making' or to active intervention in maintaining them as far as the state is concerned. [17] The distinction that Winkler makes between qualitative and quantitative intervention as marking the transition from capitalism to corporatism, appears untenable as a basis for prediction.

The definition of corporatism as state intervention and control is of course far removed from the term's historical origins in corporatist ideology where corporatism was primarily conceived as a system of functional representation designed to foster class harmony. To be sure, Winkler does point to the development of new political structures which have a good deal in common with corporatism in this sense, although these play a secondary, derivative part in his approach. Winkler argues that the corporatist state is subject to 'a twin administrative dilemma: how to deal with conflict of interest in a system where there is supposed to be one over-riding interest and how to avoid manifestations of coercion where people are supposed to cooperate spontaneously'. [18] This is indeed the old problem of corporatist ideology. For Winkler these dilemmas are basically resolved, first of all, by the state moving away from open parliamentary rule-making toward delegated and enabling legislation so that state actions are not recorded publicly except in the vaguest form; and, secondly, by the state operating, in terms of administrative enforcement through personnel and organizations which are not nominally part of the state apparatus.

Winkler's treatment of recent political developments in this respect is not without its insights. Yet a number of points must be made in respect of them. First of all, Winkler identifies as corporatist a very broad range of semi-public institutions, which, while reflective of administrative decentralization, in no sense all involve representatives of functional interest associations or the interaction of these associations in decision-making. [19] Moreover, his argument that this form of corporatism entails 'administration without bureaucracy' cannot be sustained. Delegated and enabling legislation is hardly a new development in parliamentary regimes, nor has it historically entailed a decline in the size and role of bureaucracy, but rather its expansion. Moreover, in so far as the state is seen as imposing its policy directives on private associations, especially business, it is inconceivable that this could be done without an autonomous bureaucratic arm with independent access to information and capable of supervising the operations of capital. Most important, the semi-public bodies that regulate private industry have generally been created with the purpose of obviating business fears of state control.[20] Winkler clearly believes that these bodies conceal from business contentious state activities, but he offers little evidence to show how the bourgeoisie is so easily duped, or to counter the 'captive agency' argument.[21] And since Winkler's definition of corporatism rests not on the existence of such mediatory institutions between the state and civil society but on state directive control over private capital through them, this is no small point.

Finally, although Winkler distinguishes this 'corporatism without bureaucracy' from fascist corporatism as 'the ultimate bureaucracy', he seems to believe that liberal democracy is inevitably abrogated in both forms. This is not the result of the need to repress openly the subordinate classes, however, but rather because extensive state control of the economy is inconsistent with the procedures of legal enactment. Flexibility is all and, via discretionary formulas, enabling acts and state financial control over private groups, the rule of law is destroyed under a patina of legality and formal participation. 'The corporatist purpose is to have simultaneously the substance of state control and the appearance of democracy.'[22] In this way, Winkler takes a position, which is in fact extremely common in the corporatist literature (and is shared extensively by the Marxist state monopoly capitalism theorists), that involves assuming that capital concentration and state intervention are incompatible with a liberal democratic polity of any substance. Ignored here is the fact that the extension of bourgeois democracy to the subordinate classes in the form of free association and mass suffrage coincided historically with the concentration of capital and the growing role of an active capitalist state. Capitalism was liberal long before it was democratic, and its democratic elements were introduced far more as a result of working class struggles than of the free market economy. Lurking in the corporatism literature, is the old saw (mostly commonly associated with the work of Hayek) that a polity of democratic liberty is only consistent with 'pure capitalism' as defined by the theory of perfect competition. There are indeed real dangers in corporatism, but I am hardly convinced that the best way to approach them is through this form of economic reductionism.

III

An approach to corporatism which is much stronger than Winkler's and has had much more influence, at least outside of Britain, is that of Philippe Schmitter.[23] Defining corporatism as a 'system of interest intermediation' (alongside pluralism, syndicalism and monism), this approach confines corporatism to a political subsystem and thereby avoids the pitfalls of extrapolating corporatist developments to fundamental changes in the mode of production. Yet it also exhibits, even at this level, unwarranted expansive tendencies precisely because it includes all group–state relations under an ideal-typical definitional rubric.

Schmitter's ideal-typical definition of corporatism is constructed explicitly as a paradigmatic alternative to pluralism.

> Pluralism can be defined as a system of interest intermediation in which the constituent units are organized into an unspecified number of multiple, voluntary, competitive, nonhierarchically ordered and self-determined (as to type or scope of interest) categories which are not specially licensed, recognized, subsidized, created or otherwise controlled in leadership selection or interest articulation by the state and which do not exercise a monopoly of representational activity within their respective categories.

In contrast

> Corporatism can be defined as a system of interest intermediation in which the constituent units are organized into a limited number of singular, compulsory, noncompetitive, hierarchically ordered and functionally differentiated categories, recognized or licensed (if not created) by the state and granted a deliberate representational monopoly within their respective categories in exchange for observing certain controls on their selection of leaders and articulation of demands and supports.[24]

In terms of its descriptive adequacy in relation to interest group–state relations in advanced capitalist societies, Schmitter's definition of corporatism has much to recommend it as against pluralism. However, the very fact that the concept of corporatism is constructed by Schmitter as a polar opposite to pluralism leads it to replicate many of the theoretical inadequacies of the latter. This point has already been made by Nedelman and Meier:

> The very fixation of the concept of corporatism with the previously 'dominant' model of pluralism contains a number of pitfalls. By taking over

the dimensions of the latter — such as 'numbers of organizations', 'intra-sectional monopoly of interest representations', 'degree of competition between the organizations' and so on—and just changing or inverting the empirical values of these dimensions or variables, one risks the same conceptual and theoretical difficulties already connected with the previous utilization. [25]

At a minimum, by leaving out of the definition the economic system in which corporatism (and pluralism) are located, there is not only an ahistorical quality to the definition, but little theoretical invitation to challenge pluralism's assumption of state neutrality between the groups or to address the differential power position of the groups themselves in the society.

A further example of the kind of problems that definitions based on formal parallelism between ideal-typical constructs may lead to can be seen when we examine the various sub-types of the systems of interest intermediation Schmitter introduces. He argues that there are two such sub-types of corporatism: 'societal' and 'state'. The former is characterized by spontaneous gradual development and consensual and voluntarist arrangements (as in the 'advanced capitalist, organized democratic welfare state'); the latter entails state creation or imposition over the groups and control over them. [26] His subsequent assignment of state and societal sub-types not only to corporatism, but also pluralism (and syndicalism) produces severe conceptual problems, however. His argument is that the *origins* of pluralism or syndicalism may lie in state creation or inducement. [27] But apart from the fact that if the state sets the system in motion, it is most likely to maintain continued effective influence over the groups, if not actual control, the distinction could not pertain to the *actual operation* of these sub-types, for if we had state pluralism (or state syndicalism) in practice, this would not be consistent with Schmitter's own definition of these types. State pluralism actually 'embedded in a political system' would be a contradiction in terms. This warns against formal and abstract definitions which are constructed not out of concrete analyses of actual historical examples, but out of ideal-typical combinations. Anything can be cooked out of such recipes, but how much of it is edible is another question.

These problems mainly pertain to what Schmitter himself admits [28] is the 'static' and 'disembodied' nature of his definitional approach, however, and may be overcome in historical and empirical analysis. Indeed it must be said immediately that in Schmitter's own hands these problems have been attenuated or avoided in his actual analysis of the development of corporatist structures, where he introduces 'certain basic imperatives or needs of capitalism to reproduce the conditions for its existence and continually to accumulate further resources', in a way quite uncharacteristic of pluralist theory. He argues that 'the decay of pluralism and its gradual displacement by societal corporatism can be traced primarily to the imperative necessity for a stable, bourgeois-dominant regime, due to processes of concentration of ownership, competition between national economies, expansion of the role of public policy and rationalization of decision-making within the state to associate or incorporate subordinate classes and status groups more closely with the political process'. [29] Not surprisingly, therefore, he has outlined his search for an alternative *problematique* to pluralism not only in his constructed model of corporatism *per se* but by relating it to broader theories of society such as structural functionalism, political economy and historical materialism. He clearly favours the latter, although he narrowly conceives it in terms of the Austro-German school of Marxist revisionism to the exclusion of most contemporary theorists in the Marxist tradition. [30]

A much more serious product of Schmitter's definitional approach to corporatism, which has not been resolved in his own substantive analysis, is the fact that it is founded entirely in terms of relations between singular groups and the state. This leaves out the critical dimension of co-operative mutual interaction among the groups themselves in corporatist arrangements. By leaving this dimension out, Schmitter's approach takes on a similarity with the kind of counter-pluralist argument put forward by Theodore Lowi with respect to the United States, whereby interest group–state relations are characterized by segments of the state being captured or colonized by particular groups. This stands in sharp contrast to the kind of interactive policy making at the summit among socio-economic producer groups characteristic of corporatist structures in Western Europe. Schmitter himself distinguishes Sweden, Denmark, Switzerland and the Netherlands from the United States (as well as France, Great Britain and Ireland) in terms of the former having adopted 'internal "social peace" treaties between peak associations of employers and workers in the 1930s and then move[d] rapidly towards generalized societal corporatism in the 1940s and 1950s, while the latter have proved consistently more resistant to the blandishments of corporatism.' [31] But in terms of 'generalized societal corporatism', the interactive dimensions among groups at the level of the state characteristic of the social peace treaty between labour and capital associations is not shown to be matched in other group–state relations.

This leads directly to the central criticism to be made of Schmitter's approach—his adoption of a 'group-theoretical' rather than a 'class-theoretical' approach in his definition, along much the same lines as pluralism. This allows him to cast his corporatist net much more widely (that is, include more groups) than he would otherwise, but it has, by that very fact, serious disadvantages. One of the great putative advantages of the corporatist over pluralist approach is that by using it one need not reduce all group interests, group conflicts and group–state relations to the same salience and the same plane. As an ideology corporatism has focused not on all groups and cleavages but rather, as Schmitter has himself affirmed, quoting Madison, on that 'most common and durable source of faction . . . the various and unequal distribution of property'. Schmitter's representative examples of corporatism in practice are mainly those in which capital and labour groups are centrally involved and his own *explanatory* hypotheses regarding the development of corporatism indicate a 'class-theoretical' approach. That is, he specifically relates the origins of corporatism to the 'basic institutions of capitalism and the class structure of property and power engendered by it' and distinguishes between the origins of state and societal sub-types in terms of 'the institutional development and international context of capitalism, especially as they affect the pattern of conflicting class interests'. His 'core' distinction between the origins of the two rests on 'structural conduciveness' given by 'delayed, dependent capitalist development and non-hegemonic class relations in the case of state corporatism and advanced, monopoly or concentrated capitalist development and collaborative class relations in the case of societal corporatism'.[32] All of this is not reflected, however, in the 'group-theoretical' orientation his ideal-typical definition of corporatism shares with pluralism.

Or is it? Schmitter's definition, like most others, stresses the functional basis of representation in corporatism. This would appear to refer to the constituent units of corporatism as those interest groups arising directly out of the social division of labour and out of which classes are in large part formed. As Morris and Rapp have suggested in applying Schmitter's definition:

> ·We assume here that Schmitter is referring to the various economic functional sectors such as subsistence agriculture, industrial-manufacturing, commercial, agribusiness, *empleados* (private and public), and professional groupings. The corporate definition holds that interests emanating from these sectors are represented via specific organizations, and that the particular

organizations face little or no competition within their respective sectors. Moreover, the organizations operate only within their own spheres of functional specialization and maintain/recruit their rank and file through rules and regulations that require membership in order to hold a job or participate in benefits. Under these conditions, the number of organizations should closely parallel the number of viable economic/functional sectors in the society.[33]

Yet, it would appear that Schmitter's actual understanding of the constituent units of corporatism is in fact broader than Morris and Rapp assume. For in his subsequent article, Schmitter indicates that the constituent units involved in systems of interest intermediation are the 'highly organized and specialized representatives of class, sectoral, regional, sexual and generational interests . . . complexes of specialized associations often bypassing if not boycotting, more traditional and more general partisan and legislative structures of articulation and aggregation'.[34] The various modes, it should be noted, are not distinguished on the basis of the different constituent units (for instance, with class or sector representatives assigned to the corporatist system), but rather in terms of the different *ways* in which *all* these constituent units are formed, structured and interact with the state. Although Schmitter readily admits that any given Western society exploits a mixed system of interest intermediation and that 'different interest sectors may be organized in quite different ways', he does not indicate that the corporatist mode is likely to be more salient or most suitable to any one of these sectors. Seen in this light, with a tendential possibility that sexual, regional and generational interest groups are as likely to be corporatized as class or sectoral groups based on economic function in the division of labour, it would appear that the meaning of 'functional' in Schmitter's corporatist definition has taken on a broader, and less common, meaning.

It appears that having been challenged by Nedelman and Meier[35] that it be openly acknowledged 'that only occupational and economic organizations are considered' as constituent units of corporatism, Schmitter backed away, in light of their criticisms, from his definition of interest groups in the corporatist paradigm as 'functionally specific', a tempting step since this further established the inverted parallel with pluralism. If this speculation is correct, Schmitter has erred in doing so. At least it would be necessary to offer detailed historical and contemporary evidence on the spread of corporative modes to non-economic/functional groups, which has not been offered. Of course it is hardly necessary to claim, in restricting the constituent units of corporatism to socio-economic producer groups, that other groups may not *affect* economic (or other) decisions. This is not excluded in so far as socio-economic producer groups are not necessarily seen as monopolizing all economic decision making.

How can Schmitter's 'group-theoretical' definition be made consistent with his own class-theoretical analytic framework, once the precise meaning of functional groups (that is, those based on the social division of labour) is abandoned? It can, but only at considerable cost to the value of his broader analytic framework. First of all, although Schmitter does not define what he means by 'class', he implies at one point that he sees 'the class structure of property and power' simply in terms of 'inequality of distribution'.[36] If this is so, then the unique interrelationship that structures class groups, which is a product of their *contradictory relations in production,* would be easily overlooked. It becomes easier to put unions and employers, consumers and taxpayers on the same plane, and miss the specific nature of corporatism, both as ideology and as structure, as a response to the *inevitable* expression of class conflict in capitalist society. Although this conflict is necessarily expressed in the sphere of distribution as well, the distributional struggle is inseparable from relations between the classes in the actual production process.

Secondly, it should be noted that the 'class-theoretical' analyses that Schmitter employs, and which I have quoted, pertain to the *origins* of corporatism. They are not made much use of in his description of analysis of the structure and functioning of generalized societal corporatism. In the case of state corporatism, associated with fascist or authoritarian dependent capitalist regimes, he appears much more interested in corporatism's relation to 'specific class interests'. This is perhaps why he finds Shonfield's *Modern Capitalism* so 'magisterial' a treatment of societal corporatism, despite its own systematic neglect (whatever its other virtues) of the question of bourgeois class domination in relation to the capitalist state. Schmitter, to be sure, is much more aware of this dimension and seeks to add to Shonfield a more explicit discussion 'of prior class consciousess and intensity of class antagonisms'. But this pertains, as Schmitter makes clear, to 'the emergence of societal corporatism' again.[37] Hence the use of 'prior'.

The reason for this disjuncture between concern with class analysis in examining the origins of societal corporatism and its absence in examining its actual operation appears to lie in Schmitter's more recently expressed argument against the assumption of structural functionalism, political economy and historical materialism, that changes in the mode of interest representation are primarily the product or reflection of prior and independent changes in economic and social structure . . . For the purposes of understanding initial associational responses, this economism-societalism may be appropriate, but once the new collective actors begin to acquire resources and organizational properties of their own and once the state has expanded the scope and volume of its policy interventions, the mode of interest intermediation may be molded 'from within' and 'from above', so to speak, in relative independence from the conditions of civil society, and even in disregard for the preferences and interests of the individuals and firms, sectors, classes and so on whose interests are supposedly being represented.[38]

This goes as far in dislocating interest groups from their social base as does Winkler in treating the state's 'relative' autonomy as in substance amounting to total autonomy from civil society and the balance of class forces within it. And it is this kind of posited disjuncture between groups and their membership, this kind of reification of the 'organization', which must be the basis for the absence of class analysis in Schmitter's approach to corporatism as a functioning structure.

It is also the basis for positing, as Schmitter does, the stability of societal corporatism. For once one abandons the assumption of underlying social harmony which characterizes corporatist ideology, and if one rules out the direct role of state coercion in the 'societal corporatism' of liberal democracies, one can only see corporatist structures as inherently stable if one assumes that interest associations do not in fact represent their members' interests. This is a curious assumption to see developed in the late 1970s, after a decade in which rank-and-file militancy has profoundly affected union organizations throughout Western Europe and shaken severely the stability of corporatist structures. It has been the continuing linkage between unions and their members and the continuing articulation by business associations of capital's interests that, in the context of the considerable class conflict in Western Europe in the late 1960s and 1970s, has made the 'affluent society' and 'end of ideology' theses look so jaded and worn. In the absence of the fundamental class consensus posited by such theories, and in the absence of the kind of severe disarticulation between groups and their members assumed by Schmitter, the stability of corporatist structures will depend on the state forcibly breaking the autonomous and indigenous character of the groups. This coercive dynamic contained in corporatism, based on its need to suppress the continuing expression of class struggle in capitalist society, is precisely the factor which speaks against those who would see it as the new avenue of stability for liberal democratic advanced capitalism.

IV

It should be stressed that in calling for a 'class-theoretical' rather than a 'group-theoretical' approach to the definition of corporatism, I am not suggesting that all interest groups can in some sense be reduced to classes or class fractions. This would simply be turning pluralism on its head. On the contrary, it is my contention that corporatism is specific to those groups which *are* class based. Other groups not founded on the social division of labour, or at least related to it only indirectly and through several mediations, such as issue-oriented groups, ideological groups, groups based on regional, sexual or generational bases, or groups based exclusively on the sphere of distribution such as consumers and tax-payers, will not be found to be among the principal constituent units of corporatist structures.[39] The difference between the close relations which singular interest groups have with the state in all liberal democracies and the systematic interaction among the socio-economic producer groups themselves as well as with the state which is distinctive of corporatism follows from the fact that the major classes upon which functional groups are based are *constituted in terms of a contradictory relation to one another*. Wage labour and capital, workers and capitalists, trade unions and employers' associations can only be understood in terms of the structural and historical relationship that determines their mutual behaviour and existence, in terms of the way they directly condition one another. Although all social groups may be said to be interdependent, this is true only at a general and abstract level and is only evinced in their actual behaviour in a highly mediated way or in very particular situations. The degree of interaction between groups in relation to the state is reflective of this difference.

But what about the distinction so often made in corporatist literature between *sectoral* and socio-economic (that is, class) functional groups? Certainly, in corporatist ideology, and in the formal structures of avowedly corporatist states, the constituent units of corporatism are seen as those groups based on functional economic *sectors* (that is, branches of industry, commerce, agriculture, the professions, etc.) and which include as members all those engaged in a sector's activity. Yet, at least as applied to liberal democracies, the organizational distinction between class and sector is a false one. A singular group which claims to speak for the interests of a whole industrial or commercial sector is almost invariably an association of firms in that sector, wherein the owners/managers/employers in that sector are represented, but not the non-owners/workers/employees. These are themselves organized into *separate* organizations of trade unions or employee associations, or not organized into functional groups at all. Thus, industrial or commercial sectors are not themselves 'group-homogeneous', so that they cut across class lines, but are themselves either associationally divided along class lines or only the dominant class in the sector is organized at all. (Of course, both capital and labour may be further divided in any given sector, with separate organizations, for instance, for large and small firms, or separate trade unions, often organized in accordance with occupational differentiation among the workers.) Sectors which don't fit this pattern are those which are indeed largely class homogeneous, as well as organizationally homogeneous, in terms of the social division of labour. Such sectors are those in which the traditional petty bourgeoisie are dominant, as is often the case with agriculture and the legal profession. To the extent that corporatist structures involve such sectoral associations, this does not provide evidence of sectoral *in addition* to class representation, but rather of the corporatization of petty bourgeois socio-economic producer groups.

When we speak of socio-economic producer groups as the functional groups of corporatist structures, we do not mean that these groups express the corporate interests of the whole class on which they are based, much less that they express the 'true' interests of the whole class. A trade union or trade association in a particular industry is a class organization, but not one that necessarily transcends the narrow bounds of its own industry. Indeed, this is the sense in which Marxists often speak of a 'corporativist' consciousness pertaining to the working class, and it may be thought that corporatist political structures serve in part to maintain such a limited, sectoral, subordinate class identity. It should be stressed, however, that the development of corporatist structures *at the national level* in liberal democracies has entailed the integration of the central organizations of capital and labour and encouraged their further centralization so as to be able to *overcome* sectoral divisions within each class in the application of state economic policy. This has particularly been the case with incomes policy which seeks to overcome comparability wage bargaining between sectors in the labour market. Thus, while maintaining a 'corporativist consciousness' in the sense of subordination for the working class, national-level corporatist structures do not necessarily seek to maintain the primacy of sectoral representation or identity (although their instability is in good part related to their inability to effect this.) It should be obvious, however, that corporatist structures need not necessarily be confined only to the central organizations of capital and labour or to incomes policy areas, even if their origins are clearly located there. It is entirely possible to conceive of corporatist structures developing in particular industrial sectors (conceived broadly to include even such sectors as health or education) where the state, the owning or managing authorities and the unions in these sectors interact in policy-making. This is entirely consistent with a definition of corporatism in terms of the interaction of functional socio-economic producer groups based directly on the division of labour.

But the central point remains: not all groups are functional, not all group—state relations are corporatist, not all representation/social control takes place via groups at all. All this should be borne in mind before engaging in the troubling practice of classifying total societies as corporatist (a practice which Schmitter, for instance, prudently and properly rejects.) But all this also suggests that particular spatial limits to even corporatist political structures should also be borne in mind, indeed, 'openly-acknowledged', rather than cast aside in a futile search for systemic alternatives to pluralism on its own expansive and non-discriminatory terrain.

V

It is one of the ironies of the recent literature on corporatism that even those who concentrate almost exclusively on the relations between the associations of capital and labour and the state have also offered initial definitions of corporatism which are expansive in their scope. For instance, Gerhard Lehmbruch establishes the constituent units of corporatism merely as 'large interest organizations' which co-operate with each other and with public authorities. But he goes on to identify the organizations of capital and labour as the salient groups included in corporatist structures, with other groups (even organized agriculture) largely confined to the classical pluralist pattern. And he identifies the policy areas of corporatism as economic policy formation, with particular emphasis on incomes policy. This makes 'consensus-building in liberal corporatism largely contingent on the degree to which the labour movement is integrated into the process of policy-formation'. As for trends indicating an eventual expansion of corporatist policy-making, he finds little evidence for their existence. [40]

Bob Jessop, at least in his early formulations of the concept, also tended to define corporatism broadly as a 'state form', which stands in contrast with parliamentarism as a full political system. But far from identifying the conditions for the emergence of corporatism as a state form *sui generis* and successive to parliamentarism, his work stresses how corporatism is prone to contradictions and limitations which prevent this. Its expansion is limited by its inability 'to eliminate class conflict over the labour process . . . nor every form of competition among capitals.' Moreover, 'just because corporatism is appropriate to economic intervention (since it is constituted on the basis of function in the division of labour), it tends to be inadequate in other areas' – primarily in relation to 'popular democratic struggles' pertaining to regionalism, immigration, civil rights, etc. Here pluralist pressure politics and elected parliaments continue to play a 'central political function'. He sees corporatism, therefore, as part of a hybrid system of 'tripartism,' within which corporatist and parliamentary structures coexist and where the social democratic party plays a key role in integrating the corporatist and parliamentary elements.[41]

Yet a further example of the tendency to define the scope of corporatism broadly while substantively stressing its central location in the relations between the state and the associations of capital and labour is seen in the work of Claus Offe.[42] Offe begins with a prudent warning against incorporating the defects of pluralism into research on corporatism: 'Since the concept of "group" as used in pluralist political theory is utterly comprehensive and vague, little is to be gained by quantitative indications telling us how many groups become subject to institutionalization or formal status attribution.' Yet he too casts his corporatist net rather broadly, including not only 'organized collectives representing the supply or demand sides of either labour markets or goods and service markets' (that is, unions and employers' organizations, investors and consumers), but also all those groups directly affected by state policies ('policy-takers'), amongst which he includes urban and regional governments, associations of tax-payers, welfare recipients, students, public hospitals and automobile associations. In order to take account, however, of that 'aspect of repressive discipline imposed by corporatist arrangements specifically upon the unions . . . [and] the fact that corporatist arrangements do specifically affect the terms, and institutional channels of class conflict', he proposes 'a combined explanation that neither relies on the social class or the pluralist paradigm'. This involves seeing the corporatization of working-class organizations primarily in terms of the 'restraint' it is designed to impose, while for ordinary pluralist interest groups it primarily involves 'delegation'–that is, the contracting out of state power to reduce 'administrative overload'.

Significantly, however, when he examines the structure and functioning of corporatism, Offe restricts himself to tripartite bodies of capital, labour and the state. Indeed, if his characterization of the functioning of corporatist structures is correct (as I believe it is), it is difficult to see how the other groups he mentions can be assimilated to it. For instance, the stress he places on the pattern of *inter-group* negotiations would not seem to characterize the relation of consumer groups, tax-payers or welfare-recipient organizations to public policy-making. Moreover, Offe's point that in the absence of majoritarian principles of legitimation corporatist structures tend towards fifty—fifty representation between capital and labour to avoid continual procedural wrangling, would be contradicted by the inclusion of other groups. An interesting perspective on the apparent corporatization of other groups is in fact suggested by Offe in regard to various political platforms in West Germany which call for the corporatization of interest groups in general terms. As Offe points out 'the notion of uncontrolled interest group power was clearly aimed at the "irresponsible" inflation-causing behaviour of unions'. This suggests that a better way to approach any apparent trends towards the corporatization of interest groups in general (for which Offe, like others, offers very little empirical evidence, however) might be to distinguish between the 'dignified' façade of general attribution of 'political status' to groups by the state and an 'efficient' system of corporatism involving the interaction of those groups based directly on the division of labour.

In any case, the central thrust of Offe's contribution remains his argument that far more important than searching for general attributes of 'political status' among interest groups is the search for the differential attributes among the groups in corporatist structures, as determined by the effect their class location has on their organizational structure and their relations with the state. Thus, Offe's work strongly supports our argument that corporatism is primarily about state-induced class collaboration: that far from being homogeneous in its composition and effects, corporatism is distinctly 'non-homogeneous', even with respect to the different class groups it incorporates. Research which primarily focuses on the formal aspects of corporatist structures will have little to tell us about corporatism's substantive character as a mechanism of state control over the organized working class in capitalist societies.

VI

The case that has been made here against ideal-typical expansive approaches to corporatism in advanced capitalist liberal democracies finds its echo in certain recent reactions against the application of similar approaches to Latin America. Linn Hammergren, in an attempt to confront the question raised by Schmitter of whether this 'is "still" or even "yet" the "century of corporatism" ', has argued that Latin American experience 'suggests that an emphasis on corporatist politics as a wider analytic framework may be anticipating a transition that has not yet occurred on even a very limited scale'.[43] Similarly Alfred Stepan has stressed the invalidity of ideal-typical formal models of corporatism as total systems. He shows that historically no political system in Latin America has approximated exclusive reliance on corporatist interest intermediation mechanisms. 'The theoretical and political implication of this is that there are no fully corporate systems, but rather that there are political systems in some sectors of which (usually the working class) corporatist rather than pluralist patterns of interest representation predominate. The research implications of my argument are that "corporatism as structure" is always a *partial* sectoral phenomenon in the overall political system, and that supplementary analytic frameworks must be used to study other aspects of the system.'[44] And Guillermo O'Donnell has specifically argued that corporatism's 'actual functioning and social impacts differ systematically according to changes largely determined by social class', that it is but '*one* in the set of structures or modes of linkage with civil society', and that if the concept corporatism is 'stretched' beyond these limits, 'if it is postulated as an "alternative paradigm" to resolve the present crisis in conceptualization of Latin American politics and society, then I fear it will become another contribution to the Tower of Babel we are making of the social sciences.'[45]

It would certainly appear from the review of the literature undertaken in this paper, and no less in Latin American than in Western Europe and North America, that corporatism has all the earmarks of becoming an 'essentially contested concept' in the social sciences. This occurs when 'disputes about descriptive features are so severe as to rule out any agreement over even the formal specification of the descriptive meaning' of a concept.[46] And as with all such contested concepts, their contestability extends beyond disputes over description to theoretical and evaluative disputes. Moreover, even if consensus were to be reached on a 'class-theoretical' approach to corporatism, fundamental differences would remain. For although a 'class-theoretical' approach is consistent with a historical materialist explanatory framework, it need not necessarily be located therein, given the contested nature of class itself as a social scientific concept.

This may be seen by examining two recent 'class-theoretical' contributions to the 'growth industry'. We have already seen that in the context of the Latin American disputes Alfred Stepan emphatically stresses the thrust of corporatism *vis-à-vis* working-class incorporation; and, with reference to advanced capitalist liberal democracy, Colin Crouch has explicitly rejected a definition of corporatism in terms of 'the rise of organized groups, as opposed to individuals, as the main units of civil society to which the state relates' and adopted a definition which sees corporatism as 'the hierarchical non-conflictual integration of the state and organized groups representative of capital and labour', located specifically in a strategy of class domination in the industrial relations system.[47] Stepan puts emphasis on corporatism's role in 'reducing labour's capacity to strike'; Crouch stresses the involvement of unions 'in the process whereby labour is disciplined'. But why corporatism has this primary focus is either left unexplained (Stepan) or is associated with a general model of class domination in authority terms that owes more to Weber than to Marx (Crouch). A Marxist explanation of corporatism in terms of surplus value and class struggle over the intensification of exploitation might be partially consistent with these approaches, but it would have to point in different directions in terms of the historical causes, consequences and limits of corporatist structures and the possibilities and strategies for overcoming them.

The difference between a Marxian and non-Marxian approach to corporatism, even if commonly cast in 'class-theoretical' terms, can be seen in the fact that ultimately, and despite their perceptive analyses of 'actually existing corporatism' as unequal, dominating and coercive as far as the working class is concerned, both Crouch and Stepan end up seeing corporatism positively in evaluative terms, as a goal to be strived for. Stepan accepts corporatism as a normative model (organic statism, he calls it) which in terms of the norms of 'social equity, justice and participation' appears to be preferable to him to the Marxian vision of socialism and communism, which he conflates with a crude image of authoritarian party dictatorship. It is hardly surprising that the alternative he poses to the actual Latin American corporatist structures he analyses with such perceptiveness, is a 'true' corporatism, which goes beyond 'consultation towards the power to make decisions and the capacity to work out priorities between sectors [which entails] devolution of power from the strategic state elite to the new organs of participation. This is not a logical impossibility in the model.'[48] Perhaps not, but as Stepan's own evidence suggests, it appears to be an historical one.

Crouch, for his part, remains trapped in a general model of

alternative strategies of domination, so that all he can look forward to is the least objectionable form of domination. He sees trade unions as 'the most genuine element of pluralism in the political structure of modern capitalist societies, since they are almost alone in representing relatively unambiguously the interests of subordinates within the most fundamental social relationship of the society'. He urges upon the unions, however, a system of 'bargained corporatism' in which they exchange 'the possibility of greater political influence and more and broader power for their members in the workplace . . . [for] a more obvious role for the unions in restraining their members, more state interference and fuller acceptance of the industrial order and its priorities'. His belief that unions in this process could actually 'identify more closely with the concern of their members' is only separable from original corporatist ideology by virtue of Crouch's frank admission that even bargained corporatism 'must essentially be a strategy of reinforced domination'.[49]

To end as Crouch and Stepan do is almost to return full circle to corporatist ideology as it emerged, before its association with fascism, almost a century ago. For despite their own critical treatment of actual historic corporatist structures in authoritarian and non-authoritarian regimes, they foster illusions as before about some 'ideal' corporatism. How do they end up here? It involves fundamentally, their taking a position, in evaluative terms, which rejects the possibility and/or desirability of socialism as a working-class strategy to transcend capitalism and class domination and establish genuine democracy. And on this terrain, corporatism and socialism have always been contending, as well as contested, concepts. Although the debate is today cast in social scientific terms, it replicates the century-old opposition between corporatism and socialism as two approaches to the state and society which commonly reject liberalism. The 'century of corporatism' is still inconceivable except in terms of its old nemesis—the socialist alternative.

As the growth industry of corporatism in social science continues to expand, further effort will no doubt be directed toward developing a minimal descriptive definition on which there is consensus across the ideological/theoretical spectrum, if for no other reason than to avoid sheer relativism in the handling of the concept. Yet it is doubtful that much advantage will be gained from this. For although it may be possible to achieve consensus on a core descriptive definition, the definition will have to be so formal as to be of little use in substantive social and political analysis. The debate over definitions is really a debate between different theoretical frameworks, in which normative and ideological preferences play their part.[50] Efforts to conceal these differences in a definitional consensus will only obscure rather than clarify the way corporatism is being used in social analysis. And given the immediate relevance of corporatism in contemporary society, this will not only have a social scientific effect, but a political and strategic one.

(1978–79)

Notes

1. P. Schmitter, 'Introduction' to special issue on 'Corporatism and Policy Making in Contemporary Western Europe', *Comparative Political Studies*, vol. 10, no. 1, (April 1977), p. 3.
2. G. Lehmbruch, 'Liberal Corporatism and Party Government', *Comparative Political Studies*, vol. 10, no. 1, (April 1977), p. 93.
3. Schmitter, p. 3.
4. K. Meier, 'Corporatism and Interest Intermediation: Some Comments on Areas for Research', paper prepared for the ECPR Workshop on 'Corporatism in Liberal Democracies', Grenoble, April 1978, p. 1.
5. It should be stressed that I am concentrating here on the literature on corporatism as applied to liberal democratic advanced capitalist societies. I shall not be systematically addressing myself to the burgeoning literature on corporatism in Latin American, although I shall make some reference to this literature.
6. The term is A. Wassenberg's from his 'Creeping Corporatism: A Cuckoo's Policy', paper prepared for the ECPR Workshop on 'Corporatism in Liberal Democracies', Grenoble, April 1978, p. 3.
7. J. T. Winkler, 'Corporatism', *Archives Européennes de Sociologie*, vol. 17, no. 1, (1976), p. 103, Cf, R. E. Pahl and J. Winkler, 'The Coming Corporatism', *New Society*, no. 10, 1974; J. T. Winkler, 'The Corporatist Economy: Theory and Administration', in R. Scase (ed.), *Industrial Society 1: Class Cleavage and Control*, London 1977, ch. 2; J. T. Winkler, 'Law, State and Economy: The Industry Act 1975 in Context'. *British Journal of Law and Society*, vol. 2, no. 2, (Winter 1975), pp. 103–28.
8. Winkler, 'Corporatism', pp. 119–20.
9. J. A. Clifton, 'Competition and the Evolution of the Capitalist Mode of Production', *Cambridge Journal of Economics*, no. 1, 1977, p. 143.
10. Ibid., p. 147.
11. The phrase is A. S. Miller's, applied to Galbraithian or Reichian notions of the 'corporate state'. 'Legal Foundations of the Corporate State', *Journal of Economic Issues*, 6 March 1972, pp. 59–79. Compare R. Marris, 'The Corporation, Technology and the State: Is the Corporate Economy a Corporate State?', *American Economic Review: Papers and Proceedings*, no. 62, May 1972, pp. 103–15.
12. J. Westergaard, 'Class, Inequality and "Corporatism" ', in A. Hunt (ed.), *Class and Class Structure*, London 1977, pp. 178, 183.
13. Winkler, 'Corporatism', p. 133. n. 31.
14. Winkler, 'The Corporatist Economy', p. 44.

15. See especially, R. Tarling and Frank Wilkinson, 'The Social Contract: Post-war Incomes Policies and Their Inflationary Impact', *Cambridge Journal of Economics*, vol. 1, no. 4, (December 1977), pp. 395–414.

16. Winkler, 'Corporatism', p. 105.

17. N. Poulantzas, *State, Power, Socialism*, London 1978, p. 191.

18. Winkler, 'The Corporatist Economy', p. 50.

19. For instance, institutions like the IRC and NEB are seen by Winkler as being primary examples of corporatist institutions in Britain. But while these agencies' boards are dominated by businessmen rather than bureaucrats, they are not constituted on the basis of representation from functional interest groups *per se*. Indeed in both cases, the CBI was opposed to their establishment and consequently they were set up by the state in the face of the *opposition* of the *functional* association of business. In contrast, an institution such as the NEDC is constituted on the basis of explicit parity representation of the CBI and TUC and operates in terms of the *interaction* of these functional interest groups in decision-making. To have individual businessmen occupying public and semi-public positions is not itself either *new* or necessarily corporatist. Although it no doubt serves to legitimate the activities of the state *vis-à-vis* the economy, it does not necessarily entail the integration of the *interest associations of business* in state structures. This perspective is also missed by Alan Cawson, for instance, who speaks of the IRC (established four years after the NEDC) as the first 'authentically corporatist institution in Britain'. This is the remit of his failure to distinguish clearly between individual firms and the *interest associations* of business, considering them both as functional groups ('Pluralism, Corporatism and the Role of the State', *Government and Opposition*, vol. 13, no. 2, (Spring 1978), especially pp. 179, 187.

20. One of Winkler's own sources provide considerable evidence of this. See D. C. Hague, W. J. M. Mackenzie and A. Baker (eds.), *Public Policy and Private Interests: The Institutions of Compromise*, London 1975.

21. On the ability of powerful interests 'to wrest a part of the state for its own private use' via these semi-public regulatory bodies, see A. Wolfe, *The Limits of Legitimacy*, New York 1975, ch. 5; compare Theodore Lowi, *The End of Liberalism*, New York 1969.

22. Winkler, 'The Industry Act', p. 125. Compare 'The Corporatist Economy', pp. 50–1.

23. P. Schmitter, 'Still the Century of Corporatism', *Review of Politics*, no. 36, January 1974, pp. 85–131; and 'Modes of Interest Intermediation and Models of Societal Change in Western Europe', *Comparative Political Studies*, vol. 10, no. 1, (April 1977), pp. 7–38. For Schmitter's earlier work on corporatism in authoritarian regimes see his *Interest Conflict and Political Change in Brazil*, Stanford 1971 and *Corporatism and Public Policy in Authoritarian Portugal*, Sage Professional Papers, Contemporary Political Sociology Series, vol. 1, 1975.

24. Schmitter, 'Modes of Interest Intermediation', p. 9.

25. B. Nedelman and K. G. Meier, 'Theories of Contemporary Corporatism: Static or Dynamic?', *Comparative Political Studies*, vol. 10, no. 1, (April 1977), p. 40.

26. Schmitter, 'Still the Century', pp. 103–5.

27. Schmitter, 'Modes of Interest Intermediation', pp. 11–12.

28. Ibid., p. 10

29. Schmitter, 'Still the Century', pp. 107–8.

30. Schmitter, 'Modes of Interest Intermediation', pp. 19–35.

31. Schmitter, 'Still the Century', p. 107.

32. Ibid., pp. 97, 107–8.
33. J. A. Morris and S. C. Rapp, 'Corporatism and Dependent Development: A Honduran Case Study', *Latin American Research Review*, vol. 12, no. 2, 1977, pp. 34–5.
34. Schmitter, 'Introduction', pp. 3–4.
35. Nedelman and Meier, pp. 42–3.
36. Schmitter, 'Still the Century', p. 107.
37. Ibid., pp. 114–15.
38. Schmitter, 'Modes of Interest Intermediation', p. 34.
39. 'One common denominator of corporations is that they are functional—that they define themselves by their role in society. This role is to produce goods or provide services indispensable to society. That is why . . . corporations are generally associated with the producers in society.' G. Ionescu, *Centripetal Politics: Government and the New Centres of Power*, London 1974, p. 17. It should be noted, however, that this contemporary exponent of corporatist ideology himself immediately blurs the distinction between the state and autonomous 'corporations' in society by treating territorial-administrative elements of the state below the central level as 'corporations'.
40. Lehmbruch, p. 110.
41. B. Jessop, 'Corporatism, Parliamentarism and Social Democracy', in P. Schmitter and G. Lehmbruch, *Trends Towards Corporatist Intermediation*, London and Beverley Hills 1979. This is a revised version of an earlier paper presented to the ECPR 'Workshop on Liberal Democracies', Grenoble 1978. The reference I make to his earlier work is to this version, but compare for expansive tendencies, his 'Capitalism and Democracy: The Best Possible Political Shell?', in G. Littlejohn (ed.), *Power and the State*, London 1978, pp. 10–51.
42. C. Offe, 'The Attribution of Political Status to Interest Groups– Observations on the West German Case', in S. Berger (ed.), *Interest Groups in Western Europe*, Cambridge 1981.
43. L.A. Hammergren, 'Corporatism in Latin American Politics: A Re-examination of the Unique Tradition', *Comparative Politics*, 9 July 1977, p. 455.
44. A Stepan, *The State and Society, Peru in Comparative Perspective*, Princeton, NJ 1978, pp. 70–71.
45. G.A. O'Donnell, 'Corporatism and the Question of the State', in J. M. Malloy (ed.), *Authoritarianism and Corporatism in Latin America*, Pittsburgh and London 1977, pp. 48, 81, 47.
46. R. Plant, 'Community: Concept, Conception and Ideology', *Politics and Society*, vol. 8, no. 1, (1978) p. 83.
47. C. Crouch, 'The Changing Role of the State in Industrial Relations in Western Europe', in C. Crouch and A. Pizzorno, *The Resurgence of Class Conflict in Western Europe since 1968*, vol. 2, London 1978, p. 197; compare his *Class Conflict and the Industrial Relations Crisis*, London 1977 and *The Politics of Industrial Relations*, London 1979.
48. Stepan, p. 316; compare pp. 17–40, 302.
49. Crouch, *Class Conflict*, pp. 269 ff; 'The Changing Role', p. 263; and *The Politics of Industrial Relations*, p. 188 ff.
50. See Plant, p. 83 ff.

7.
Trade Unions and the Capitalist State

It is a matter of considerable irony, as well as a cause for concern, that the otherwise valuable and exciting development of Marxist theorizations of the capitalist state in the past decade have only tangentially noted, and have largely failed to address systematically, one of the most significant political developments pertaining to the working class in the modern period: the emergence within the democratic capitalist state of new political structures which articulate trade unions with state administration and business associations in a broad range of economic policy-making. The fact that this development occurred in a period of trade-union industrial strength, and of increasing expression of class conflict via official and unofficial trade-union struggles, only served to underline the relative weakness of Marxist theorizations of the nature of trade unionism in advanced capitalism and its relationship with the bourgeois-democratic state.

Over the course of what might be called 'the decade of the theory of the state', Marxist theorists clearly attempted to move beyond the abstract formalism and high level of generality that tended to characterize earlier work. In particular, texts such as Therborn's *What Does the Ruling Class Do When It Rules?* and Poulantzas's *State, Power, Socialism* explicitly concerned themselves with tracing and delineating the changing patterns of bourgeois-democratic rule in the monopoly capitalist era. The significant changes were broadly seen to entail: a shift in the locus of decision-making from parliament to the technocratic/executive apparatus of the state; the fusion of the state at this level with the top echelons of capitalist enterprise; and the general breaking down of the public—private boundaries that previously characterized bourgeois democracy. Although these observations taken in themselves were by no means new, either within or without the Marxist problematic, their systematic location within a Marxist theory of the state was much to be applauded.

Nevertheless, the pivotal role of trade-union integration within the network of policy-making apparatuses linking the state executive and bureaucracy with private corporate management was either elided or merely treated in passing as a subsidiary aspect of the general development of an interventionist state under monopoly capitalism. At most, we saw a rather mechanical extension of the dynamics that connect the state with monopoly capital to the integration of working-class organizations. The specific dynamics and the particular importance (for the attenuation of liberal democracy)[1] of the incorporation of trade unions, and the contradictions (for both unions and the state) of this incorporation, were not elucidated. However important the general attention that has been paid to what Poulantzas called in his last work, 'the statization of social life' overcoming the 'institutionalized dissociation between public and private which is the cornerstone of traditional representative democracy',[2] this is a phenomenon which cannot be examined only in terms of its implications for parties and civil liberties, while leaving aside the specificity of trade union structures. A distinction surely needs to be drawn between the statization of bourgeois-dominated spheres of civil society and the statization of working-class organizations. For Marxists, the latter process might be thought to be a matter of central strategic importance requiring separate and extensive theoretical disquisition and empirical research.[3]

Unfortunately there has been traditional failure amongst Marxists to address the relationship between trade unionism and the state in a rigorous dialectical fashion. Therborn's valuable perception, for instance, that as a collective mass organization, 'the labour movement is organized in a fundamentally different way from the state bureaucracy or a capitalist firm', was not carried over to examine the contradictions that arise when trade-union representatives join state personnel and capitalist management in 'institutionalized joint bodies'.[4] For his part, Poulantzas made little attempt to clarify the significance of his passing observation that ' "reformist" trade unions are now directly inserted in the (state) administrative structure'.[5] Particularly in light of his generic definition of the capitalist state as already including (as 'state ideological apparatuses') the trade-union movement, and given his simultaneous belief that even a reformist organization remains a 'working-class phenomenon, with its own special links to the working class',[6] one might have expected an elaboration of this tension and its implications for the development of the class struggle. In fact I think Therborn's and Poulantzas's attitudes are symptomatic of a broader 'politicist' syndrome which has characterized Marxist theorizations of the state and which has tended to see trade unions as 'less important' because they are geared to short-term demands which are neither explicitly political nor revolutionary.[7] Particularly in a period when the class struggle has been *increasingly* industrial in form, and when industrial militancy has accompanied the incorporation of trade unions in the state apparatus, this 'politicist' syndrome forecloses the possibility of a full analysis of the balance of class forces in the contemporary conjuncture and of an assessment of the contradictions arising from changes taking place in the bourgeois-democratic state.

Corporatism and Marxism

Despite the weakness of Marxist theories of the state in dealing with the contradictory phenomena of trade-union incorporation in the contemporary phase of capitalism, this question has not gone totally unexamined by Marxist writers. In particular, an increasing number have sought, under the rubric of the concept of 'corporatism', to examine both the 'statization of civil society' in general and, more specifically, the dynamics of trade-union integration and the contradictions to which it is subject.[8] The employment of corporatism in this sense certainly marks a break with conventional Marxist discourse, which has tended to define corporatism in three quite different ways. It has, first of all, been commonly employed to characterize, in Gramscian fashion, a certain *ideological* condition of the working classes, whereby a defensive, sectionalized class exhibits a subordinate ideology and practice in polar contrast to a hegemonic orientation. Alternatively, the term is often employed to connote an actual political structure, but one confined exclusively to fascist regimes.[9] Finally, corporatism is often treated by Marxists entirely as a (false) ideological construct, which cannot be dissociated from its origins in corporatist ideology. In this last usage, any attempt to employ corporatism as an analytical tool to capture the reality of a given society is seen as inevitably tainted by corporatist ideology, carrying with it the assumption of the desirability and possibility of securing class harmony under the aegis of a neutral state within capitalism. This would rule out the possibility of employing the term within Marxist discourse to denote an actual process or structure which reproduces class domination on these premises.

In so far as recent theorizations of corporatism mark a significant break with the past, and employ the term descriptively or analytically to refer to a specific form of state-induced class collaboration in capitalist democracies there is no necessary normative connection between the use of the concept in Marxist analysis and those aspects of corporatist ideology which originally constituted the term. The questions of whether, why and with what consequence corporatist structures develop within the bourgeois-democratic state becomes a matter not of definitional *fiat,* but of concrete historico-empirical investigation. To be sure, such questions need not be inserted into a Marxist problematic: just as 'democracy' and 'class' are contested concepts in social science, so too with 'corporatism'. Thus, although corporatism has been universally contrasted with pluralism to emphasize the weakness of the latter's assumptions of multiple group competition *vis-à-vis* a neutral state, it has remained encumbered in various bourgeois theorizations with assumptions of equivalence of power and influence between labour and capital in corporatist political structures. More recently its use has involved the argument that state intervention in the economy entails the actual replacement of capitalism with a corporatist economic system defined by 'state control over profit'.[10] Obviously, as located in such approaches, the concept of corporatism is incompatible with a Marxist problematic. But the definitions of corporatism offered by Marxist writers do *not* assume equivalence of power or influence between the groups or the classes based on them, nor the neutrality of the state *vis-à-vis* them. Nor do they assume that corporatist political structures are in any sense desirable, or even stable. On the contrary, by situating corporatism *explicitly* within the parameters of advanced capitalist society, they invite investigation of the manner in which corporatist structures reflect, mediate or modify the class struggle.

The Locus of Hegemony

Thus a Marxist conception of the development of corporatist structures *within* the bourgeois-democratic state raises significant questions for the theory of the state under advanced capitalism. It opens, first of all, the question of whether and in what sense parliamentary structures need to be seen as the *linchpin* of hegemonic domination, constituted on the basis of the mediation 'between the ruling and ruled classes in universalistic (i.e., not overtly class-specific) terms'.[11] For it would appear that the very preservation of bourgeois democracy in the context of extensive state intervention and a strong labour movement under monopoly capitalism entails a supplementation (but not a displacement) of parliamentary and party forms of representation/mediation (which formally dissociate state and class) with corporatist forms of representation/mediation *which are explicitly class-based*. Corporatism is a mode of representation/mediation appropriate to certain forms of state intervention in the economy since it is constituted on the basis of groups arising directly on the social division of labour. Jessop sees it as a system of representation which is particularly suited to state economic intervention because it 'entitles the political organs of capital and labour to participate in the formulation and implementation of policies concerned with accumulation so that responsibility for such intervention is placed on those immediately affected rather than mediated through parliamentary representation and rational-legal administration'.[12] Corporatist structures are prone to contradictions and limitations, however, due to their inability to eliminate class conflict over the labour process and distribution. For this reason, and because of the concentration of corporatist structures on economic intervention, parliaments, elections and pressure-group politics continue to remain important sites of representation and hegemonic control.

Secondly, Marxist approaches to corporatism lay the basis for distinguishing the different consequences of corporatist integration for trade unions versus business associations, determined by the effect their class location has on their organizational structures and their relations with the state. This is not only a product of the design of state policy *vis-à-vis* the two classes, but also a product of the different internal structures of the respective organizations.[13] As Claus Offe has argued, trade-union power is based on the effectiveness of its collective organization. But the power of capital is based on control of the means of production, and this control is not transferred to the interest associations of business by individual firms. This means that these associations' incorporation via state structures is less significant for capital than is the incorporation of trade unions for labour, precisely because these associations play a less critical role for their class as agencies of struggle, of representation and of social control than do trade unions for their class, not least because of the role of the capitalist state itself in cementing a common interest among capital's competing fractions.

Finally, and perhaps most importantly, a Marxist approach to corporatism within bourgeois democracies suggests that the debate over the scope of the state among Marxists in recent years has been fundamentally miscast. Two static positions were originally put forward: either the state was defined according to the constitutional legal distinction between public and private (Miliband), or all institutions engaged in the *function* of reproducing class domination ideologically and politically were identified with the state (Althusser, Poulantzas). When cast in these static terms, Miliband's position was unassailable, maintaining the notion of separation of state and civil society characteristic of bourgeois-democratic as opposed to fascist regimes, and viewing the state not as a functional activity pervading all society (including the family) but as a specific *instance*. [14] To be sure, by the late 1970s this debate had largely been 'resolved', and the static dimension cast aside, by a common approach on the part of Miliband and Poulantzas towards identifying a process of statization under monopoly capitalism whereby the distinctions between state and civil society are increasingly blurred. This is what theorizations of corporatism have been identifying for some time. But it would be a mistake to see the process as a *linear one*, inevitably the product of monopoly capitalism, as implied by most Marxist theories of the state and by many theorists of modern corporatism. An examination of the development of corporatist structures within bourgeois democracy suggests, at least as regards the incorporation of trade unions, that the scope of the state is not something which can be defined *a priori* nor its expansion predicted in a linear fashion. Rather the scope of the state *is an object of struggle itself.* As I shall attempt to show in the following sections, even when corporatist structures are established they remain unstable in face of repeated struggles about whether trade unions are to become mere agencies of the state or preserve their role as autonomous working-class institutions. It is precisely the *open and unresolved* nature of this conflict over the scope of the state as pertaining to corporatist political structures that distinguishes them from their brethren in fascist regimes. [15]

A Socialist Corporate State?

The failure to recognize the capitalist dynamic entailed in the growth of these new corporatist structures (however many new contradictions they may sow) has produced its own misguided political corollaries. For there has been an increasingly visible tendency to extrapolate the struggle *over* the incorporation of working-class organizations into the capitalist state, into a struggle *within* corporatist forms, if not to *transform* the state, then to enhance considerably working-class power. In this sense, it has been suggested that in so far as the union leadership 'maintains close ties to the working class and remains a legitimate instrument of real working-class organizations', this not only 'undermines the planning functions of corporatism' but 'brings class struggle into the administrative heart of the state apparatus itself'. [16] From this it is but a short step to the kind of view put forward recently by the British Marxist economist and left-Labourite, Geoff Hodgson:

> Corporatism means state control. It therefore raises the question of who controls the state . . . It is important, therefore, to develop the struggle for working-class control of production at the workplace level, and working-class control of planning and investment policy, at both the local and national level. It is also vital to defend and extend existing civil liberties, democratic rights and democratic institutions, even if this means the defence of institutions which could be regarded as bourgeois-democratic. Such questions of strategy could determine the precise flavour of a future corporatist state. And that, after all, is a vitally important question. For upon it depends the possibility of mobilising the forces for the socialist transformation of society and the eradication of a system which has meant alienation, conflict and misery from its birth to its death. [17]

It is precisely this image of a *socialist corporate state*—which returns full circle to a purely instrumentalist view of the state, whereby the state apparatuses can be 'captured' intact by the working class—that has made many Marxists rightly wary of employing the concept of corporatism for analysing the bourgeois-democratic state. It not only assumes that the working class can unify itself hegemonically on corporatist terrain, but fails to understand that corporatist political structures (there can be no such thing as a 'corporatist state' given the necessarily partial nature of corporatist structures in both bourgeois democracies and fascist regimes) are a form of capitalist domination. Long before power can be won on this terrain, the structures will either be dismembered by the state and the bourgeoisie, or they will be turned into repressive facsimiles of their fascist counterparts. As I attempt to show in the following sketch of the development of contemporary corporatist forms, one of their paramount characteristics is precisely their dissonance with rank-and-file activity or working-class power.

The Parameters of Modern Corporatism

The development of political structures which integrate trade unions with the state executive/bureaucracy and associations of business in framing, legitimating and administering public policy cannot be read off directly from the advent of monopoly capitalism and the necessarily enhanced role of the state in fostering capital accumulation. Were monopoly capitalism itself a sufficient condition for explaining the emergence of corporatist structures, one would have expected to find such structures most highly developed precisely in that society which has been the world centre of monopoly capitalism in the modern era—the United States. Instead corporatist structures in the United States are comparatively *least* developed. Conventional interest group lobbying *vis-à-vis* the legislature still plays a major role, and labour representation *vis-à-vis* bureaucratic policy making is largely confined to the Department of Labour, a site which occupies a lowly place in the hierarchy of state apparatuses. However great the incidence of class collaboration in America, its practice is little elaborated in the institutional field of the central administrative apparatus of the state, where trade unions are largely excluded from participation in policy-making. Similarly, were the incidence of state intervention in the economy itself the determining variable, one would have expected France, with its extensive state economic planning, or Italy, with its extensive public ownership, to exhibit highly developed corporatist state structures. Instead, these societies are precisely marked by the comparative distance of the trade-union movement from the state apparatus.

Arrighi has argued recently that the central dynamic of the monopoly stage of capitalism is located in the contradictory effects which capital accumulation has on the working class. While increasingly subordinating labour to capital, capital concentration simultaneously increases the strength of the working class by concentrating and centralizing it and thus developing its collective industrial power and solidarity. The value of this mode of analysis, as I have argued before, is that the tendency to capitalist crisis is not located abstractly in mechanical formulations of the changing organic composition of capital, but is located centrally in the class struggle in the form of the capacity of the working class to resist increases in the rate of exploitation. But in so far as we are attempting to explain concretely the factors generating capitalist crisis and the changing form of the bourgeois-democratic state as it tries to counteract them, we are still operating at too great a level of generality. As Arrighi himself admitted in a postcript to his article, his presentation of the 'trend towards a long-term structural reinforcement of the working class' suffered from its 'linear and uniform character', by failing to introduce distinctions which would identify the uneven development of working-class strength and medium-term oscillations of that strength. [18] As regards the establishment of corporatist structures, where and when this occurs can only be explained in terms of such uneven development and medium-term oscillations.

The Role of Labour Markets

The critical factor accounting for the development of corporatist state structures, at least in the first two decades after the Second World War, appears to have been the level of employment, and relatedly the commitment of the state to maintaining a high-employment fiscal and monetary policy. This in turn largely reflected the extent of the *political* strength of the working class and its allies on the question of 'full employment', although the conditions favouring rapid economic growth set the framework for the extent of this victory. [19] Within the context of the general trend towards the structural strengthening of the working class in the monopoly capitalist era, it was the attenuation of the reserve army of labour as a result of nearly full employment in particular societies that critically further strengthened the organized working class at the industrial level. And as the state intertwined with corporate management to facilitate the restructuring of capital necessary for accumulation and economic growth, what largely dictated the absorption of trade unions into this policy-making network was the extent to which high employment closed off the possibility of securing the necessary rate of exploitation via labour market mechanisms alone. Where the labour movement was too weak or too divided to secure an effective commitment to full employment from the state, the expansion of the state's role in the economy occurred *without* the unions' participation.

This was the case in the United States where the 1946 Employment Act was passed only after the commitment to maintaining full employment was emasculated from the originally proposed 'Full Employment Bill', and where unemployment throughout the post-war period (until the 1970s) ran at almost twice the rate of Britain or the Scandinavian countries. A similar situation prevailed in Italy, France and Germany until the beginning of the 1960s, although for somewhat different structural and political reasons. In each of these countries a deflationary programme was pursued in the immediate post-war period. In Italy unemployment hovered between 10 and 15 per cent throughout the 1950s. Corporatist proposals for union integration only surfaced after the emergence of the tight labour market and the widespread militancy and wage gains of 1961–2. In West Germany throughout the 1950s state economic policy was conducted as though Keynes had never been heard of and the demands of the West German confederation of trade unions (DGB) for participation in economic policy making were largely ignored. It was only after unemployment fell dramatically in the early 1960s (to below 1 per cent) and the bargaining position of unions was strengthened considerably (with irregular but notable expressions of strike activity) that the state turned towards 'concerted action' (in the year *before* the Social Democratic Party (SDP) entered the Grand Coalition). And although France had the most elaborate indicative planning system in the world, the unions were effectively excluded from this state-business network, under conditions where unions were extremely weak at the level of collective bargaining and where rural unemployment and short-term work prevailed through the 1950s. Again it was only in the early 1960s, with the establishment of the basis for CGT–CFDT common action under conditions of a tight labour market and renewed industrial militancy, that overtures were made to incorporate the unions in economic planning. As usual, it was the question of incomes policy that dominated state thinking in this regard. In each of these countries, capitalist economic strategy was predicated on the labour market weakness of the working class until the 1960s and the expansion of the state's role in the economy occurred without the unions' participation. [20]

In direct contrast, it was in those societies in which the labour movement had been strong enough to secure an effective commitment by the state to Keynesianism and full-employment policies in the immediate post-war period, and at the same time were industrially well organized and thus able to take advantage of full employment via wage pressure (with its attendant effects in terms of inflation), that trade unions were drawn into the state's economic apparatus. This was the situation in Britain, Sweden, Norway, Austria and Holland—and in each case incomes policy was the central mechanism of incorporation. It was thus trade-union *economic behaviour* (wage pressure) and the particular *mode* of state intervention necessary to deal with it, that was the basis of the establishment of corporatist political structures. There were, however, additional facilitating factors. Two of these were a pre-existing high degree of union centralization *and* a legal framework for collective bargaining, both of which established suitable conditions for the uniform application of wage restraint while constraining counter pressures (unofficial strikes) arising in the labour movement. The absence of these conditions in Britain were factors accounting for the relative hiatus in corporatist developments from 1950 to 1960, but attempts at incorporation since that time, as we shall see, have entailed the concurrent attempt to establish these conditions. Another facilitating factor was social democracy. It was not only social-democratic governments which pursued corporatist structures, nor was political loyalty to a social-democratic government the only factor in inducing union co-operation. But the readiness with which unions were willing to look at corporatist integration seriously was conditioned by the effects of social-democratic ideology on the labour movement, with its rejection of the Marxist concept of class struggle, its belief in the neutral state and its promulgation of 'planning'. In contrast, Communist unions, as in Italy and France, rejected involvement in economic planning bodies and incomes policies explicitly on the grounds that they were corporatist.[21]

The Implications for Unions

What are the effects of corporatist political structures on trade unions? The primary *organizational* effect is to articulate the collective mass organization with centralized state apparatus, by encouraging the *centralization* of the union movement so that union policy is increasingly made not at the level of local or individual unions but via the permanent apparatus of confederal centrals. The evolution of centralized wage bargaining was thus facilitated and encouraged by the state. Ironically, the readiness with which union movements have undertaken this development 'voluntarily' in the modern era has to a large extent been a function of the threat made by the state to intervene directly by regulative/coercive means in the collective bargaining process.

In Sweden, for instance, this took the form of joint centralized wage regulation by the Landsorganisationen (LO) and the Central Employers' Federation (SAF) in the late 1930s under the direct *threat* of legislation by the newly-elected social democrats. The state acted as only a silent partner in this bargaining structure throughout the post-war period, but the continued threat of direct government intervention served both to establish explicit corporatist state structures and to ensure moderate wage agreements. Thus the unions' promotion of, and integration into, the system of tripartite labour market boards took place, according to the LO's Rudolf Meidner, in part because of 'worry . . . about the effects of a permanent over-full employment economy on the ability of the union organizations to act as free negotiating parties independent of the government.' Similarly, moderate wage increases were negotiated under the central agreements between the LO and SAF in the 1950s and 1960s in part because they 'assigned the highest priority to preventing government intervention in collective bargaining in general and wage determination in particular'.[22] Thus, while centralized bargaining and a corporatist Labour Market Board were encouraged by the LO to avoid 'state control over the pricing of labour services' and as a 'reaction against the strong pressure to have a policy of wage restraint',[23] wage moderation via these structures was secured due to the fear of further state intervention.

To take another case, the participation of the Trades Union Congress in Britain in the establishment of national wage-norms in the mid 1960s, and the development of an internal TUC Incomes Policy Committee to vet the wage claims of individual unions in light of these norms, was acquiesced in by the powerful individual member unions on the grounds that in this way statutory wage control would be avoided. When a statutory incomes policy under the administrative aegis of the tripartite National Board for Prices and Incomes was nevertheless introduced, the union argument for co-operation with it was based on the hope that by demonstrating compliance the statutory policy would be temporary. Similarly, when the Labour government's proposed legislation in 1969 to control unofficial strikes, 'In Place of Strife', was met with implacable hostility in the labour movement, the government responded with the explicit argument that 'If the General Council (of the TUC) would agree to legislate, the Government would agree not to legislate.' The attempt by the government to force a change to this effect in the TUC rules, and the resistance of the TUC to this, turned into a fundamental argument on the question of whether the TUC and its affiliated unions could become bodies which would exercise discipline over their members with the degree of reliability that the state could expect from one of its own agencies. The government went so far as to propose to back up TUC rulings by state sanctions against strikers who refused to accept these rulings. The TUC successfully resisted these pressures and this constituted a substantial victory against fuller incorporation in the state. Nevertheless, the public agreement struck between the government and the TUC to close the controversy committed the union movement, at least formally, to a TUC role in monitoring and vetting unofficial strikes 'in the national interest'.[24]

In terms of the effect on trade-union *policy* of corporatist political structures, the most general is the introduction of capitalist growth criteria within the formulation of union wage policy, the central aspect being the recognition that profit is the condition for future economic growth, including that of wages. Of course, to cast the matter simply in terms of profit is too narrow. Macro-considerations for the economy as a whole enter into the formulation of wages policy via union participation in corporatist structures. Thus the maintenance of full employment, the avoidance of inflation, even the rationalization and concentration of industry, became explicit concerns of unions in formulating wage demands. As Meidner has put it, the full acceptance in the 1940s of the idea of the co-ordination of wage bargaining among the unions in Sweden, an idea originally developed to increase the solidarity of the working class, was 'forced upon the unions by outside forces and circumstances' and 'admittedly on different grounds from those originally advocated . . . Full employment and the preservation of economic stability were now regarded as a stronger argument for co-ordination than a wage solidarity policy.'[25]

This is not to say that all concerns related to an *autonomous* working-class wages policy are lost in the process. Indeed, in so far as the redistributive aspects of collective bargaining *between the classes* taken as a whole are largely foregone in the context of a corporatist wage restraint policy, there is an added impetus for a 'socially conscious' and centralized labour movement to evolve policies that redistribute the total wage 'pool' going to the working class to the benefit of the lower paid. This is what might pejoratively be called 'socialism in one class'. In Sweden, this became the linchpin of trade-union incorporation as the LO explicitly evolved a policy of pursuing higher wages for the low paid in the context of an overall wage policy of 'responsibility', and articulated this with the state via the Labour Market Board to obviate the effects of redundancy in the low-profit sectors affected. In this way, the Swedish labour movement attempted to cope with the official hypocrisy of 'justice to the low paid' that so regularly attends incomes policies, but in the process it also enmeshed itself further in corporatist state structures.

The Contradictions of Corporatism

The development of corporatism in the bourgeois-democratic state, however, is by no means linear. It is subject to repeated strains and even ruptures, which emerge from the contradiction contained in the attempt, not to smash, but to incorporate those very working-class organizations which, however reformist, are the vehicle through which class struggle is waged, day by day and year by year. The very legitimation that corporatist structures are designed to give to state policy is contradicted by the 'delegitimation' that these structures produce over time. This is not primarily due to a popular-democratic resentment against the incorporation of labour and business associations to the exclusion of other 'non-functional' interest groups. Nor is it in the main a product of a developing political rejection on the part of workers of the principle of union collaboration with the bourgeois state. It is rather that the concrete form in which trade unions legitimate/mediate state economic policy is via their promulgation of wage restraint 'in the nation interest' and their administration of it to their members. Because it is not just the trade union (conceived as some abstract form of organization), or the union bureaucracy, which 'quantifies' workers' demands under capitalism, but the workers themselves who do so, the application of wage restraint undermines what Adam Przeworski calls the 'material basis of consent.'[26] This need not happen on a large scale immediately, of course, although incomes policy is continuously breached surreptitiously by sectoral or local negotiations outside the control of centralized bargaining, which are the basis of 'wage drift'. This is only a partial breach, however, and in so far as wage restraint is practised continually or intensified to the point of producing falling real wages, there is an increasing likelihood that, through the mobilization of opposition within union organizations at the policy or union elections level, or through the expression of unofficial strikes on a large scale, trade unions will withdraw from, or at least attempt to renegotiate their place in corporatist political structures.

Thus, what characterized the development of corporatist structures, no less than their persistence, in certain bourgeois democracies, is their instability. The corporatist-structured incomes policies of Britain and Sweden in the late 1940s were defeated by the labour movement at the turn of the decade and although resuscitated quickly in Sweden, in Britain they were not really revived until the Conservative government established the tripartite National Economic Development Council in 1961 to secure trade-union participation in an incomes policy. (In Holland, the initial post-war policies of corporatist economic planning structures lasted longer, but rank-and-file pressure led to a renegotiation of the basis of incomes policy in 1959 and the rejection of centralized wage controls by 1963.) But it was the outbreak of rank-and-file militancy throughout Europe in the late 1960s that really demonstrated the fragility of corporatist political structures. This militancy, being a general phenomenon after the recession of 1966–7, cannot, of course, be attributed only to the resentment against corporatist wage-restraint policies. But where they existed, resentment against them certainly fuelled militancy and became a focal point for mobilization.

The effect on the union leadership was readily visible, as they ran after their members, not merely in a cynical attempt to retain organizational control, but often as a genuine response to their base. The consequences for corporatist structures were, at a minimum, a substantial decline in the authority of the centralized wage bargain (Sweden) and, at a maximum, the actual, albeit temporary, withdrawal of the union leadership from certain corporatist structures (Britain and Holland). Even in West Germany, where 'concerted action' had but recently got off the ground, the effect of the 1969 strike wave was notable: 'The sudden revision of the unions' restrained wage policy due to the dissatisfaction on the part of their members was a decisive turning point for the state incomes policy. Since this revision, "concerted action" and the guidelines have had only limited influence on actual wage policy.'[27]

The Failure of Coercion

The immediate response of the state to these developments was in most cases a coercive one, designed to weaken the union movement in general or a particular sector of it. This was seen in Britain in terms of industrial relations legislation directly concerned with constraining the right to strike, both by making unofficial strikes in most critical circumstances illegal and by legally requiring unions to police them. In Holland, the state undertook to invalidate wage agreements which it considered detrimental to the national interest. In Sweden, the coercive response was also there, but it was more balanced: the right to strike for public employees was suspended and the 1971 wage agreement was struck only after the threat to impose an agreement (favouring the LO's position) upon the employers. In West Germany, the threat of a statutory incomes policy reared its head.

Coercive measures had little impact, however, in resuscitating corporatist integration. This was both because rank-and-file militancy did not dissipate in the face of these measures and because union leaders feared for their own autonomy as a consequence of legislation and, having been once burnt, became more responsive to rank-and-file demands. Thus, in the early 1970s official strikes became more common and a significant radicalization was seen in both the industrial and political programmes of the union movements. This development also reflected the unions' response to the new economic situation of the 1970s, above all, the concurrent and dramatic rise of unemployment and inflation. For in so far as wage restraint could no longer be legitimated on the grounds of full employment and price stability, the rationale upon which post-war corporatist structures had rested was effectively removed. Corporatism now had to be legitimated on the grounds that wage restraint would *restore* full employment and price stability, or, even more difficult, on the grounds that it would prevent the situation from getting worse. While trade-union leaders were certainly open to such arguments, it was hardly surprising that they treated them with caution, not least because not only their own, but clearly the bourgeoisie's faith in the 'mixed economy' was somewhat shaken. In this situation, union leaders were bound to 'up the ante' for reintegration. This was seen in the 'socio-political' turn of the DGB, in the Meidner Plan in Sweden and in the 'social contract' in Britain.

Indeed, the question posed by high unemployment for corporatist structures in the 1970s was why they should, apart from inertia, continue to exist at all. Their development, after all, was predicated on the need to cope with wage pressure resulting from near-full employment. And the unemployment of the 1970s was both an economic reflection of, and a state response to, the earlier inability of the state, *pace* Poulantzas, to assimilate effectively even 'reformist' trade unions into 'the institutional materiality of the [state] administrative structure.'[28] But the role for corporatist structures would only have been obviated in so far as unemployment had the effect of undermining working-class militancy. Although it is difficult to predict what its long-term effect will be, and to deny there may be some threshold of unemployment yet to be reached which would cow the working class into submission, it is certainly the case that this did not happen, except for very temporary periods, in the 1970s. The long-term structural strengthening of the working class identified by Arrighi itself made unemployment a less potent phenomenon in the 1970s than in the 1930s, or even in the late 1940s and 1950s. Moreover, whereas the mass unemployment in the 1930s followed the *defeat* of working-class militancy in the 1920s, the rise in unemployment in the 1970s followed the successes of the wage and strike explosion of the late 1960s and early 1970s which increased courage and organizational capacity for further struggles. Finally, the very coexistence of rapid inflation with unemployment (due in good part to successful wage pressure, if much else as well) increasingly impelled workers towards further militancy to defend real wages.

Corporatism in a New Guise

Under these conditions, corporatism still had a role to play in bourgeois democracies. But the resuscitation of corporatist structures took a new turn in light of the effective decentralization and radicalization of the union movements. Rather than persist with coercive measures to strengthen corporatist structures and run the risk of endangering bourgeois democracy altogether, the state, especially where social democratic governments were in office, set about, partly in response to the new demands coming from the unions themselves, to integrate lower levels of the movement—right down to the shop-floor—more effectively. This took the form of progressive legislation and state-fostered managerial practices designed to facilitate union recognition in unorganized sectors and extend union membership in organized sectors; to foster workers' participation schemes in company boards and works councils (this time under the direct aegis of the unions); to institutionalize local level bargaining and shop steward committees; and to provide a legal framework for qualitative issues (for example health and safety), unfair dismissals and redundancy. In one way or another this was the direction of social democratic state industrial relations practices in Sweden, West Germany and Britain in the early and mid 1970s. [29] These reforms were progressive, but they further enmeshed the trade unions in the legal apparatus of the state and institutionalized and juridified conflict on the shop-floor. Moreover, combined with the eschewing by social-democratic governments of *statutory* incomes policies, and the programmatic bow made by social-democratic parties to some form of 'investment planning', these reforms constituted the new *quid pro quo* for wage restraint under resuscitated corporatist political structures.

It was on the basis of these developments that certain Marxist theorists began to envisage the possibility of corporatism being the field on which class struggle would be brought 'into the heart of the state apparatus'. The naivety of such prognoses is made clear by observing the effects of corporatist arrangements precisely in those countries where conditions were most favourable for waging such struggles—for example, where social democratic governments were in office. In Sweden the 1973–4 central wage negotiations 'reversed the trend from 1964 through 1966 and 1969 to 1971 of increasing difficulty and conflict. The 1973–4 negotiations were the fastest since the early sixties and the only ones since then not requiring mediation'. [30] This outcome was enhanced by the government using its taxation policy to shift the burden of pension contributions from worker to employer, on the condition that wage demands during the negotiations would be correspondingly reduced. But this did not alter the overall impact of wage moderation in these negotiations, and in so far as it led to the reduction of conflict in centralized negotiations, it acted as a break in sustaining in a unified way the previous mobilization. Similarly in West Germany, after two years of unofficial and official strikes which had secured a growth in real wages outside the guidelines established in the incomes policy, 'union wage policy once again acquiesced to the recommendations of the Federal Government and its Council of Experts. Contractual wage increases were kept within the guidelines of incomes policy, which provided only for an adjustment of wages to price increases and also planned a redistribution favourable to corporate earnings.'[31] And in Britain, the resuscitation of corporatism via the Labour Government—TUC 'social contract' wage-norm negotiations in 1975–6, introduced the most sustained and draconian reduction of real wages (by 8 per cent from 1974–5 to 1976–7) in the post-war period. Strikes correspondingly fell to their lowest levels, after the intense mobilization of industrial struggle over the previous six years, for well over a decade. As in Sweden, this demobilization occurred in the context of a wage norm designed to benefit the low paid and the tying of the reduced wage demands to decreases in taxation. But in the context of rising unemployment and falling wages in general in Britain, this at best had the effect of redistributing very marginally the burden of increased exploitation.[32]

Each of these corporatist wage policies was negotiated in years of national economic crisis of proportions unknown in the post-war period. And corporatist political structures became the vehicle for engineering, legitimating ('in the national interest') and administering the increase in exploitation which was necessary to sustain capital in the crisis. The sacrifice undertaken by the working class in the context of the crisis would have been one thing had the respective governments implemented those reflationary policies and structural reforms which the union movements had promulgated earlier in the 1970s. That they were undertaken rather in the context of policies which were designed to restore the profitability of private capital and which depended on *this* to reduce unemployment is an indication that only class collaboration, not class struggle, can be practised in the corporatist 'heart' of the state apparatus. In so far as class struggle was practised it was not within, but outside of an implicitly or explicitly against, corporatist structures, as seen most clearly in the strikes of 1978–9 in West Germany and Britain, and of 1980 in Sweden.

That certain Marxists have nevertheless identified the possibility of class struggle occurring in the corporatist 'heart' of the state apparatus has much to do with the fact that the corporatism of the 1970s involved the unions in tripartite discussions on 'investment planning'. This occurred extensively in Britain where the Labour government, as an alternative to undertaking the direct impositions on capital which had been the core of Labour's 1974 election manifesto, established an 'industrial strategy' based on tripartite sectoral working parties to 'plan' investment industry by industry. The emptiness of this planning exercise—apart from its legitimation value—can be seen from the comments of Jack Jones, the main union architect of the Social Contract. Speaking in 1977 to a TUC conference, he said: 'I have yet to see . . . any firm evidence that the efforts of the sector working parties . . . have produced any significant increase in investment or in employment, and that is the test . . . In my view, an industrial strategy which relies only on the deliberations of sector working parties, on polite talks with industrialists and trade associations . . . is not a strategy at all, but an excuse for one.'[33] As Lehmbruch put the matter, regarding corporatist arrangements in West Germany and Austria: 'Enlarging the field of corporatist economic decision-making beyond incomes policies (or, more exactly, control of wage policies) would have meant, among others, control of profits and of investment and hence, a considerable structural transformation. This would have necessitated a shift in power relations which certainly could not be obtained within a corporatist system.'[34]

It will be argued that the extension of conclusions based on the British and West German experience to other countries is invalid. Particularly, some will say that Sweden, where the LO, the Social Democratic Party and the Labour Market Board are reputedly animals of quite another breed, shows the way to the 'socialist corporatist state'. To be sure, that the outcome of corporatist structures would have been exactly the same in Sweden as in West Germany and Britain in the late 1970s cannot be entirely clear. The defeat of the Social Democrats in 1976 foreshortened the relevant period in which the new testing of the limits of social democratic reform could be undertaken (although the new government maintained the corporatist structures in place). But James Fulcher's reading of the situation on the eve of the 1976 electoral defeat appears apt:

the government's decision to allow the investment of state pension funds in private industry has made possible the covert extension of state ownership.

State intervention may well, however, create more problems for the organizations of the working class than it solves. It seems unlikely that, in a climate of intense international competition, any government, whatever its character, will carry out measures which might seriously threaten the profitability and competitiveness of industry. Indeed, state-owned industries in Sweden, as elsewhere in capitalist societies, tend to be operated according to capitalist principles. Thus the Social Democrat government's political need to meet the demands of LO may be expected to conflict with its need to maintain economic competitiveness and the 'labour' government in Sweden may not be able to avoid the dilemma that has so afflicted Labour governments in Britain.[35]

Conclusions

What conclusions can we draw from this discussion? Despite their instability (marked by the withdrawal from time to time of active union cooperation in these structures), it remains clear that, once established, corporatist structures exhibit a tenacious durability, spanning the rise and fall of particular governments. (In Britain, for instance, the National Economic Development Council has withstood not only Heath's 'Selsdon Man', but also the more extreme ideological and policy shifts of the Thatcher regime; while in Sweden, the new governing coalition retained the corporatist structures inherited from the long period of Social Democratic rule, in particular the Labour Market Board.) Nevertheless, it does seem to be the case that it is incorrect to see the institutionalized network of state-business-labour collaboration as *displacing* party/parliamentary activity or, as Poulantzas seemed to think, as obviating the need for striking 'political compromises on the political arena—that is, of publicly elaborating the hegemonic interest in the form of a national interest'.[36] The salience and the viability of trade-union integration in corporatist structures in any given conjuncture depends in large part on its articulation with complementary party/parliamentary activity, and on the public legitimation which trade unions accord to the 'national interest'. The resuscitated corporatism of the 1970s was very much dependent on the bargains struck between social democratic parties and trade unions; involving the promise that the compromise made by the working class in corporatist structures would be compensated for via the parliamentary process, whether through the 'social wage', industrial relations legislation or direct impositions on capital. In so far as corporatist structures are now a major locus for legitimating and administering working-class sacrifices 'in the national interest', and in so far as compensation for these sacrifices cannot be secured by unions directly from capital within corporatist structures themselves, they need to be provided in the party/parliamentary arena (where the costs of these compensations, in any case, can be made diffuse, that is, born by the 'public' in general). Social democratic parties play a critical role in articulating the two arenas: they offer to win compensations for the working class in parliamentary institutions which dissociate state and class in representation/mediation, in exchange for compromises made by the working class in corporatist institutions where representation/mediation is explicitly class-based. The strength of the link provided by social-democratic parties is often the test of the degree to which the organized network of state-business collaboration extends to the effective incorporation of unions.

It should be noted again, however, that this link does not prevent the recurrent instability of corporatist practices. If trade unions are readier to co-operate within corporatist structures when social democratic parties are in office, they still are unable to escape indefinitely the central contradiction of remaining responsive to their base while administering corporatist wage restraint. To be sure, this contradiction is aggravated because the actual compensation offered the working class in the parliamentary arena for the sacrifices obtained in corporatist structures usually falls considerably short of the promises made by social democratic parties, particularly given the restrictions which the current crisis imposes on the capitalist state's social expenditures and its willingness to challenge the nostrums of 'business confidence'. But whereas the party/parliamentary arena is protected from instability by its universalistic, non-class constitution in general, and by regular elections in particular, the trade unions' very function of representing the immediate material interests of their members creates a much more difficult role for them in promulgating and administering the 'national interest' within corporatist structures. Hence trade-union incorporation in the state is marked by far more discontinuities in the corporatist policy process than is the case with social democratic parties in the parliamentary process. These discontinuities influence, but do not exactly parallel, the electoral fortunes and intra-party controversies of social democratic parties. It should be noted, moreover, that attempts by the state to overcome the instability of corporatism by weakening the responsiveness of unions to their memberships are themselves likely to emanate (as was the case in the late 1960s and early 1970s) from parliamentary legislation which seeks to reorganize the industrial relations system. Thus, here as well, corporatism should be seen not as *displacing* Parliament, but rather as depending on it for the conditions necessary for its success.

As for the question of corporatism bringing class struggle into the administrative heart of the state apparatus, such conceptions would indeed appear to be particularly barren. They involve an insufficient appreciation of the role corporatist structures necessarily play, as arenas of top-level bargaining, in forestalling or constraining working-class mobilization. Perhaps this is best illustrated by the following example. At the height of the wave of strikes in Britain in 1979, the TUC and the Labour government issued a joint statement on 'The Economy, the Government and Trade Union Responsibilities'. Its theme was this: 'There is no answer in confrontation. Solutions to our problems have to be found in agreement. But agreement will only be possible if our people all recognize that we are all part of a community of interest.' And it went on: 'The Government, business, and financial institutions, and the trade-union movement, by their actions help to decide how the economy performs. This has fundamental implications for the proper handling of the relationship between these great interests . . . It also imposes on the TUC, with its broad and undisputed representative capacity, the need to accept that its expanding role carries with it wider responsibilities.' On this basis the General Council of the TUC issued, as an annex to this public document, restrictive guidelines to its affiliated unions on negotiating and disputes procedures, on the conduct of strikes and picketing, on the maintenance of emergency services in strikes and on the 'flexible operation' of the closed shop. [37]

The importance of this document was not that it laid the basis for the TUC's own restrictive administration of strike activity. This is presently far beyond its capacity. It was rather that on the basis of the document the TUC General Council *publicly* legitimated, and associated the working class with legitimating, the general interest of the bourgeoisie and the government regarding the strikes then taking place. *This is the corporatist field of class collaboration,* and in such situations corporatist structures operate more effectively as a hegemonic apparatus than do parliaments, precisely because representation/mediation under corporatism is class-specific rather than universalistic. At the same time, some of the very members of the General Council of the TUC who were associated with this document were leading their individual union's *official* strikes against which the document was directed. *This is the field of industrial class struggle.* That the two hats may sometimes be worn at once bespeaks precisely the contradictions between trade unionism and corporatism in bourgeois democracies. But this is not a basis for confusing a field of class collaboration with a field of class struggle.

The Fate of Trade Unionism

Corporatism must be seen as a system of state-structured class collaboration. As such, its extension poses not an opportunity, but a danger to working-class organizations. Based on communitarian premises and collaborative practices which articulate the interests of capital with the state, corporatist structures require of trade unions, as their contribution to the operation, *not that they cut their ties with their base, but rather that they use those ties to legitimate state policy and elaborate their control over their members.* This would alleviate their function of working-class mobilization, albeit on 'economistic' premises, against capital and the state. The reason we are able to speak of the development of corporatism *within* bourgeois democracy is that corporatist structures have not yet entailed the abrogation of freedom of association which is the first task of the 'authoritarian state'. The network of corporatist institutions has not yet subsumed trade unions, as Middlemas aptly puts it, 'into a pyramid of authority, within fixed limits of activity, exercising power only in so far as it has been delegated by the state'.[38] They still remain, as 'collective mass organizations' distinctive to the working class, in a fundamentally different relation to the state than the conventional state apparatus, participating in the 'institutional materiality of the administrative structure', yet not reducable to it. To be sure, the consistent clamour that their participation in state policy making needs be balanced by an extension of their disciplinary control over their members bespeaks the dangerous dynamic of corporatism. And this remains the warning light to the need to maintain clarity over the importance of struggles within unions and between unions and the state over limiting the scope of the state as pertains to trade-union organization and practice. The danger in Marxist theorizations of corporatism is that they may fall prey to the romantic notion that the central contradiction of corporatism can be swept away in formulations that rhetorically combine invocations to retain the maximum responsiveness to membership with programmes for further assimilating unions into corporatist political structures.It is perhaps worth noting that no less an authority on the matter than the LO's Rudolf Meidner has admitted that the elaborated reform strategy of the Swedish unions in the 1970s, precisely in proposing to widen the scope of corporatist arrangements, was at the same time implicitly 'threatening in its most far-reaching manifestations to undermine the whole basis of the trade-union movement's independence from the state'.[39]

To warn against the dangers of further trade-union integration into the capitalist state is not to return to a syndicalist position. Far from it. It is rather to take the position that one of the reasons that a socialist transformation is impossible via participation in corporatist structures, apart from the function of these structures in the bourgeois state, is that trade unions by their very nature cannot undertake such a transformation on their own, being constituted, as they are, on the basis of mobilizing workers for short-term gains *within* capitalism. This does not negate their role as agencies in class struggle, but it does account for the relative low ordering in their operative priorities usually given to public ownership and controls over capital, let alone to the project of bringing the working class to power in the sense that the bourgeoisie is in power in capitalist society. For this a revolutionary working-class party is a vital necessity. But for this project to be a meaningful one—even if it is directed at a democratic transition via the parliamentary structures of the bourgeois state—it requires above all that the mobilizing institutions of working-class struggle—both the extra-parliamentary party organization and the trade unions—retain their autonomy from the bourgeois state and constitute as such the main basis for building working-class hegemony. Corporatist political structures are incompatible with this basic requirement. The Euro-Communist project, taken seriously, is a hazardous enough project in itself, given this requirement (as was seen in Italy in 1976–9).[40] The social democratic variant of it (Euro-corporatism?) is another thing altogether, although it should serve as a warning light in the construction of revolutionary strategies for a democratic transition.

(1979–80)

Notes

1. As such, Adam Przeworski's definition of democracy is appropriately broader than those of Poulantzas and Therborn, who concentrate on elections and parties: 'Capitalist democracy is a system in which the institutionalization of surplus as the form in which a part of the product becomes withheld from the immediate producers forms the basis for somewhat indeterminate struggles over the distribution of product. The indeterminacy of struggles over the realization of short-term material interests is the condition of hegemony since it leads to the organization of wage-earners as participants in the struggles over distribution and allows their interest to be realized within some limits. Capitalist democracy at the

same time reduces class struggles to struggles over the realization of immediate interests and generates struggles over the immediate interests.' (A. Przeworski, 'Toward a Theory of Capitalist Democracy' (1977) revised and republished in *Capitalism and Social Democracy*, Cambridge 1985, see esp. p. 145.

2. N. Poulantzas, *State, Power, Socialism*, London 1978, p. 238.

3. It is perhaps indicative of the *generality* of the problem here (to avoid appearing partisan) that when Miliband in his latest book also discusses the 'statization' of civil society, the example he concentrates on, like Poulantzas, is the communications industry—already a bourgeois-dominated sphere. See R. Miliband, *Marxism and Politics*, Oxford 1977, pp. 56—7.

4. G. Therborn, *What Does The Ruling Class Do When It Rules?*, London 1978, pp. 57, 89, 107—8.

5. Poulantzas, pp. 224—5.

6. Poulantzas, 'The Capitalist State: A Reply to Miliband and Laclau', *New Left Review*, no. 95, January—February, 1976, p. 69.

7. Cf., in this respect, Giovanni Arrighi's comments on: 'the traditional Marxist point of view that, in the long run, capitalist accumulation tends to engender a progressive weakening of the bargaining position of labour *vis-à-vis* capital—a weakening that can be countered only by a *political* advance of the working class. It is my view that the events of the past decade contradict this point of view. Neither the strength exhibited by the workers' movement during the struggles of the second half of the sixties, which precipitated the crisis, nor the capacity of resistance to the blackmail of unemployment demonstrated as the crisis unfolded during the seventies, can be easily ascribed to factors of *political* consciousness and organization. One can do so only on the basis of the truism that the class struggle is always a political struggle. Otherwise it must be observed that the transformation of the political organizations of the working class into instruments for the containment rather than stimulation and support of industrial conflict has been most rapid and evident precisely during this past decade—without a *significant* simultaneous growth of alterative political organizations'. G. Arrighi, 'Towards a Theory of Capitalist Crisis', *New Left Review*, no. 111, September—October 1978, p. 23.

8. See Ch. 5 above, 'The Development of Corporatism in Liberal Democracies', C. Offe and H. Wiesenthal, 'Two Logics of Collective Action', *Political Power and Social Theory*, no. 1, 1979, and C. Offe, 'The Attribution of Political Status to Interest Groups', in S. Berger (ed.), *Interest Groups in Western Europe*, Cambridge 1981; B. Jessop, 'Corporatism, Parliamentarism and Social Democracy', in P. Schmitter and G. Lehmbruch, *Trends Towards Corporatist Intermediation*, London and Beverly Hills 1979, and 'Capitalism and Democracy: The Best Possible Political Shell?', in G. Littlejohn (ed.), *Power and the State*, London 1978; Nigel Harris, *Competition and Corporate Society*, London 1972; G. Esping-Anderson, Roger Friedland and Erik Olin Wright, 'Modes of Class Struggle and the Capitalist State', *Kapitalistate*, nos. 4—5, Summer 1976.

9. Poulantzas, *State, Power, Socialism*, p. 233. Thus Poulantzas limits the term, *qua* political structure, only to various examples of fascism and corporatist-type military dictatorships. For him 'a corporatist state . . . is an exceptional form of bourgeois state' in which the dominant political role is played by a repressive apparatus ('the fascist party, the army, the political police') distinct from a corporatist bureaucratic administration.'

10. I undertake a critique of these positions in 'Theories of Corporatism: Reflections on a Growth Industry', ch. 6 above. Cf. J. Westergaard, 'Class, Inequality and "Corporatism" ', in A. Hunt (ed.), *Class and Class Structure*, London 1977.

11. The quotation is from Therborn, p. 170. But see in particular Perry Anderson 'The Antinomies of Antonio Gramsci', *New Left Review*, 100, November 1976–January 1977, p. 28.
12. Jessop, pp. 199–200.
13. This point is particularly well made in Offe and Wiesenthal.
14. E. Laclau, *Politics and Ideology in Marxist Theory*, London 1977, p. 21.
15. Keith Middlemas, whose important book on the development of corporatism in Britain tends far too much towards portraying the power of labour and capital as balanced in corporatist structures, has nevertheless come close to capturing the significance of defining the state in terms of struggles over its scope. Referring to the TUC and CBI as 'governing institutions', he writes: 'The modern state is composed not only of government and the state apparatus but includes the governing institutions . . . [But] the governing institutions are not subsumed into a pyramid of authority, within fixed limits of activity, exercising power only in so far as it has been delegated by the state. The state exists effectively in these fields only because they have associated themselves with it; yet they retain . . . freedom always to respond to their own membership (a factor which vitiates, in advance, the "corporate state").' And regarding the continuing struggle over the scope of the state implied in this arrangement he writes: 'Only if that struggle is abandoned is there need to fear the thing which was not buried by the military verdict of 1945, renewed, under another name by governments whose skill at harmonizing clashing wills would ignore or subordinate the institutions' responsiveness to membership which, in the last resort, as much as that of parties, sustains democracy.' *Politics in Industrial Society: The Experience of the British System since 1911*, London 1979, pp. 460–61, 463.
16. G. Esping-Anderson et al., p. 197. Offe and Wiesenthal, and Jessop offer virtually identical formulations.
17. G. Hodgson, *The Economic Background to Unemployment: The 1930s and the 1970s*, A Clause 4 Pamphlet, 52 Dovey Street, Liverpool, n.d.
18. Arrighi, pp. 23–4; compare Ch. 3 above: 'Profits and Politics: Labour and the Crisis of British Capitalism'.
19. A remarkable comparative analysis of post-war bourgeois democracies in these terms is Nixon Apple, 'The Rise and Fall of Full Employment Capitalism', *Studies in Political Economy*, no. 4, Fall 1980. Cf. Bill Warren, 'The State and Capitalist Planning', *New Left Review*, no. 72, March–April 1972.
20. On the US, see especially R. B. Duboff, 'Full Employment: The History of a Receding Target', *Politics and Society*, vol. 7, no. 1, 1977; J. D. Straussman, 'Employment Policy and Job Rationing in Advanced Capitalism', paper delivered at the 1976 Annual Meeting of the American Political Science Association, Chicago 1976; on Italy, see especially V. Foa, 'Incomes Policy: A Crucial Problem for the Unions', *International Socialist Journal*, January 1964; on Germany, see A. Shonfield, *Modern Capitalism*, Oxford 1965, Ch. 12, and W. Müller-Jentsch and Jans-Joachim Sperling, 'Economic Development, Labour Conflicts and the Industrial Relations System in West Germany', in C. Crouch and A. Pizzorno (eds.), *The Resurgence of Class Conflict in Western Europe Since 1968*, vol. 1, London 1978; and on France, see especially J. E. S. Hayward, 'Interest Groups and Incomes Policy in France', *British Journal of Industrial Relations*, no. 4, July 1966.
21. At the same time, however, these unions have been (until recently in Italy, at least) notoriously weak in terms of collective bargaining potential, and their militancy—even at the level of bread and butter demands—has often been more

political in form (one-day general strikes directed at the state) than industrial. Hence, the degree of wage pressure they put on capital—which is the critical factor leading to corporatist political structures—has apart from all else, been weak in any case.

22. Both quotations are from J. Fulcher, 'Class Conflict: Joint Regulation and Its Decline', in R. Scase (ed.) *Reading in the Swedish Class Structure*, Oxford 1976, p. 55.

23. Berndt Ohman, LO *and Labour Market Policy Since the Second World War*, LO Research Report, Prisma 1974, pp. 25–6; see Appendices 1 and 3 for the phenomenal growth of the Labour Market Board.

24. I discuss these events extensively in my *Social Democracy and Industrial Militancy: The Labour Party, the Trade Unions and Incomes Policy 1945—1974*, Cambridge 1976, especially Ch. 7.

25. R. Meidner, *Co-ordination and Solidarity: An Approach to Wages Policy*, LO Research Report, Stockholm 1974, pp. 16–18.

26. Adam Przeworski, 'Material Bases of Consent: Economics and Politics in a Hegemonic System', *Political Power and Social Theory*, no. 1, 1979.

27. Müller-Jentsch and Sperling, pp. 286–7.

28. Poulantzas, *State, Power, Socialism*, p.225.

29. See W. Streek, 'Organizational Consequences of Corporatist Co-operation in West German Labour Unions: A Case Study', Berlin 1978; Fulcher, 'Class Conflict'; and R. Hyman, 'British Trade Unionism in the 1970s', *Studies in Political Economy*, no. 1, 1979.

30. Fulcher, p. 83.

31. Müller-Jentsch and Sperling, p. 292.

32. See Ch. 4 above, 'Socialists and the Labour Party: A Reappraisal', and R. Tarling and F. Wilkinson, 'The Social Contract: Post-War Incomes Policies and Their Inflationary Impact', *Cambridge Journal of Economics*, vol. 1, no. 4, December 1977.

33. Another union delegate, and later a left-Labour MP, Ernie Roberts, came to this conclusion on the basis of his experience with investment planning: 'It is not enough for us to meet and to have generalized discussions in Sectoral Working Parties . . . to be given a mass of paper work, much of which it is difficult enough to find time to read, and the information never really getting down . . . on to the shop floor . . . Competition between employers and industries causes them, by their very nature, to be secretive and uncooperative', TUC, *The Trade Union Role in Industrial Policy, Report of a Conference of Affiliated Unions*, Congress House, London 1977, pp. 33, 43. See also the evidence contained in *State Intervention in Industry: A Workers' Enquiry* (Coventry, Liverpool, Newcastle, N. Tyneside Trades Councils), Newcastle-Upon-Tyne 1980.

34. G. Lehmbruch, 'Liberal Corporatism and Party Government', *Comparative Political Studies*, no. 1, April 1977, p. 109.

35. Fulcher, p. 86.

36. Poulantzas, p. 223.

37. *The Economy, the Government and Trade Union Responsibilities: Joint Statement by the TUC and the Government*, London HMSO, February 1979.

38. Middlemas, p. 460.

39. Meidner, p. 28.

40. Limitations of space have made it impossible here to discuss recent developments in countries which had not by the 1970s developed corporatist structures. Particularly, some authors have asked whether developments in Italy in the 1970s (and not least the participation of the PCI in the 'parliamentary majority' which sustained the

214

Andreotti government between 1976 and 1979) involved laying the foundation for the integration of Italian trade unions in corporatist arrangements. See especially P. Lange, 'Unions, Parties, The State and Liberal Corporatism', *Il Mulino*, 28 November–December 1979; and 'Neo-corporatism in Italy? A Case in European Perspective', paper prepared for the Workshop on Neo-corporatism and Public Policy, Cornell University, Ithaca, New York, April 1980. These should be set in the general discussion offered in P. Lange and S. Tarrow, (eds.), *Italy in Transition: Conflict and Consensus,* London 1979; S. Tarrow, 'Historic Compromise as Popular Front: Italian Communism in the Majority 1976–1979', in H. Machin (ed.), *The End of Eurocommunism?*, London 1981; and I. Regalia et al., 'Labour Conflicts and Industrial Relations in Italy', in Crouch and Pizzorno.

8.

The Importance of Workers' Control for Revolutionary Change

Workers' control, workers' participation, workers' self-management: the vast array of meanings that have been attached to each of these terms, ranging in substantive content from revolutionary to reformist to corporatist conceptions, bespeaks an ambiguity characteristic not merely of a lack of scholarly consensus with regard to these terms, but, more importantly, a lack of common motivation on the part of people who employ them. Often the literature in this field and the debates at conferences on the subject remind one of the strange world which Alice encountered in *Through the Looking Glass*.

> 'I don't know what you mean by glory,' Alice said. Humpty Dumpty smiled contemptuously. 'Of course you don't—till I tell you. I meant there's a nice knock down argument for you!'
> 'But "glory" doesn't mean "a nice knock down argument",' Alice objected.
> When I use a word,' Humpty Dumpty said, in a rather scornful tone, 'it means just what I choose it to mean—neither more nor less.'
> 'The question is,' said Alice, 'whether you *can make words* mean so many different things.'
> 'The question is,' said Humpty Dumpty, 'which is to be master—that's all.'

If one had the freedom of Humpty Dumpty in the use of words, the deliberate employment here of workers' control in counterposition to workers' participation would make little sense. But given the way workers' participation has been used most often in the literature and given the nature of the projects that have been initiated in its name, it becomes clear that this term cannot be bent at will to make it consistent

216

with revolutionary change. For the real question is not who is to be master over words, but who, or rather which class, is to be master in the production process and in the society as a whole. Whatever the good intentions of those who originally employed the term, workers' participation has become absorbed by the capitalist class as part of its own ideology, as an expression of its intention to secure class harmony within capitalism, and it has become recognized as such not only by those associated with revolutionary movements, but also by the more industrially militant sections of the working class. Indeed, one is now reminded almost daily of the validity of the suspicions that many trade unionists have always had of worker's participation as symbolizing the attempt to integrate the working class into capitalist authority structures, limiting the autonomy of indigenous working-class organizations, blunting the thrust of workers in the class struggle. To take but one example close at hand, a foremost advocate in Canada of workers' participation, ex-Postmaster General Bryce Mackasey, not long ago promised to initiate an experiment where postal workers would be allowed to run their own postal plant. 'There is ample room in the Post Office,' he said, 'for a greater degree of participation in the decision-making to a certain degree by the workers.' What is particularly significant about this statement is not the cautious and obvious qualification to participation suggested by 'degree', but rather the *context* in which the statement occurred. The *context* was that of a major attack by Mackasey on the militant Montreal local of the Canadian Union of Postal Workers, which had been engaged in both official and unofficial strike action against the Post Office's hiring of casual labour and its unilateral introduction of new technology which entailed the elimination of jobs and the imposition of lower rates of pay, but which was not subject to negotiation. The context for Mackasey's participation scheme was his suspension of eighty militant workers, his broader attack on 'hoodlum' and 'radical' elements in the union whom he considered responsible for 'the erosion of managerial rights', and his warning that until these workers were 'weeded out of the Post Office and the managerial rights are once more enforced . . . we will continue to have trouble in that particular area'.[1] Workers' participation is safe, it appears, because it is granted from above, not taken from below.

This particular example of workers' participation as a cover for the consolidation of 'managerial rights' through the concurrent suppression of the most militant sections of the working class is of course symptomatic of a general development in post-war capitalist societies. It perhaps reached its crescendo in Gaullist 'participation' to counter the spontaneous and potentially revolutionary occupation of the factories during the French May 1968, but its origins go back much further. A most candid and concise definition of the capitalist, and hence in our societies, of the *dominant* meaning of workers' participation, was offered as early as 1950 by Aubrey Jones, then a British Conservative MP, who became more widely known fifteen years later as one of the key architects of the British Labour government's notorious incomes policy. 'Authority remains with the employer; it is he who still controls. But those who are controlled are taken into his confidence; their views are solicited; and so the control, by becoming less of an imposition, is made to operate more effectively.'[2]

Capitalist interest in workers' participation at the workplace level in the post-war period is in fact closely associated with the emergence within liberal democracy of neo-corporatist structures at the national level, such as indicative planning and incomes policies, designed to induce trade unions to act as agencies of social control over their members. The origins of this neo-corporatist development can be generally traced to the potential dislocations in capitalist economies which attended the introduction of Keynesian reforms, particularly the problem that arose with the 'guarantee' of full employment and the apparent consequent loss of the socio-economic functions performed within capitalism by the reserve army of labour. For instance, a prescient article in *The Times* of London (23 January 1943) contended that the fear of unemployment was an 'essential mechanism' of the private-enterprise economy, which maintained 'the authority of master over man'. During the war a substitute for this mechanism had been found in 'appeals of patriotism' but 'in peacetime with full employment the worker would have no counterweight against feeling that he is employed merely to make profits for the firm, and that he is under no obligation to refrain from using his newly found freedom from fear to snatch every advantage he can'. As a solution to the problem, the article recommended a 'middle course' between 'fascism and socialism', whereby a range of policies including some nationalization, price and profit controls, social security programmes, and workers' councils would combine 'to produce a situation in which workers would be prepared to accept discipline to a necessary and reasonable extent'. In the form of union participation with business and government representatives in economic planning and incomes policies at the national political level, and in the form of workers' minority representation on the boards of public corporations and 'human relations' techniques on the factory floor, this course has been followed with varying scope and emphasis according to the requirements and conditions of different capitalist countries. Nevertheless, although this neo-corporatist thrust no doubt contributed to blunting revolutionary trends, it has not secured the economic stability which was its aim. The continued struggle for higher wages and income redistribution via collective bargaining (increasingly sanctioned by unofficial rank-and-file strike action), the repeated breakdown of incomes policies and the repudiation of union leaders associated with them, the rejection or indifference on the part of workers to *Mitbestimmung* and its sorry variants, are indicative of the impossibility of achieving class harmony within and through corporatist structures. The neo-corporatist project has proven inherently unstable, a testament to the continuing contradictions of a society where even the best-intentioned of reforms must be accommodated to the primary needs of maintaining and fostering private capital accumulation.

In a conscious attempt to divorce themselves from the neo-corporatist element in workers' participation, many proponents of workers' control have adopted the term 'workers' self-management' to indicate their belief that workers can take over the running of production only in the context of a socialist society. This has given rise to a significant and large literature on possible models for a self-managed socialist economy, reflecting a desire to offer a vision of a democratic socialist future and a commitment to examining the theoretical requirements of such a system. To the extent that this literature examines rigorously what is certainly one of the key problems of socialist praxis—how comprehensive planning can be married to grassroots autonomy—the contribution it can make is immense. Where it seeks not to counterpose socialism to democracy but to achieve theoretically a synthesis between the two, so that one is inconceivable without the other, it may be located squarely in the finest tradition of Marxism. For, as Hal Draper has recently observed:

> The characteristic answer to the problem [of democracy] emerging from Marx's theory was already located in his notebook critique of Hegel's philosophy of right, where he sought to show that 'true democracy' requires a new social content—socialism, and it will be rounded off with his analysis of the Paris Commune, which showed that a state with a new social content entailed truly democratic forms. Marx's theory moves in the direction of *defining consistent democracy in socialist terms, and consistent socialism in democratic terms.* The task of theory, then, is not to adjudicate a clash between the two considerations (a hopeless job once the problem is seen in that light), but rather to grasp the social dynamic of the situation under which the apparent contradiction between the two is resolved.[3]

There is, however, an inherent danger in writings on self-management, a danger that any discussion of post-revolutionary structures must avoid — that of utopianism. What even the most sophisticated discussions of the relationship between state, party and self-managed enterprise must guard against is a tendency to theoretical abstraction, above all a failure to consider the role that the actual revolutionary process and the relationship between party and producer groups in that process will have in post-revolutionary structures. There is, in this sense, a certain idealist current running through models— even 'transitional' models—of self-management which omits the historical dynamic so central to Marxist analysis and fails to examine whether and how the contradictions of existing society and the political forces operating within them will facilitate self-managed socialism. If self-management is to come about as a real phenomenon it will require a social base to support it; it will have to grow out of the concrete activity of the working class. There must be, at a minimum, a leading element of the rank and file that will infuse the revolutionary process with workers' control, that will have the strength to fight for it within the revolutionary party. Without this, all the models of 'pluralism' within post-revolutionary structures are of little worth, as is a theoretical insistence that socialized property not be state property.

This is not simply a critique of work on self-management for leaving out certain questions which might be answered in terms of one writer not being able to cover everything. The point is rather that unless the question of revolutionary praxis is addressed, the discussion of post-revolutionary structures is like drawing figures in the air. In so far as the discussion is concerned with new structures only, and omits the question of how revolutionary praxis changes the men and women who occupy them, it will often appear that certain attributes of our present society are endemic to all history. Before assuming, for instance, that the conflict between producer, consumer and citizen roles, which are so symptomatic of the alienation of our present-day existence, is the key question to be resolved through post-revolutionary structures, one ought to consider the integration that might take place in this respect in the course of revolutionary practice by the working class. Indeed, unless one takes this into consideration, the prospects of disillusionment are particularly great. This was exemplified in the historic exchange of open letters between Edward Thompson and Lesjek Kolakowski, where Thompson upbraided Kolakowski for his cynicism regarding the socialist project in the United States. 'Let us imagine', Kolakowski suggested with acerbity, 'what the dictatorship of the proletariat' would mean if the (real not imaginary) working class took over exclusive political power now in the United States.' To which Thompson countered:

> The absurdity of the question appears (in your view) to provide its own answer. But I doubt whether you have given to the question a moment of serious historical imagination: you have simply assumed a white working class, socialized by capitalist institutions as it is now, mystified by the news media as it is now, structured into competitive organizations as it is now, without self-activity or its own forms of political expression: i.e., a working class with all the attributes of subjection within capitalist structures which one then 'imagines' to achieve power without changing either those structures *or itself*: which is, I fear, a typical example of the fixity of concept which characterizes much capitalist ideology.[4]

In so far as the literature of self-management considers new structures, it avoids this tragic pitfall; in so far as it *fails also* to consider how the working class changes itself in the struggle to establish these new structures, it falls into it as well.

The defects of both workers' participation and workers' self-management can be avoided through a conception of workers' control that places it within the context of the revolutionary process and understands that process as involving a change in the working class itself through its struggle for hegemony. This view of workers' control was the one taken by André Gorz for whom 'workers' control is not an end in itself. It is mainly a means or method, a means whose true significance can be understood only if we place it in a strategic perspective of social and political revolution'. Thus ongoing workers' struggles for obtaining sufficient power on the factory floor to refuse speed-ups, arbitrary redefinitions of work rules, skills, and rates, etc., must be treated as more than a negation of capitalist authority structures. They must be practically connected with a revolutionary affirmation of workers' power. Today's struggles against the authoritarian factory system must become one moment in the broader assertion 'of the capability of workers to take control of the process of production and to organize the working process as *they* think best. To organize the work process in such a way as to stop it from being oppressive, mutilating, soul-destroying and health-destroying; to organize it to allow for the maximum display of each worker's initiative, responsibility, creativity; to organize it to replace forced labor and authoritarian division of labor by free cooperation.'[5]

Among the 'classic' Marxist writings of this century, the work of Antonio Gramsci stands out precisely because of its recognition of the importance of workers' self-education and self-change *through* the assertion of workers' control. Although most people versed in the workers' control literature are best acquainted with Gramsci's early articles on the role of factory councils, Gramsci's later work, although more explicitly oriented toward the need for a disciplined revolutionary party, did not depart from this focus, placing particular stress on the necessity for working-class cultural hegemony *before* the revolution, and on overcoming the gap between revolutionary intellectuals on the one hand and workers on the other through the medium of the 'organic' working-class intellectual.[6] Gramsci's view, moreover, was that this process, which had to begin in the factories, would not remain confined there, but would extend beyond it to the working-class neighbourhood to overcome the alienating division of the individual into producer, consumer, and citizen. He proposed, therefore, the creation of ward committees composed of delegates of all categories of workers residing in a ward. This 'knits together and centralizes all the proletarian energies of the ward' and 'should be an expression of the whole working class living in the ward'. This indigenous system of workers' democracy within, and in counterposition to, capitalism, 'whose power will be delegated by free election, not imposed in authoritarian fashion', would not only 'give a permanent form and discipline to the masses', but would also be 'a magnificent school of political and administrative experience'. The task of workers' control was thus not just economic and political, but *cultural* in the deepest sense of that word: 'Assemblies held within the workshop, and ceaseless propaganda and persuasion by the most conscious elements, should radically transform the workers' psychology. It should increase the readiness and capacity of the masses for the exercise of power, and diffuse consciousness of the rights and duties of comrade and worker that is concrete and effective, since it has been spontaneously generated from living historical experience.'

Gramsci placed such emphasis on the cultural and education factor precisely because he realized long before the tragedy of Stalinism made this readily apparent, that there was a dangerous tendency in Communist theory and practice to divide the revolution into two separate elements: the destruction of the bourgeois state first, and *after* that the creation of a new liberated social order. But for Gramsci the revolution was indivisible: 'The revolution is not necessarily proletarian and Communist if it proposes and obtains the overthrow of the political government of the bourgeoisie . . . [or] even if the wave of popular insurrection places power in the hands of men who call themselves (and sincerely are) Communists.' Instead:

> The revolution as the conquest of social power for the proletariat can only be conceived as a dialectical process in which political power makes possible industrial power and industrial power political power . . . The factory council, as a form of producers' autonomy in the industrial field and as the basis of Communist economic organization, is the instrument of a mortal struggle against the capitalist regime insofar as it creates the conditions in which class-divided society is suppressed and any new class division is rendered 'materially' impossible . . . To the extent that it can be achieved by party action, it is necessary to create the conditions in which there will be not two revolutions, but in which the popular revolt against the bourgeois state will be able to find the organizational forces capable of beginning the transformation of the national apparatus of production from an instrument of plutocratic oppression to an instrument of Communist liberation.

As this suggests, those who take inspiration from Gramsci would be wrong to counterpose the movement of workers' control to the need for a revolutionary party. Without a revolutionary party to catalyse, generalize and raise to the national political level the struggle for workers' power, demands for workers' control at the industrial level will suffer the same problems as trade-union activity; that is, they will remain sporadic, defensive, and localized. Factory consciousness may represent a 'higher' level than trade-union consciousness, but it too must be distinguished from class consciousness. There has been an unfortunate tendency among many, given the failures and betrayals of working-class parties, to glorify spontaneity and ignore leadership. Yet recent examples of spontaneous shop-floor action only underline the classic case for a revolutionary party which can integrate the totality of working-class experience and demands. What one must ensure, as Gramsci was concerned to ensure, is that it will be 'a party of the masses who want to free themselves from political and industrial slavery autonomously, by their own efforts, through the organization of the social economy, and not a party which uses the masses for its own heroic attempts to imitate the French Jacobins'.

This is much easier to say than do, of course, and to speak of the need for a mass revolutionary party is not to suggest that we abandon all else to rush headlong into party formation. Such a conclusion, particularly in the context of a society without a strong proletarian sub-culture, would only lead to the further proliferation of political *groupuscules*.

Before the task of party formation is addressed in immediate terms rather than as an orienting goal, we must ask with Gramsci whether

> a Communist Party [can] really exist (one which is an active party not an academy of doctrinaires and petty politicians who think and express themselves 'well' where Communism is concerned) if the masses do not have the spirit of historical initiative and the aspiration toward industrial autonomy that should be reflected and synthesized in the Communist Party? Since the formation of a party and the emergence of real historical forces of which parties are the reflections do not occur all at once out of nothing, but according to a dialectical process, is not the major task of the Communist forces precisely that of giving consciousness and organization to the essentially Communist productive forces that must be developed and by their growth will cause the secure and lasting economic base of the political power of the proletariat?

One must, perhaps, move even one step further back than this at our present stage. Gramsci's efforts, in the context of Italy in 1919, to foster the development of workers' councils preliminary to the formation of a revolutionary party, made hard sense and his proposals were taken up with alacrity by the workers. But in the present context of Western societies, such a programme would certainly fall on deaf ears, its adventurist air would be clear, its presumptuousness obvious. Where the conceptions of workers' control and of a mass revolutionary party require much development to take root among the mass of workers, it is imperative for revolutionary socialists to locate themselves and their deliberations in the concrete activities and struggles of the working class. This means supporting workers' control demands when they arise, aiding spontaneous rank-and-file action, working with militant workers to overcome organized false consciousness in the official union movement. It does not mean, however, writing off all traditional union activity. A recognition of the limitation of trade unionism as a structural reflection of capitalist authority relations, which seeks to bargain over the price of wage labour but not overcome it, is a *sine qua non* of revolutionary socialism. Equally imperative, however, is a recognition of the dialectical nature of trade unionism, of its position as an indigenous working-class oppositional structure within capitalism. As the shop stewards' movement in Britain and its effect on official trade unionism has shown, the parameters of militant trade-union action are broader than was thought to be the case by many post-war theorists of union integration. While admitting the structural limitations of even militant trade unionism, we must also perceive that it is the soil in which movements for autonomous rank-and-file organizations and mass revolutionary parties can take root.

When we seek to understand workers' control as part of the revolutionary process, when we try to locate the concept in the tradition of the classic Marxist debates on spontaneity and leadership, mass and party, appropriately sober and modest conclusions emerge. The most important of these is that workers' control groups must not merely engage in abstract or future-oriented discussion, but must take their place in the concrete ongoing struggles of the working class. The contribution such groups can make to these struggles and the experience they can gain from them will help lay the basis for the day when workers' councils and mass revolutionary parties will not be orienting goals but immediate tasks to undertake.

(1975)

Notes

1. *The Globe and Mail*, Toronto, 26 May 1975.
2. A. Jones, *Industrial Order*, London 1950, p. 31.
3. Hal Draper, 'Marx on Democratic Forms of Government' in R. Miliband and J. Saville (eds.), *The Socialist Register 1974*, London 1974, p. 102. For a similar view of this question as 'perhaps the central problem of socialist theory and practice' compare in the same volume, Richard Hyman, 'Workers' Control and Revolutionary Theory', especially p. 253.
4. Edward Thompson, 'An Open Letter to Lesjek Kolakowski', in R. Miliband and J. Saville (eds.), *The Socialist Register 1973*, London 1974, pp. 99–100, n. 69; emphasis added.
5. André Gorz, 'Workers' Control Is More Than Just That', in Gerry Hunnius and G. David Garson (eds.), *Workers' Control: A Reader on Labor and Social Change*, New York 1973, pp. 326–39. For a distinction similar to that employed here between workers' participation, workers' self-management, and workers' control, compare in the same collection, John Case, 'Workers' Control: Toward a North American Movement', especially p. 444. (It must be noted that Gorz's own views on the potential of the working class have changed markedly over the past decade. See his *Farewell to The Working Class*, Boston 1982.)
6. For his early articles see 'Soviets in Italy, *New Left Review*, no. 51, September–October, 1968, pp. 28–58; later writings are collected in *Selections from the Prison Notebooks*, London 1971. The quotations used here are all from 'Soviets in Italy'.

9.
The State and the Future of Socialism

I

In being asked to initiate a discussion on the role of the state in the future of socialism in Europe, one is immediately put in the position of having to decide whether one ought to address the question of the devil or the question of the deep blue sea. That is, should one concentrate on the role of the bourgeois state *vis-à-vis* the future of socialism, that is, its role in seeking to foreclose or forestall that future? Or should one address the question of the socialist state of the future, of the role of the state in the transition to socialism and under socialism? For a number of reasons it is tempting to discuss the devil we know, that is, the existing bourgeois state, rather than embark upon the deep, uncharted waters of the socialist state, even the transitional socialist state, of the future. For one, in terms of personal capacities, my own research and writing has heretofore been much more concentrated on the state of advanced capitalism. For another, the recent advances that have been made in Marxism on the theory of the state have almost exclusively been concerned with the bourgeois state. Thirdly, in the immediate future, the pressing question before revolutionary socialists remains how to combat the bourgeois state, or how to operate within it, if we follow the Eurocommunist perspective, until such time as sufficient mass support is created to embark on a socialist transition. Yet however tempting this course of approach to the topic, it would be a mistake to stop at this. This is not only because our hosts clearly intended that this colloquium begin to chart those deep, blue waters, but also because it is of great importance that this be done both in the interests of Marxist political science and in the interests of the working-class revolutionary movement. However much more needs to be done in addressing the question of the bourgeois state, the very progress that has been made has underlined the great lacunae in Marxism of systematic theorization of the state under socialism, both of the nature of the state in 'actually existing socialism' as Rudolf Bahro has appropriately called the societies of Eastern Europe, and of the possible 'institutional forms of *socialist democracy* in the West'.[1] Nor is this, of course, simply a theoretical requirement, it is also a strategic one. For if the socialist movement in the West is to move effectively towards a socialist future it has to distinguish itself from 'actually existing socialism' in terms of concrete possibilities and expectations. The choice of a democratic road towards state power over an insurrectionary one, as in the case of so-called Eurocommunism, is in this sense but a minor step. Beyond it lies the enormous question of the mode of proletarian rule after the stage of participation of communist parties in the bourgeois state via the 'historic compromise'. If the democratic socialist alternative is to be an effective one, it will have to address itself credibly to this question. With all of these considerations in mind, I will talk both about the devil and the deep blue sea, well aware that in the process I may deal with neither satisfactorily. I will restrict myself to Western capitalist countries, and to the future of socialism in these countries.

Let us turn first to the question of the role of the capitalist state in forestalling or foreclosing the future of socialism. Here one is really addressing not simply the repressive role of the state at the moment of a particular or hypothetical revolutionary conjuncture, but much more broadly, the general mode of operation of the state in capitalist society: the way in which it sustains accumulation, integrates or represses class conflict, reproduces social relations, represents the dominant classes, in short, the role of the state in maintaining the capitalist mode of production. If, in the outpouring of Marxist writings on the capitalist state in the last decade, there is one concept above all that has gained general currency in this respect, it is the concept of 'relative autonomy'. This concept embodies the notion that the state is not a mere agent of the ruling class, but has to be seen as acting independently on its behalf, uniting its various competing fractions, and is itself situated not in relation to the ruling class alone but within the entire field of class struggle. Although this conceptualization can be shown to have been constructed to a substantial extent out of Marx's own writings (not least in *Capital* as I have argued before),[2] most people would probably agree that it is the concept of 'relative autonomy' that has above all stood out as marking a break, or at least an advance, between recent Marxist theories of the state and the traditional approach to the subject, which interpreted Marx in terms of seeing the state as an instrument, a tool of the bourgeoisie.

Yet, there is, I think, a far more significant common departure from classical Marxist notions of the state in the recent theorizations. And that is the tendency away from seeing the state primarily, or at least in its predominant aspect, as consisting mainly as Lenin, after Engels, put it, of 'special bodies of armed men'.[3] There can be no doubt that Marx and Engels laid very great stress not only on the state as a class organization, but on the state as a *repressive* class organization, stressing the *overtly* coercive aspect (a standing army, prisons, police, 'institutions of coercion of all kinds') as the salient instruments of state power. Not just domination by one class over another, but actual physical force, is at the centre here. When Marx and Engels speak of the withering away of the state, as we shall see below, it is not to public authority they are referring, but to *repression* as a mode of rule. To use the currently fashionable functionalist terminology among Marxist theoreticians of the state (now shared by Mandel, Miliband, Poulantzas, O'Connor, and Offe), the accent in classical Marxism clearly falls on the 'coercion function' of the state, as opposed to the 'legitimation' or 'accumulation functions'.

The accent in recent theorizations on the other hand, falls clearly on 'legitimation', or 'consent', in contrast to coercion. The reason for this is not hard to find; it lies in the periodization of these theories, in their evolution in the context of the emergence in this century, and especially since the First World War, of the liberal democratic state system as, in Anderson's terms, 'the normal mode of capitalist power in the advanced countries'. There remains considerable disagreement, of course, as to the primary means by which this consent is created. Some stress the role of cultural institutions in fashioning ideological hegemony, whether those are seen as part of the state (as with the ideological state apparatuses) or more properly as extra-state agencies facilitating the state's legitimation function. Others would stress the integrative role served by welfare reforms; still others the direct incorporation of legitimation within the state's expanded accumulation function in the form of accumulation providing its own legitimation via promises of growth and full employment. Anderson has, in my view, gone to the core of the matter in his argument that 'the novelty of this consent is that it takes the fundamental form of a belief by the masses that *they exercise an ultimate self-determination* within the existing social order'.

> The general form of the representative state—bourgeois democracy—is itself the principal ideological lynchpin of Western capitalism, whose very existence deprives the working class of the idea of socialism *as a different type of state* . . . The economic divisions within the 'citizenry' are masked by the juridical parity between exploiters and exploited, and with them the complete separation and *non-participation* of the masses in the work of parliament. This separation is then constantly presented and represented to the masses as the ultimate incarnation of liberty: 'democracy' as the terminal point of history. The existence of the parliamentary state thus constitutes the formal framework of all other ideological mechanisms of the ruling class. It provides the general code in which every specific message elsewhere is transmitted. The code is all the more powerful because the juridical rights of citizenship are not a mere mirage: on the contrary, the civic freedoms and suffrages of bourgeois democracy are a tangible reality, whose completion was historically in part the work of the labour movement itself, and whose loss would be a momentous defeat for the working class.[4]

The importance of this formulation is that it locates the production of cultural domination at the very centre of the state system itself. Coercion is not left out, but it is displaced from a central role in the day-to-day functioning of the state to the revolutionary conjuncture, at which point coercion, via the army, becomes both 'determinant and dominant in the supreme crisis', including any serious, albeit naive, attempt to legislate socialism peacefully from Parliament. In this last respect, Anderson is much more categorical than Marx, who admitted the possibility of a peaceful transition in the exceptional conditions of America and England, or contemporary theorists like Althusser who suggest that where the balance of class forces is particularly favourable 'a peaceful and even democratic transition becomes possible and necessary'.[5]

It is not my brief at this point to adjudicate between these positions. It is rather to point out that the general stress laid in recent Marxist theorizations on the legitimation function of the state, when taken together with the current debate on the Eurocommunist strategy, may have the effect of limiting our perception of the coercive function of the state solely to the question of the revolutionary conjuncture, to the detriment of our perception of the role state coercion is again coming increasingly to play in the normal day-to-day operation of the capitalist state.

The stress that Anderson and Therborn have recently put on the representative nature of the bourgeois state, and on the labour movement's role in securing this, is consistent with Marx's and Engels's approach to the question of democratization in the bourgeois republic. They too stressed the need for the labour movement to work towards the 'maximization of the weight in the government structure of the representative system',[6] while continuing to develop revolutionary strategy to pass out of this state system. But if the representative form has become the general mode of capitalist rule in our time, as it was not for Marx and Engels, it must also be recognized that the same intrastate dynamic that Marx and Engels observed for the particular representative forms they encountered has been replicated now *generally* in the capitalist states: that is, the domination of the executive arm of the state *over* the legislature. The reasons for this are too complex to be gone into here; they have to do with the concomitant emergence of mass parties with extensive party discipline, and with the development of the state's accumulation function which places emphasis on direct ties with business and technical bureaucratic 'expertise' in capitalist planning. In any case, the objective 'decline of Parliament' within the state system must have implications for the centrality of Parliament in cultural domination. The extent to which this has been the case may be seen in the widespread emergence of corporatist structures within liberal democracies, whereby legitimation for state policy is secured through the attempted integration of the industrial class organizations of labour with the state. Here the juridical equality between citizens in the state is supplemented by the formal equality of status granted to the central organizations of labour and capital *vis-à-vis* the state. But these corporatist structures have proven within recent years to be unstable, as the unions have repeatedly been forced to opt out of co-operative behaviour within them in the face of rank-and-file militancy. The fact that these corporatist forms have been tied to the state's accumulation function, particularly in terms of union co-operation in incomes policies, has served to delegitimate the union leadership in so far as they participate actively in wage restraint.[7]

Increasingly, the state's response to this development has been a coercive one *vis-à-vis* unions as free associations, at least in the form of repressing rank-and-file actions and legally insulating union leadership from its effects. In the face of strong union opposition, this trend to coercion against the freedom of unions as indigenous class organizations has not yet been effective. To make it stick, in the face of an organized working class mobilized against these coercive measures, would involve the extensive use of police powers, and probably severe limitation of free speech and assembly. Capitalist states have refrained from this heretofore, but in the face of the continued economic difficulties of advanced capitalism, particularly the simultaneous experience of high wage pressure, unemployment and inflation, and in the absence of political movement which would incorporate and transcend rank-and-file industrial militancy, an authoritarian turn toward the 'strong state', even while maintaining the shell of liberal democracy, seems a likely development.

It is possible, in other words, that the accent placed on the legitimation function over the repression function of the modern bourgeois state will come to be seen not as characteristic of the normal mode of bourgeois rule, but as corresponding only with a very specific period in capitalism's history. Of course, the scenario we have sketched applies less to countries like Italy and France, where the main arena of working-class integration *vis-à-vis* the state is the parliamentary one, than to countries like Britain and Sweden, where parliamentarist integration has been supplemented by the corporatist structures of the state. The difference is clearly a product of the relative dominance of social democracy; although it is at least arguable that the eventual entry of Communist parties into governments of the bourgeois state would establish a basis for corporatist developments in Italy and France, if the socialist project were not to be carried through. In both cases, however, it appears that the state's response to the contradictions posed by class struggle of a dimension which threatens the stability of the system is a coercive one. In the Eurocommunist case, this appears in the form of the likely response of the state to an attempt actually to carry through the socialist project via Parliament. In the social democratic case, it appears in the form of a state response to a tenacious industrial militancy which becomes the main channel of struggle in the absence of effective *political* representation of the working-class interests. In the former case, the turn to coercion will likely be more spectacular when it comes; in the latter, it will come more gradually and insidiously.

The timing and the actual successful accomplishment of such a shift back toward coercion as the dominant aspect of the state will, of course, entirely depend on the particular balance of class forces in each country, as well as internationally. It is thus by no means a foregone conclusion. But to stress again the coercive function of the capitalist state in the face of intractable working-class pressures serves at least as a warning against simplistic assumptions about the ease of a transition to socialism via either the parliamentary or corporatist structures of the advanced capitalist state. It is a reminder of the state's coercive role in forestalling or foreclosing the future of socialism. This does not obviate the need to theorize about the institutional framework of the democratic socialist state of the future, for the reasons already given, but it does serve, as we move to consider this, to place it in an appropriate context.

II

There are two grave dangers—one utopian, the other cynical—which must be avoided in undertaking any consideration of the institutional forms of the socialism of the future. There is first of all the danger, represented not only in traditional utopian thought, but also, I believe, in a great deal of the socialist self-management literature, of drawing models of democratic socialism, blueprints of the future, without consideration of the revolutionary process which will give rise to them and will compose their indissoluble elements in a transitional period. They tell us that people change and institutions change and that relations among them change, but they rarely tell us how, and thus ignore the question of what constraints the process of change will impose on their abstract, even if detailed, models. A second danger is seen in the tendency to assume a revolution, but in constructing a vision of the post-revolutionary social and political matrix, to assume that people and their institutions have not changed in the process of making the revolution.

It will been seen that what both utopian and cynical conceptions of socialism leave out is the *political* process of revolution itself. The great contribution of Marx in this respect was not only (as the economic determinists would have it) to have located the economic contradictions of one mode of production which will lead to its replacement by another which grows out of these contradictions, but also to have laid particular stress on the role of *struggle*, making the possibility of socialism *contingent* on struggle, rejecting the idea of transition from one form of society to another as an automatic process without revolutionary intervention. For Marx the very *definition* of socialism is only completed in the process of struggle: 'What we have to deal with here is a communist society, not as it has *developed* on its own foundations, but, on the contrary, just as it *emerges* from capitalist society; which is then in every respect, economically, morally and intellectually, still stamped with the birth marks of the old society from which it emerges.'[8] Moreover, a pre-condition for socialism is a particular kind of consciousness, which cannot be developed outside the struggle for socialism itself. 'Both for the production on a mass scale of this communist consciousness, and for the success of the exercise itself, the alteration of men on a mass scale is necessary, an alteration which can only take place in a practical movement, a *revolution*: the revolution is necessary, therefore not only because the *ruling* class cannot be overthrown in any other way, but also because the class *overthrowing* it can only in a revolution succeed in ridding itself of all the muck of ages and become fitted to found society anew.'[9]

If we are going to begin seriously addressing the question of the institutional forms of socialist democracy, therefore, we will have to do it not abstractly but in direct relation to the organizations and strategies of the working class with the allied groups who are engaged in the revolutionary process. It is with this in mind that the remainder of this paper will examine the three main conceptual elements of the Marxist theory of the socialist state: the smashing of the bourgeois state, the dictatorship of the proletariat and the withering away of the state. There are those who consider each of these inviolable and unproblematic scientific concepts. It will be immediately apparent that I do not.

Let us begin not at the beginning, but at the end, with the withering away of the state. We begin here not because it is easiest to deal with, being the furthest removed and the most contingent on unforeseeable actual historical developments, but because the acceptance of the ultimate stateless character of communism has fostered an unfortunate tendency to consider the question of the state in the transition of only secondary importance, and has thus interfered with rigorous consideration of the socialist state at all in Marxist theory. In my reading, at least of Marx and Engels in their maturity, the withering away of the state had a very special meaning which is not adequately captured by the phrase in question. It meant not the end of public authority in society but the end of class *repression* as embodied in the state. A great deal depends here on definitions of terms and on translations from the German, of course. But it seems to me incontrovertible, despite various inconsistent and loose usages of terminology, that Marx and Engels did not see the state as simply a repressive and coercive apparatus, but as also encompassing other functions, which would continue to be exercised by public authority in a fully communist society. These common functions are encompassed by 'the state of class society'; it colours them, absorbs them, structures them in the context of its primary role of maintaining ruling class domination, but it nevertheless contains them. A basic example of this may be seen in the state's role in the prevention and containment of epidemics. The state's action in this regard is structured by the form of production of medical goods and services, by the inequality of access to them, by the great differences in living conditions among the classes, all of which the state helps to reproduce while dealing with disease. But the particular function remains none the less and will remain in communist society.

No other interpretation can be given to the many, albeit largely incidental, references in Marx's and Engels's writings to the 'legitimate functions of the old government power' (*The Civil War in France*) or to the 'social functions [of the state in communist society] that are analogous to present state functions' (*Critique of the Gotha Programme*).[10] In the third volume of *Capital*, Marx explicitly refers to how even in 'despotic states, supervision and all-round interference by the government involves both the performance of common activities arising from the nature of all communities, and the specific functions arising from the antithesis between the government and the mass of the people'.[11] And as Draper has pointed out in this regard, even Engels's approach to the origins of the state contains this perspective. The state arises 'only after the division of society into classes, and because of this division: but it does not arise out of the whole cloth. It has its roots in activities and *offices* in non-class society.'[12] The 'special bodies of armed men' do not arise out of nothing, but on the basis already established in the primitive community whereby, as Engels put in *Anti-Dühring*, the safeguarding of common interests ('adjudication of disputes: repression of abuse of authority by individuals; control of water supplies', even 'religious functions') were 'handed over to individuals, true, under the control of the community as a whole . . . They were naturally endowed with a certain measure of authority and are *the beginnings of state power.*'[13]

One could go on, but there is no need to further belabour the point. The question remains, however, of what institutional form this public authority of full communist society is to take. Marx properly refused to be drawn into detailed blueprints for this, but it is arguable that general phrases like the 'simple administration of things', and the 'superintendance of production' or the refusal to consider this public authority as political in order to distinguish it from class rule, obscured rather than clarified the basic point involved. At one point at least,

Marx, in his disputation with Bakunin, did refuse to quibble over words
and suggested the issue should be formulated precisely: '. . . what form
the administrative function can take on the basis of this workers' state,
if he wants to call it that.'[14] And when one comes to examine Marx's
impression of the framework of this 'workers state', it soon becomes
clear that what is involved is not so simple. There are offices of public
authority involved. They are highly decentralized, elective, their occupants are not career bureaucrats but there is none the less a public
authority embodied in actual institutional forms, and based on a highly
sophisticated set of electoral devices, although the 'election has none of
its present political character'. Engels makes the point even clearer: 'on
the one hand, a certain authority, no matter how delegated, and, on the
other hand, a certain subordination, are things which, independently of
all social organization, are imposed upon us with the material conditions under which we produce and make products circulate'. To be
sure, 'the social organization of the future would restrict authority solely
to the limits within which conditions of production render it inevitable',[15] but this does not alter the basic point. Marx and Engels clearly
had the impression that this authority and subordination could be non-
repressive and based on fully voluntary consent in a non-class communist society. In this sense, it would be 'in the interests of society' and
not separated from society. But politics and the state, understood as
representative public authority, and not as class repression, remains.
  Althusser has properly made the same point with regard to ideology:

> it is clear that ideology [as a system of mass representations] is indispensable
> in any society if men are to be reformed, transformed and equipped to
> respond to the demands of their conditions of existence . . . In a class society
> ideology is the relay whereby, and the element in which, the relation between
> men and their conditions of existence is settled to the profit of the ruling
> class. In a classless society ideology is the relay whereby, and the element in
> which, the relations between men and their conditions of existence is lived to
> the profit of all men.[16]

So it must be with politics and the state, and Marx's and Engels's
general refusal to use the terms as applied to communist society only has
obscured our understanding of this. It has contributed, moreover, to
failing to ask of the transition to socialism, not only how the political
forms appropriate to it will render a non-class society, but how they will
in turn develop institutions appropriate for the exercise of public
authority in non-class society itself. With this in mind, we may turn to

the questions posed by the 'dictatorship of the proletariat' and 'the smashing of the bourgeois state' in the transitional period.

The 'dictatorship of the proletariat' has been much in the news recently by virtue of its rejection by the Twenty-Second Congress of the PCF (French Communist Party) and its abandonment by 'Eurocommunism' generally. Yet it must be said that it is the core concept in the Marxist theory of the transitional state. The question is, to what extent is it true, as Althusser has argued,[17] that this is a scientific concept which cannot be abandoned by Marxism in theory or practice? The dictatorship of the proletariat expresses two fundamental aspects of Marxist theory, both of which are essential to mark it off from social democracy. The first is that it expresses the idea of the working class coming to power in the same sense that the bourgeoisie is in power in capitalist society, as a hegemonic class. Social democracy rejects this above all in Marxism, defining socialism not in terms of the conquest of power by the working class, but rather in terms of class co-operation. Although it was by no means apparent at the turn of the century, the immortal words of Ramsay MacDonald have come to express fundamentally the perspective of social democracy as we now know it: 'Socialism marks the growth of society, not the uprising of class. The consciousness it seeks to quicken is not one of economic class solidarity, but one of social unity. The watchword of socialism therefore, is not class consciousness but community consciousness.'[18] The dictatorship of the proletariat, expressing hegemonic working-class rule, and a working-class state, in the same sense as we speak of the bourgeois state, is not in this light to be readily abandoned.

The concept expresses more than simply class domination, however. It also refers to the fundamental nature of the state as Marx and Engels saw it in a class society. The accent, from the point of view of class struggle in the transitional socialist society, falls on the repressive, coercive function of the state, just as it did in their conception of the capitalist state. The reason for this, as Marx again and again pointed out, was to 'gain time', to 'appeal for a time to force', which was 'the first *desideratum*—for permanent action'.[19] Engels again made it crystal clear: 'A revolution is certainly the most authoritarian thing there is; it is the act whereby one part of the population imposes its will upon the other part by means of rifles, bayonets and cannon—authoritarian means if such there be at all; and if the victorious party does not want to have fought in vain, it must maintain this rule by means of the terror which its arms inspire in the reactionaries.'[20] As expressing a mode of class rule, the accent of the dictatorship of the proletariat falls, as it did for their

theory of the bourgeois state, on repression, not consent, on the
'coercion function', not on the 'legitimation function'. Coercion is both
dominant and determinant, at least in the initial stages of the
transitional state.

In Marx and Engels (and Lenin), these two aspects of the dictatorship
of the proletariat are indissolubly linked. The problems with the
concept arise, however, precisely out of this linkage. There are three
such problems. First, how can the accent on coercion in the initial stage
effectively be married with the democratic forms described by Marx in
The Civil War in France? Secondly, is the concept of dictatorship
appropriate to the further development of the transitional society, in
which the state still expresses the class rule of the proletariat but in
which consent becomes *dominant* after the armed threat of the
reactionary forces in the immediate post-revolutionary period is
suppressed? And finally, can we dissociate the two elements of the
concept so that we retain the conquest of power by the working class,
but in the context of a peaceful transition to socialism, jettison the
dominance, even in the short run, of the coercion function?

It is the last question that is directly posed to the dictatorship of the
proletariat by Eurocommunism, although it will be seen to encompass
the first two as well. Those who would retain the concept to express
the actual political form of a fully democratic state in the transition
to socialism can only do so by sleight of hand. Althusser, following
in a long tradition, contended that 'the *political form* of this class
dictatorship or class rule of the proletariat is "social democracy" (Marx),
"mass democracy", "democracy taken to its limits" (Lenin)'.[21] But in
order to make this view stick, one has to empty of all meaning the term
dictatorship, so that it loses not only its rhetorical effect, but also its
theoretical import. The basis for distinguishing between political forms
which are authoritarian and coercive and those which are democratic and
consensual becomes lost. Why, as modern Marxist theoreticians of the
state are generally agreed, is it insufficient and inadequate to designate
liberal democracy merely as the 'dictatorship of the bourgeoisie'?
Precisely because it does not give us a basis to distinguish between
fascism and liberal democracy as political forms. Indeed, one can only
consistently employ such a concept *vis-à-vis* the socialist state by
rejecting the idea that capitalist democracy has any substance at all.
This is the way Lenin approached the matter in *State and Revolution*. He
made light of bourgeois democratic forms (something he was not always
wont to do *viz. left-wing Communism*), saying they exclude the
exploited from participation in democracy. In turn the dictatorship of

the proletariat would exclude the exploiters from its democracy.[22] This makes good rhetoric, but poor theory. Are the exploiters to be allowed to maintain indigenous class organizations, as can the working class under capitalist democracy? If not, we are talking of two very different forms of exclusion here, which cannot be grasped through the same prism, as Lenin would have had it. And are the opinions of the exploiters to be allowed to be circulated openly? What of the opinions and organizations of their supporters in the middle classes and even in the subordinate classes (of which there will be many, or else the exploiters would not constitute a serious political force)? And what of formal participation in the elective organs of 'mass democracy'? On what basis is exclusion to be established? Is it to take place culturally and economically as in bourgeois democracy with many of the exploited, or by political fiat? For Lenin, the answer was absolutely clear, and understandably so, writing even as utopian a tract as *State and Revolution* at the outset of the civil war: 'there is no freedom and no democracy where there is suppression and where there is violence.' Yet in the same breath, Lenin speaks of 'democracy for the vast majority of the people'. Can the two be so easily married? In so far as the main accent falls on dictatorship *vis-à-vis* the field of class struggle, can one envisage a vast exercise in democratic decision-making by the working class and its allies? Does it not involve, above all, discipline, with the appropriate political forms for the popular forces as against the reactionaries in the struggle?

The question is so very difficult and momentous, not because it involves abstract moral principles of democratic rights for all in all conjunctures, but because the different political forms involved are of no little moment to the working class itself and the transition to socialism. There is, again, general agreement among modern Marxist theoreticians of the state that the dictatorial capitalist state has much greater relative autonomy from the bourgeoisie than does the liberal democratic state. Dictatorship as a political form cannot permit extensive political self-activity for the bourgeoisie as a class. As Poulantzas pointed out in consideration of some of these instances of authoritarian capitalist rule, they entail serious costs for the bourgeoisie in that they do not enable 'contradictions to be regulated by the organic representations of these various fractions [of the bourgeoisie] within the state apparatus', with the result that 'conflicts within the power bloc [are] . . . settled by sudden blows, jerkily and behind the scenes', eventually even threatening 'the organized hegemony of the bourgeoisie as such'.[23] Dictatorship in the proletarian state will have more serious effects in terms of the consequences of great 'relative autonomy' of the political apparatus from the working class. In *State and Revolution,* this problem is not really addressed, but it becomes inescapable once the question of the role of the Leninist party is introduced (which it is not at all in *State and Revolution*). The point was of course made by Rosa Luxemburg, who deserves in this context to be quoted at length:

> Lenin says: the bourgeois state is an instrument of oppression of the working class; the socialist state, of the bourgeoisie. To a certain extent, he says, it is only the capitalist state stood on its head. This simplified view misses the most essential thing: bourgeois class rule has no need of the political training and education of the entire mass of the people, at least not beyond certain narrow limits. But for the proletarian dictatorship that is the life element, the very air without which it is not able to exist . . .
>
> Socialism by its very nature cannot be decreed or introduced by ukase. It has as its prerequisite a number of measures of force—against property, etc. The negative, the tearing down, can be decreed; the building up, the positive, cannot. New territory. A thousand problems. Only experience is capable of correcting and opening new ways. Only unobstructed, effervescing life falls into a thousand new forms and improvisations, brings to light creative force, itself corrects all mistaken attempts. The public life of countries with limited freedom is so poverty-stricken, so miserable, so rigid, so unfruitful, precisely because, through the exclusion of democracy, it cuts off the living sources of all spiritual riches and progress . . .
>
> In place of the representative bodies created by general, popular elections, Lenin and Trotsky have laid down the soviets as the only true representation of the labouring masses. But with the repression of political life in the land as a whole, life in the soviets must also become more and more crippled. Without general elections, without unrestricted freedom of press and assembly, without a free struggle of opinion, life dies out in every public institution, becomes a mere semblance of life, in which only the bureaucracy remains as the active element. Public life gradually falls asleep, a few dozen party leaders of inexhaustible energy and boundless experience direct and rule. Among them, in reality only a dozen outstanding heads do the leading and an élite of the working class is invited from time to time to meetings where they are to applaud the speeches of the leaders, and to approve proposed resolutions unanimously—at bottom then, a clique affair—a dictatorship, to be sure, not the dictatorship of the proletariat, however, but only the dictatorship of a handful of politicians, that is, a dictatorship in the bourgeois sense.[24]

The problem, which is present in Marx and Engels as well as in Lenin, is a matter of trying fully to reconcile irreconcilables, of perfectly balancing the need for coercion and the need for discipline, on the one hand, with the need for maximum mass democracy and the need to mimimize the power of the executive, on the other hand. At the theoretical level, the problem is only seemingly swept aside by incorporating democratic forms into the dictatorship of the proletariat, for in this formulation the accent must fall on coercion and discipline. For Lenin 'the formula "dictatorship of the proletariat" is merely a task of "smashing the bourgeois state machine"'.[25] It seems to me that the obverse is, however, true. The historically concrete and scientific (if there is such) way of addressing the problem is to begin with the concept of 'smashing the bourgeois state'. For it is through this concept that Marx and Engels really approached in detail the question of political forms appropriate to socialist democracy, while retaining within it the notion of working-class hegemony, in the transitional period. Only here do we not have an *a priori* decision that coercion is to be 'dominant' as well as 'determinant'.

The formula 'smashing the bourgeois state', although unfortunately cast in negative terms, contains the most *positive* of Marx's political formulations. The image that is brought to mind of seizing a hammer and getting to work is entirely contradicted by its substance. For what is involved is the creation of new forms much more than the destruction of old. There is not the space here to lay out in any detail Marx's treatment of this question in *The Civil War in France* and elsewhere in his political tracts of the 1870s.[26] The principal elements of the pattern of political power to be created are these: the standing army is replaced by a popular militia; a career bureaucracy is replaced by election to administrative posts, with officials paid the average worker's wage; the elected deputies, like the administrators, (40 million people rule only in the sense that 'the whole thing begins with the self-government of the commune')[27] are subject to recall in order to limit the independence of government (deputies also have administrative functions); factories are handed over to workers to be run as co-operatives with production regulated by a national plan. Much here is unclear and inadequate, of course. If all state offices are to be elective and their occupants subject to immediate recall, this contradicts the need for discipline and efficiency, and not only in the immediate post-revolutionary class struggle. Is the national plan to be composed and administered under the aegis of the communally elected deputies or representatives of the co-operative factories? How are the two repositories of popular authority to be co-ordinated; is this a case of 'parcellized sovereignty'? Above all, with Marx and Engels no less than with *State and Revolution,* where are the unions, and where is the party, the main embodiment of the struggle which is in the Marxist theory of revolution the essential transformative linkage between the old society and the new?

The fact that so little serious attention has been given in this century to the positive substance of the concept of 'smashing the bourgeois state' is to be much lamented. And this poses all the more pressingly the immensity of the theoretical, let alone practical, tasks before Marxism today. I have already suggested that advances can be made only through the explicit recognition that the tension between coercion and consent, between discipline and democracy, cannot be swept aside in theoretical formulations for the sake of political expediency. The state in the transition to socialism is to be largely defined by this tension, and if it is attenuated by too great emphasis on one to the detriment of the other, the socialist society of the future will suffer at the hands of its state. The tension is, of course, already presaged in the revolutionary party, via the theory and practice of democratic centralism. Any advance towards understanding and demarking the political form of the future socialist state, whether one follows the insurrectionary or the democratic strategy, will thus have to take into account the structure and practice of the revolutionary party.

To focus on the questions raised by 'smashing the bourgeois state' means, in other words, not crystal-ball gazing, but conceiving institutional forms of struggle and control which presage socialist democracy. Practically, this means not only a highly politicized, critical and initiatory mass party membership, but also an openness in party structures to relations with and input from non-party members. If the tension between discipline and democracy is structurally resolved to the sole benefit of the former in making the revolution, one is chasing a chimera in thinking this will be overcome in the even more difficult period of post-revolutonary rule. Moreover, the party cannot be seen as the only institutional midwife in the revolutionary process. Workers' control structures in industry are another, and in this respect and with particular regard to the state, the question arises of workers' control not in industry alone but in the apparatuses of the state itself. It will in my view be impossible for all administrative posts to be elected and to be subject to immediate recall in the socialist state. But a limitation on executive power may be sought via the creation of state workers' councils in government departments themselves, linking the organizations of state workers today with a new role in the socialist state beyond defence of their immediate, sectional interests in the highly politicized society of the transition to socialism. Therborn has properly addressed this recently, and without falling into the utopian perspective characteristic of much socialist self-management thought:

we have contrasted the cadre administration of existing socialist states to the *bureaucracy* and *technocracy* of the bourgeois states. In order to function effectively as instruments of collective working-class supremacy, the cadres must simultaneously belong to a labour movement independent of the state and exercise powers of non-commanding direction over bureaucrats and managers. Recent Western strategic formulations have emphasized only the first aspect. But the advanced democratic and socialist state will also need to employ political and ideological weapons against bureaucratic-managerial reproduction of the subordination of the workers. Some of the political cadre functions may be fulfilled by unions of state employees, such as those already developed in the monopoly capitalist state, and through devolution of central powers to elected regional and local assemblies. However, state bureaucrats and managers will not thereby disappear, and problems of popular control will remain. Under Social Democratic and liberal pressure, the present conceptions of socialist democracy have largely evaded the serious and complicated questions of bureaucracy and technocracy. In the end, sweeping theses on *autogestion* [or self-management] may prove as misleadingly utopian as the picture of the dictatorship of the proletariat drawn in *State and Revolution*.[28]

The questions raised in this paper barely skim the surface, and the answers are excruciatingly inadequate. Above all, I have avoided speaking directly to the question of finding the means of transition from the bourgeois state of the 'historic compromise' to the socialist state. It is troublesome, to say the least, that there is apparently little serious open discussion of *this* question in the Eurocommunist parties today. A facile identification of Eurocommunism with social democracy is in my view indefensible. The abandonment of the 'dictatorship of the proletariat' does not make these parties social democratic so long as they retain a definition of socialism in which the proletariat becomes the hegemonic class. Whether 'parliamentary illusions', to use Luxemburg's apt litmus test (not to be confused with an immediate and dominant parliamentary strategy), are being created among the supporters of Eurocommunism remains, however, a central question to be asked. For even if communist parties come to governmental office in certain Western liberal democracies, this does not rule out the factor of coercion in subsequent developments. Engels's warning of the 'insane cruelties of revenge [to which the bourgeoisie] will be goaded the moment the proletariat dares to take its stand against the bourgeoisie as a separate class, with its own interests and demands'[29] remains worth heeding, particularly in a conjuncture today which reveals certain tendencies toward a reassertion of the dominance of the coercion function in the advanced capitalist state.

It is to be borne in mind, in other words, that the tension between coercion and consent, which will be the defining characteristic of the transitional socialist state, cannot be easily passed over in strategic preparations. Revolution is going to be, as it always has been, an affair in which force plays a considerable part. In this regard, it is perhaps fitting to conclude by considering a quotation from a speech by Norman Bethune in the city of Montreal in 1935, upon his return from visiting the Soviet Union.

> Isadora Duncan, in the story of her life, describes her confinement . . . 'There I lay', she wrote, 'a fountain of spouting blood, milk and tears.' What would a person think, watching for the first time a woman in labor and not knowing what was happening to her? Would he not be appalled at the blood, the agony, the apparent cruelty of the attendants, the whole revolting technique of delivery? He would cry: 'Stop this! Do something! Police! Murder!'
>
> Then tell him he was seeing a new life brought into the world and that the pains would pass, that the agony and ugliness were necessary and always would be necessary to birth. Knowing this, then, what could he say truthfully about this woman as she lies there? Is she not ugly? Yes. Is she not beautiful? Yes. Is she not pitiful, ludicrous, grotesque and absurd? Yes! Is she not magnificent and sublime? Yes! And all these things would be true.
>
> Now, Russia is going through her delivery, and the midwives and obstetricians have been so busy keeping the baby alive that they haven't got around as yet to cleaning up the mess, and it is this mess, this ugly and uncomfortable mess, which affronts the eyes and elevates the noses of those timid male and female virgins suffering from sterility of the soul, who lack the imagination to see behind the blood the significance of birth.
>
> Creation is not and never has been a genteel gesture. It is rude, violent and revolutionary. But to those courageous hearts who believe in the unlimited future of man, in the divine destiny which lies in his own hand to make of what he will—to these Russia presents today the most exciting spectacle of the evolutionary, emergent and heroic spirit of man which has appeared on this earth since the Reformation. To deny this is to deny our faith in men—and that is the unforgivable sin, the final apostasy.[30]

Some will take this as apologetics, and understandably so. Yet, I do not believe it should be left at that. It does not minimize the blood, the cruelty, the agony, and in speaking to the confusion of the observer it captures the mixture of revulsion and hope that still largely characterizes Western Marxist attitudes to new revolutionary regimes today. If Bethune's faith in the particular socialist experiment in Russia up to the 1930s was stronger than ours, (and if his use of the generic "man" seems today grating and misplaced), this has to be understood in relation to our vantage point half a century later. To carry his metaphor on, it has for a very long time been clear that Stalinism, far from cleaning up the mess, stifled the 'child's' growth and deformed its personality, so that it is now a very different person from the one the Bolsheviks had hoped to bring into the world. The point that remains universally relevant in Bethune's observation, however, is that the act of creation is not to be shunned because it is a messy business. Those who would look forward to the future of socialism only on the condition that it be a tidy and clean process, and those who would reject advances toward that future because of the practice of 'actually existing socialism', are precisely those who deny our faith in humanity, who commit today the final apostasy.

(1978)

Notes

1. Rudolf Bahro, 'The Alternative in Eastern Europe', *New Left Review*, no. 106 November–December 1977: 5; Perry Anderson, *Considerations on Western Marxism*, London 1976, p. 108.
2. See 'The Role and Nature of the Canadian State', in L. Panitch (ed.), *The Canadian State, Political Economy and Political Power*, Toronto 1977, pp. 3–5.
3. V. I. Lenin, *The State and Revolution*, in *Selected Works*, vol. 2, Moscow 1970, p. 292.
4. 'The Antinomies of Antonio Gramsci', *New Left Review*, no. 100, November 1976–January 1977, pp. 28, 30.
5. See 'Speech in Amsterdam, 1872', in David McLellan, *Karl Marx: Selected Writings*, London 1977, pp. 594–5, and Louis Althusser, 'On the Twenty-Second Congress of the French Communist Party', *New Left Review*, no. 104, July–August 1977, pp. 13–14.
6. Hal Draper, 'Marx on Democratic Forms of Government', *Socialist Register 1974*, London 1974, p. 111.
7. For an elaboration of this argument, see ch. 5 above, 'The Development of Corporatism in Liberal Democracies'.
8. 'Critique of the Gotha Programme', in Marx and Engels, *Selected Works*, vol. 3. Moscow 1970, p. 17.
9. 'The German Ideology', in Marx and Engels, *Collected Works*, vol. 5, 1845–1847, New York 1976, pp. 52–3.
10. Marx and Engels, *Selected Works*, vol. 2, p. 221: vol. 3, p. 26.
11. *Capital*, vol. 3, Moscow 1959, pp. 376–7.
12. Hal Draper, 'The Death of the State in Marx and Engels', *Socialist Register 1970*, London 1970, p. 298.
13. Quoted in ibid.
14. Karl Marx, 'Conspectus of Bakunin's *Statism and Anarchy*', in *The First International and After: Political Writings Volume 3*, (ed. D. Fernbach), London 1974, pp. 336–7.
15. Engels 'On Authority', *Selected Works*, vol. 3, pp. 378.

16. L. Althusser, *For Marx*, Harmondsworth 1969, pp. 235–6.
17. 'On the Twenty-Second Congress', p. 10.
18. Ramsay MacDonald, *Socialism and Society*, 6th edn, London 1908, p. 144.
19. Marx, in McLellan, pp. 594–5.
20. Engels, 'On Authority', p. 379.
21. Althusser, 'On the Twenty-Second Congress', p. 13.
22. *The State and Revolution*, pp. 349–51.
23. *The Crisis of the Dictatorships*, London 1976, pp. 30, 49–50.
24. 'The Problem of Dictatorship', in R. Luxemburg, *Selected Political Writings*, London 1972, pp. 244–7.
25. Quoted in G. Therborn, *What Does the Ruling Class Do When It Rules?* London 1978, p. 25.
26. For a recent account, see B. Ollman, 'Marx's Vision of Communism: A Reconstruction', *Critique*, no. 8, Summer 1977, pp. 5–41.
27. Marx, *The First International and After*, p. 335. Cf. Draper, 'The Death . . .' p. 296.
28. Therborn, pp. 279–80.
29. Engels, Introduction to *The Civil War in France*, Marx and Engels, *Selected Works*, vol. 2, p. 180.
30. Quoted in T. Allen and S. Gordon, *The Scalpel, the Sword*, Toronto 1971, p. 87.

Index